2⁰⁰

D1029446

DOVES

AND DOVE SHOOTING

By

BYRON W. DALRYMPLE

NEW WIN PUBLISHING, INC.

In Memory of J. D.

◇◇◇

ACKNOWLEDGMENTS

W HEN THE IDEA of *Doves and Dove Shooting* was first conceived, I was immediately eager to begin the necessary research. But after it was once launched, I began to be appalled at the task I had taken on. This, I discovered, was not only to be a subject never tackled before in the field of sports books, but a subject hardly touched in scientific literature. My personal experience with doves over a gun barrel was one thing; the background for "the dove story" on a world-wide basis another— a most obscure matter, with only bits of information never complete and widely scattered.

I have never found people more eager to assist, however, and I am therefore greatly indebted to many sources. Two of those sources of inestimable value were books: the Bible and the grand collection of quotes from authorities of another generation, and of personal knowledge, titled *The Passenger Pigeon*, by the late Wm. B. Mershon. Several others were bulletins by wildlife biologists who have made intensive dove studies: the numerous published reports of my good friend Elliott McClure, who made the Cass County, Iowa, mourning dove study mentioned in some detail in my chapter titled "Mourners for Tomorrow"; the bulletin acquired from the Fish and Wildlife Service covering the work of biologists Moore and Pearson, titled "The Mourning Dove in Alabama"; the excellent bulletins by Johnson Neff, Fish and Wildlife Service biologist, covering his long and detailed studies of the band-tailed pigeon on the

Acknowledgments

West Coast and in Colorado; "The White-winged Dove in Arizona" by Lee W. Arnold, a remarkable bulletin that adds much to the knowledge of a bird little known sciencewise.

The Fish and Wildlife Service and the various state conservation departments were without fail most congenial and patient with my many requests. Frank Dufresne and W. F. Kubichek of the Fish and Wildlife Service helped me to locate much valuable information. My correspondence with Johnson Neff, Elliott McClure, O. N. Arrington of the Arizona Game and Fish Commission brought me not only much personal pleasure, but many desperately needed facts and further contacts as well. There were dozens of others who were helpful, and to whom, herewith, I wish also to extend my thanks.

The magazines—*Field & Stream, Outdoors, Sports Afield, Outdoor Life*—all generously allowed me to quote from items appearing in their pages, and Alfred A. Knopf, publisher, extended the same courtesy regarding several books.

Photographs, which had worried me no end, were heaped upon me when my written pleas went out. For that favor I wish especially to thank and credit the following: Nancy C. West of the National Audubon Society; W. F. Kubichek of the Fish and Wildlife Service; O. N. Arrington of the Arizona Game and Fish Commission; Charlie Elliott, Mabry Anderson, Charles Niehuis—all outdoor writers who could probably have used to their own better personal advantage photographs that they tendered to me.

To all others—and there were dozens—who had some part in this work, my sincere gratitude. There are in particular several persons of the sort who seldom get any credit when a book finally finds its way into print, and I want them to know that their work was just as important in its way as mine: my stanch friend and agent, Gideon Kishorr; Wallace Hanger of G. P. Putnam's, who first recognized that the doves deserved their chance on the printed page; the Caffrey family, who prodded me and encouraged me to get the book done; Ellen Christoffers, who started out to do the tedious job of getting my scratched-up manuscript ready for the publisher—and wound up as Mrs. B. W. Dalrymple!

B. W. D.

UP-DATE-OCTOBER, 1991

B EHIND OUR RURAL HOME in the Texas Hill Country we built a large, graveled patio. The fine gravel covering was purposeful. In the center of the patio stands a pedestaled concrete bird bath, and my wife, Ellen, scatters bird seed over the gravel. Birds attracted have to work for their meal, and consequently remain for longer periods than as though the seeds were easily found. This gives us more time to enjoy their visits.

The chief impetus for this arrangement was the abundance of doves, especially in winter, that flock to the patio. Occasionally we've had as many as fifty mourning doves at one time, up to twenty of the diminutive, non-game scallop-feathered Inca doves, and a whitewing or two. Doves, as anyone who reads this book will know, have fascinated me for a lifetime.

It was a half century ago when I began planning this book, and it has been forty-two years since it was first published. My strong penchant for observing, hunting, and photographing the elegantly fashioned doves and pigeons is thus given new life and gratification by seeing it in print again.

During the years in between, I have never missed a season without hunting, or the enjoyment of observing, one species or another. There were exciting days in the thorny jungles of eastern Mexico after red-billed pigeons—*paloma morada,* literally the mulberry-colored pigeon. There were numerous times of standing, gun in hand, but not shooting, awed by flights of tens of thousands of whitewings passing over head, moving out from their mesquite forest quarters to feed in vast grain fields, also in Mexico. There was the fall the hunting closure on bandtailed pigeons was lifted in Arizona and New Mexico after many years, and I drove a thousand miles to savor these birds in this high-forest setting new to me for this endeavor.

Meanwhile, of course, the ubiquitous mourning dove was the main fare, my pursuit of this shooting covering numerous states and terrains, from mid-country grain fields to plains with scarce perching trees, from swampy southern locations to the seemingly barren deserts of the Southwest, and to my own Hill Country, Texas, bailiwick where wild croton and sunflower patches offer superb sport.

The sleek, swift mourning dove was the presiding celebrity of the dove-pigeon tribe when this book was written, and it is the same today. It was the nation's Number One game bird half a century ago, and still is. It is the only one that nests in all of the contiguous states, and indeed far south of our borders. The annual hunter harvest within the U.S. is estimated at perhaps 50 million birds, yet populations remain stable and undented.

The main reason the mourning dove has so fascinated me since boyhood is that unlike other game birds, it is the epitome of total freedom. It is tied to no exacting specifics of latitude, longitude, terrain, or living conditions. It is the classic of free spirits, roaming at will and by whimsy wherever and whenever it chooses. It gathers its living at random, and without temperamental tastes, taking every seed from corn to ragweed, peanuts to sorghum to milkweed, wild millet and grasses.

Indeed, the dove is tied to nowhere, to nothing. It drinks from a lake or a mud puddle. It perches in any available tree or bush. Although mourning doves gather in large numbers at certain especially ample feeding locations, these are not truly flocking birds. They're not dependent on others of their kind, as are the colonial whitewings. They don't mind being solitary, or with others. They even nest well separated.

If a deluge disturbs them, or a drastic switch in temperature, they simply fly off to a more congenial area. They may move in any direction, and any distance, from ten to a hundred or two hundred miles in a day, hurtling along with a tail wind at a mile-a-minute clip or more.

This total freedom, this vagabonding spirit is the attribute of the mourning dove which has always mesmerized me, perhaps because of a deep-lurking kindred feeling. Waterfowl are inexorably tied to water. The uplanders such as quail, grouse, pheasants, are sedentary homebodies. Nothing ties a mourning dove down. Its home is everywhere, anywhere, as it happens to feel the urging. It makes do admirably with whatever is at hand that offers forage and reasonable comfort.

Writing those words, I think of a particular hunt I made some years ago in New Mexico which succinctly illustrates the complete freedom of spirit of the mourning dove. At that time I had formed a small film production company, specializing in producing TV films for manufacturers of sports related equipment. We'd done films for such firms as Remington Arms, Redfield Scope, American Motors Jeep. We were headquartered for a few days in a small New Mexico village on this job, in a most non-scenic area of flat, scrub, partially abandoned ranch lands.

One day was so overcast we couldn't shoot film. Bored, a New Mexico game department employee who was helping us, and was an old friend of mine, suggested we see if we could find a few doves. There were only a few days of season left, and shooting was virtually over, birds scarce and scattered. We drove out some miles from the village, turned onto a narrow, rutted sideroad. Wind was from the north and chill. The rough trail led to a huddle of tumbledown, abandoned ranch buildings, a scattering of scrubby, ribby cattle showed distantly, perhaps belonging to a pasture lessee. By the dismal look of the land, no wonder the cattle were thin.

Just as we approached the buildings a dove flushed beside the vehicle. We stopped, got guns out, looked the place over. There were some tall trees on the north side of the buildings area, obviously planted years ago as a windbreak. An ancient windmill creaked and rattled nearby. Its trough overflow had muddied ground cut by cattle tracks, each track filled with muddy water. Here were water and roosting trees for doves, but what could they, as well as the cattle, possibly find to eat?

As we milled around, another dove flushed. We noticed scattered, dry yucca stalks lightly stippling the depressing looking landscape. These were of the yucca variety often called by Mexicans "the Lord's Candles." The whorl of stiff leaves grows close to the ground. The slender flower stalk rises in spring some four or five feet, bearing a welter of lovely white flowers along the last foot or more. When the flowers wither, fat seed pods form. In fall and winter as they dry, they break open, dropping black seeds. The last bird had flushed from below a yucca stalk.

Widely separated, we began walking slowly into the wind to cover our sounds. Presently a dove burst from the ground below a yucca stalk, wings emitting that thrilling whistle. Every fifty yards or so one of us flushed a bird. Some we collected, some we missed. What a novel, coverless location to find doves, and what a novel experience, jump shooting in such a place.

Toward dusk we sat in the car, drinking thermos coffee, watching doves swirling in to the windmill, drinking from cattle tracks, then flying off to the old windbreak roost trees. Here indeed in this dismal place was a delightfully classic example of the total freedom and pioneering vagabond spirit of the mourning dove. I remember the thought of my old book crossing my mind, the countless hours of library and travel research that went into it. How nice it would be, I thought, if a new generation of readers might share with me what went into it, and the fascination of the dove as both a unique species and game bird.

Without counting, I presume that experience occurred at least twenty years ago. But I wondered often about a reissue of the book. How nice it would be to acquaint today's readers with the book that grew from a plan conceived fifty years ago.

Byron W. Dalrymple

CONTENTS

1. Dove of Dissension   3

2. Whistling Wings   33

3. Ebb Tide of Empire   63

4. The Gray Bullet   97

5. Shooting the Breeze   133

6. Mourners for Tomorrow   161

7. Pacific Mountaineer   185

8. Dove of the Desert   219

9. And Lo, in the Evening—   235

*A section of illustrations will
be found following page 54.*

DOVES AND DOVE SHOOTING

Chapter 1

DOVE OF DISSENSION

IT WAS A GRAY late December afternoon, nippy and threatening rain. It was the kind of day when doves are restless and high flying, when they waste no time winging lazily but slice down the sky in crazy patterns, each bird hell bent on feeding full before the early dusk draws down. When we were within a half mile of the field, hidden away in the pines that mask most such southern valleys, we could see wisps of birds swiftly making toward the rendezvous, each small group knowing exactly where it was headed, but swinging and shifting, now high, now low, zigzagging wildly, so that when you thought of them in terms of shouldering your gun they seemed to have no direction at all.

This was a typical southern shoot. A hogged-down cornfield of perhaps forty acres, with a pond nearby, and everywhere pines for roosting. Already there were some twenty guns slamming away at the field. We could hear them as we swung off the pavement and curved along the narrow red-mud road. There was one of our group who was about to have his first experience with the mourning dove.

"Lord," he said, "shove it along, will you? By the sound of that barrage they'll have every dove knocked down before we get there!"

We laughed. When the peanuts have been harvested in the southern Georgia dove country, so that the feed is concentrated in smaller areas, doves flock in to their favorite fields not by tens, or fifties, or hundreds, but by thousands. It is a sight to make a Yankee disbelieve his eyes, not only the number of the birds, but their appalling wing speed and insane flight patterns.

"You don't want to believe all that noise you hear," our host said. "A dove shoot is just about what it says. More shoot than doves. You're not going to be pointing your gun at any *easy* bird this time, mister. These fellows are gray bullets, and that's a fact. The mourning dove, I reckon, is just the damnedest game bird—but never mind, wait and see."

Fifteen minutes later I stood beneath a tall pine at the edge of the field and wondered how a man was supposed to pick a target here. I watched fifty birds sweep in from the far end of the field, dropping over the tall pine tops, slashing down close to the broken corn, skimming, sideslipping—and all the way, from the moment their ragged formation had shown above the pines, the lead had been cutting futile swaths around them. Thirty shots I counted, and not a bird nicked, no feather floating, no spiraling clean kill plummeting. But as I watched, there was a swish and whistle like bombs falling. Two—three—a single—six birds close huddled went by me within twenty feet, catching me with my gun down, and before I could get over that surprise there were several flocks of what looked like a hundred or more following that far fifty in. And yonder, at the most distant corner of the big field, a long gray line went weaving down against the stormy horizon, five hundred birds in one flock.

Then I quit wondering and gaping, and went to work. This was duck shooting on a high pass, only better. This was all the hunting excitement I had ever known, rolled into one experience. My gun was hot from high misses, and satisfied a bit with a connection it made now and then on a skimmer. My fingers fumbled as I tried to reload fast enough to try for the next one wheeling and flaring as he caught sight of me. This was quail, pheasants, grouse, prairie chickens, all in one package, tougher by far than any or all. More frantic, heady action than a gunner could pack into a week. More *shooting* than a whole season might bring with other game. The constant barrage, the continuous stream of "gray bullets" dashing helter skelter over the field and along the horizon, and me, comfortably standing beneath that pine. Sweating! And the day a nippy one!

I don't know just how long it had been when I reached into my shell bag and found it empty. I won't tell you how many shells had been in it when I left the car. I don't like to lie, and I don't like to make excuses just because the little mourners were flying high and wild that day. Suffice to say that when I tallied up I lacked one bird of my limit, and being something of an old hand at dove shooting, I matched that against my expenditure of shells and felt satisfied with my gun pointing.

It was about then that the Yankee we were initiating came puffing up out of the pines, holding a single dove in his hand and with a most apologetic expression on his face. "Have you got any extra shells?" he asked. "You know, for some reason I just can't hit them little things. Just this one—" He extended his hand, showing it to me, grinning sheepishly. Then, "But gad, man," he said, "now *that's* shooting! If anybody had told me a mourning dove could—why, these little things are the damnedest game birds—"

"You're stealing the native line," I said. . . .

But so they are, and of that fact I'm convinced. The mourning dove, without question, is one of the finest, if not *the* finest game bird flying the U. S. today! And it is the game bird least known, least appreciated by the average American gunner. Our forgotten game bird. It was the shoot just described that made me want to do something as big as I possibly could to remedy that situation. For there was a shoot which added up to everything the dove is and has to offer before the gun. It was too good to contain. And so, since my business is with words, it seemed to me a book was the answer to doing something for the dove. Whatever it does for the dove it will do for the hunter also, I'm sure. For those who know this bird for what he is will applaud this effort in the dove's behalf, no matter how poorly I have constructed it. And those who come to know him for the first time through these pages, and afterward in the field, I feel certain will do likewise. For what gun toter lives who doesn't like the best?

The first question that has always been asked of me whenever I went about blowing the dove's horn for him is this: "Why has he gone so long with so few loud songs of praise to his credit?" The answer is not readily obvious, but in its rather complicated and obscure facets it is intensely interesting: the dove is and long has been a bird of fabulous dissension. Let me, then, introduce you to him, and to the realm of dissension which has always surrounded him in his relations with man-kind, by relating what might be termed a "three-pronged" anecdote from my boyhood. It has always appealed to me as a typical illustration of the many opposites of attitude among people, regarding the doves.

There are three characters in this little drama, my good friend and shirttail relative, Ross McGuigan, my mother, and myself. There is probably no kinder gentleman on earth than Ross, nor one more emotionally erratic in his likes and dislikes. This bothers my mother at times, though just why I'm not sure since she has been known to lay a sharp tongue worthily to a favorite dislike now and again.

My mother, you must understand, loves mourning doves. They delight her, during late spring's first explosion of blooming and greenery, as they go singly or in pairs—not abundantly in the Thumb-of-Michigan section which was my boyhood bailiwick, but in scattered nesting numbers substantial enough to be daily observed—grayly hurtling across the green-sprouting, even-rowed brown cornfield next our vegetable garden, low and erratically twisting and turning, bent on some top-important dove mission.

I have seen her stand by our back-stoop pump to watch a pair of doves sweep with a quick, audible swish of wings over our ancient apple orchard just outside the kitchen door. They burst up and over the orchard edge, boring through bough openings headlong, dipping, rolling, swerving, ruddering in a never-hesitant, never-slowing display of streamlined, now coasting, now powerfully pulsating, rocket flight, like artistically molded wind splinters from some lost and shattered gray hurricane, directionless, and at once perfectly controlled.

At those times she might turn and say simply, "Aren't they

wonderful!" And I, itchy fingered for fall and the cool walnut of a gunstock thrown against my cheek, would answer, "What a flight to watch and follow—over a gun barrel!" Meaning this, of course, but straight faced purposely just to see it rile her, and then laughing when she rose to it. My mother, the mourning dove, and I have been fighting a triangular battle for years.

Her special pleasure, I think, is of an early, dew-fresh dawn, when these mourning doves sit concealed in the apple trees and empty out the half-rhythmic, unliquid sounds from which their Christian name derives.

"Isn't it pretty," my mother will say, stirring the early-morning oatmeal, and trying to look out into the dawn-speckled orchard to locate the sound exactly. "Poor, mournful little birds. Sad birds. So pretty and sad."

"Bosh," I answer. "You make it up. You make up a character like you'd fashion a dress, and then you slip it over their heads and tuck it in around their pink feet. What's sad about it? The fact is, that sound is a sound of plain old back-alley passion. The only thing that will make that stubborn little devil sad is if the gal he's working on doesn't see things his way!"

She wants to be angry, but can't, and laughs with me and says I'm a "caution." But one day the matter got down to something quite different.

That day I was patterning my gun. Fall, it was, a long time ago, with a few migration-gathered mourners doing feverish groundwork beneath the lightly frost-nipped, seed-dropping sunflower row beside the garden. Fall, and pheasant season about to roll up several old roosters' numbers.

My mother passed by, going to pick up pears from beneath a frost-touched tree. A full-flight dove winged over. "Next one that close is mine," I needled her, grinning.

"You leave them alone," she commanded. "You've birds enough to shoot besides those dear little doves."

Well, I wouldn't have done it for the world, I guess. But a little later, when I caught a gray flash out the tail of my eye, I was instantly a gunner, with the old thrill at swift wings leaping up in me, blotting out everything else—you know how it is, you wing shooters. Impact of many remembered experiences whirling together. A bright, sudden explosion in your mind.

I swung, of course not meaning to hit him—*of course*. He was not even legal there. Just making as if, you know. I swung and laid the blue nose of the barrel behind, along, across him, swiftly, still swinging, ahead, and when the *feel* inside me said *"now!"* I crossed his forty-yards-out, forty-mile-an-hour path with a long-spread pattern—*lucky*, understand, not expert —and watched him tumble, exploding feathers flowering gray and tawny, drifting in the spot above him where he'd been.

Coming back with the pears, my mother saw me handling the bird, admiring it. Her blue Irish eyes blazed at me. "I see you killed it anyway," she said quietly. "If you were a youngster instead of a grown man who should know better, I'd take your gun away for good. I'd trounce the pants off you, believe me!" Then grimly, passing on, "When you're through being proud of yourself, clean it and I'll cook it for you."

She added something else under her breath, something that sounded like, "—so you'll remember eating it a long time." In fact, I wouldn't be surprised if that's exactly what she said.

For she cooked it. Indeed. She even stuffed it. And brother, when I licked the last of the meat from my chops and bit into that delicious-looking little ball of stuffing—I'll remember it a long, long time. I'll recall it and run for water to quench the blazing-hot, solid black-pepper fire in my throat!

So that's how it is with my mother and the doves. But with old Ross McGuigan it's a different matter. He pauses often to listen to the empty-jug blowing of a mourner along the roadside. But what comes after, when he starts talking, is in no way sentimental.

"Byron," he'll say in the overly precise, subdued accents he saves for such fanatic discourses, "it would please me immensely if every damnable dove in the entire world was to be struck dead at this instant!" His voice rises almost imperceptibly, becomes stilted as he builds his inner rage. "I should like, indeed, to see each and every one of them piled here before me in a huge pile. Dead. In fact," he spreads his hands, "I should like to wring their bloody necks individually."

Ross was in the hospital some years ago, very ill, very restive of nights, and apparently very irritable. At the time, several mourning doves sat outside his window each dawn, carrying on their interminable cooing. "I called upon the Almighty to force them to stop such nonsense. I forced myself to try to sleep. When I finally began to doze they stopped—and I immediately woke up again, wondering what was missing. Then they'd start again. The same routine. Over and over. I was on the verge of insanity. I was truthfully, Byron, make no mistake about it. They'd stop and start and I'd wake and doze and wake, going through it over and over again. Byron, I utterly detest those doves. In fact, God have mercy on me, I truly *hate* the devils!"

The foregoing tale serves to illustrate the widely diversified attitudes so common toward doves. But there's nothing unusual about them as compared to the scenes we're about to review. For the result of the relationships of the doves and pigeons versus mankind, especially as it is evidenced in our modern attitudes toward these creatures as game birds, has created the most unique situation of its kind ever to occur. No group of birds has in all history been so variously united with, so variously utilized and loved by, and at the same time so often and sadly forgotten, neglected, and sometimes brutally treated by mankind as the doves and pigeons. Nor has factional feeling regarding any group of birds ever been so varied, pronounced, or belligerent.

Oddly, each faction has loved and admired identical qualities and attributes of these birds—their streamlined shape, their speed of wing, their charm, their inoffensive qualities—but each faction for its own specific reasons. And each faction has, therefore, because of the wealth of tradition founded on these reasons, built up a dove character of its own. Indeed, in all bird history, there is nothing to compare with the story of the doves.

To avoid confusion it should be explained that the terms *dove* and *pigeon* are entirely interchangeable. Most of us think of the word *dove* as relating to the smaller species of this large bird group, and the word *pigeon* as relating to the larger. This is not true. No actual distinction can be made, nor would it be possible to point out one species as being a pigeon and another as a dove, except as common usage dictates in any particular section. Supposedly, dove is Anglo-Saxon, while pigeon is Norman. Specifically, pigeon is French, from Italian *pipione* or *piccione,* by way of Latin *pipio,* while dove is closely allied to such words as the Dutch word *duif.* An excellent example of the way the two words are interchanged is evident with the common domestic pigeon, which is almost identical with, and stemmed ancestrally from, the wild rock dove.

Let us now begin the strange story of dove dissension by dragging out a few random exhibits.

Here, first, is a bookshelf in the book department of the country's largest sporting-goods store. You cannot think of a single outdoor subject which is not covered here before you in great detail. Or can you? See if you can find a book about the wild doves and pigeons of America, either for hunters or for nonhunters. To the best of my knowledge you cannot.

Here, in a large library, are the back issues of all the half-dozen-odd outdoor magazines published in the United States. Would you like to find out a little something about doves and dove hunting? I warn you that for the most part a search here will be a tedious, time-consuming waste. You will find a few scattered articles, to be sure. A very few.

Well now, you may say, what is so odd about that? Publicity is bound to be given to those game birds which are most hunted, which have a sporting tradition of many years standing behind them. Wait now. Don't get into any arguments on the matter. Did you know that it has been estimated by competent authorities that since this country was settled a greater number of wild doves has been killed than of *any other game bird?* Think about that a bit.

Here, now, is a parade of our game birds: the quails, the grouses, the pheasant, the woodcock, the waterfowl. They are known by even the most ill-informed individuals as game birds. You could not stop any person on the street who would not know that these birds fall into that category. What do you think would happen if you questioned people at random about doves? I can tell you. One will say, "Don't be silly. Doves aren't game birds." Another will say, "What! You mean to tell me people actually *hunt* those tiny song birds? I don't believe it!" If you happen to stop a New England grouse hunter and extol the dove to him as a game bird, he will scoff at you. If you hinted that the ruffed grouse isn't even in the same class with the dove, you would be inviting a fight. Yet you can take him down to Georgia on a hunt, after he has sharpened his eye to the limit on his fall grouse and woodcock, and "those little things," as he previously and cynically will have labeled them, will make a perfect fool of him!

He has seen them sitting tamely all summer in the apple tree by his porch, during nesting season. He now sees flocks of thousands upon thousands, and he discovers with awe and utter disbelief that since he last saw them they have changed their personality along with their address!

Here, however, is a Deep South village on the opening day of dove season. Practically every male has deserted the village. Every one of them, man and boy, is raking the rice fields and the kaffir corn patches with bird shot, doing his damnedest to outwit by swift swing of gun the gray lightning of dove hordes slicing the sunny sky.

Such completely opposed opinion exists with no other game bird. Even those people who do not hunt, or are opposed to hunting, still think of all other game birds as game birds.

So, you say, that is how it goes. In restricted sections undoubtedly it is true that doves do furnish sport. But the grouse, the pheasant, the quail, remember, are birds for *everybody*. That's why there's never any question as to their status.

Again let me caution you. Don't gamble on that opinion. The mourning dove, for example, is the only U. S. game bird that breeds in every state in the union. It is readily available to more gunners than any other, and more states as a rule have open season on it each year than on any other single indigenous game-bird species. Think about that a bit, too.

Let us now watch state conservation organizations, and our federal conservation agencies, spending millions to assist the continuance of those fine game birds the quail, the grouse, the pheasant, the waterfowl. Almost any one of these agencies can furnish men to tell you anything you want to know about any of those birds, from detailed descriptions of diseases which affect them, to their most minor preferences in food. Ask them, now, about the doves.

Top men of all these organizations will admit to you that they do not actually know anywhere near so much about our doves as they wish they did. There have been, and are, a few study projects. But in comparison to other game birds, little solid and complete scientific knowledge exists about the whistle-winged gray ghosts who make you swing your gun faster than any winged target we know. What has gone to assist the doves financially, to make it possible for them to hang on all these years? Practically nothing.

And yet, strangely, while the other game birds decline—even with all the millions poured into their causes—the doves have fairly well held their own. This, mind you, not for one year, but for decade after decade. If we asked any other species to do what the dove has done, it would have been gunned into extinction in a half-dozen seasons or sooner!

But, you say, one has to remember that tremendous numbers of pheasants, of quail, of grouse are killed each year. These birds have to have help, while those with less gun-mortality can better take care of themselves.

You would lose your money on that statement, too. The mourning dove, that little speedster beloved by the ammunition companies because of the powder burned in his behalf with endless misses, is today, and long has been, by numbers legally killed each season, our third most popular upland game bird! That, too, will bear thinking about. It is a fact that not one gunner in a hundred realizes.

So here is an upland bird (not even counting the other legal dove species) the annual legal kill of which is exceeded only by quail and pheasants, and by not very great margins at that, and yet we neither know so very much about methods of conserving his numbers nor have we so far tried very determinedly to learn. Here is a bird available to a major share of us, a bird that has shown itself capable of holding its own almost unassisted against great odds, at a time when others constantly decline while getting the best of care, one that will very likely be here long after civilization has squeezed the others out of existence—and he even has a rough time of it getting himself permission from the copyright owners to use the name "game bird"! There indeed, I believe you will agree, is a strange situation.

I do not wish to give the impression that I think the lack of publicity and assistance on behalf of the dove is anyone's fault in particular. I do not blame the grouse, woodcock, or pheasant hunter who has not experienced a dove shoot, for raising an eyebrow at the suggestion that in the dove he will find something far surpassing what he has already experienced. The point is, the story of the doves is so extraordinary that it is virtually impossible to avoid taking what might be termed a mildly belligerent stand in order to get the story across at its dramatic best.

Do you suppose it might be that the reason the dove has received so little public acclaim as a game bird is that in reality he is only a so-so target? If you have hunted him, you will know better. If not, let me quote for you what a few writers and gunners have said.

Major Charles Askins writes in *Sports Afield:*

Many of us can remember when the dove was not considered a game bird, and there were persons who threw up their hands in horror when it was referred to as such. However, since boyhood I have considered it as belonging in this category ... and have enjoyed some splendid sport while matching my shooting skill against their speedy flight. No matter what some may think ... when listening to its mournful notes ... I am bound to say that I like dove shooting. It taxes the skill of the best shots. ... You ... must hold right, otherwise you go home light in both shells and birds. However, one is likely to go home light in both respects, no matter how cute the hold. ... The dove is a miniature waterfowl. He has the same speed of wing ... and can swerve and duck and dodge in a way no mallard can imitate.

Hal Spencer writes in *Outdoor Life:* "There is no bird in America so difficult to generalize about as the dove, for at one time or another he calls for almost every kind of shooting there is."

William Brent writes in *Outdoor Life:* "There's no greater shooting thrill... than connecting with these fast-flying, elusive gray targets."

Colonel H. P. Sheldon writes in *Outdoors:* "Dove shooting is one of the most agreeable occupations known to sportsmen. It is the equivalent of duck shooting, or... walked up in standing corn, much like woodcock with the... flavor of bobwhite thrown in."

Ray Holland writes in *Field & Stream,* speaking of the band-tailed pigeon: "There is no sportier pass-shooting than that furnished by these birds. Many experienced gunners claim there is no target more difficult."

Jack O'Connor says in his book, *Hunting in the Southwest*:

Those hunters who live in the North ... miss one of the finest of all scattergun sports: shooting at mourning doves. I say "shooting at" purposely, for attempting to hit a mourning dove in flight is about the most exacting and difficult feat possible. The dove is one of the swiftest and most agile birds that flies ... for most hunters, the hardest of all birds to hit consistently. I can bring home about twice as many ducks for each box of shells as I can doves.

H. L. Betten writes in his book *Upland Game Shooting,* speaking of the band-tailed pigeon of the West:

I doubt if there is another game bird on the continent that is so difficult to hit as the band-tail. This is because the range is not estimated properly by the hunter, and because the bird flies at super-speed. Quite recently in one small district in California, an actual count showed that 350,000 shells were expended by sportsmen in bagging approximately 21,000 band-tailed pigeons during an open season of two weeks.

Hart Stilwell writes in his book, *Hunting and Fishing in Texas,* speaking of the whitewing of Texas and Arizona:

* Reprinted by permission of the publishers, Alfred A. Knopf, Inc.

The whitewing is a noble bird in flight, one of the finest game birds to be found anywhere. I don't believe there is any bird harder to hit than a whitewing that has been shot at and missed. There is really no other hunting exactly like it, and I don't blame hunters who come by the thousands from places as far as a thousand miles away to get two or three days' shooting at the whitewing. It is spectacular hunting and worth the trip even though you get to hunt only a day or two.

It is not just the writer-expert who is ready to vouch for the facts. Recently I clipped, from the letters-to-the-editor department of *Outdoor Life* magazine, the following: "No man living can tell you how to hold on a dove in flight. After you have shot dove forty years, and have it figured down to a fine point, you will go out some day and miss 90% of your birds." Signed, Sid Schultze, Louisville, Kentucky. And again: "Aside from being one of America's gamest birds, the dove is also one of the very finest that ever graced a dinner table." Signed P. R. Lilly, Valdosta, Georgia.

I recall an advertisement from the excellent shooting preserve, Ivy Lodge, at Lumber City, Georgia, a place which is long on its feature of quail and turkeys, but which stated somewhat as an afterthought: "Join several other sportsmen on a dove field, the toughest test for any wingshot marksman. When they come to feeding grounds at top speed, there is probably no other game bird that stimulates an equal excitement in the hunter."

Indeed, this is no bill of goods I have to sell. Several years ago, I ran across a piece by Jules Ashlock, in an old issue of *Sports Afield* magazine, which pleased me immensely. Here is an excerpt from it:

Why the long winged dove is not classed as America's finest upland game bird has always been a source of mystification to me, and to the thousands of sportsmen who know this beautiful creature for the extraordinary sport he annually affords. What strange reasoning has placed this wondrous feathered projectile below his inferior rivals surpasseth all understanding, unless it may be due to plain ignorance. These graceful gray fellows tower over the timid ground dwellers just as clearly as the trout outglamours the catfish, or the tarpon the shark.

While any game bird might duplicate one or two of the dove's extraordinary qualities, none comes anywhere near combining his rare mixture of charm, showmanship, beauty, and personal daring. He boasts to an unbelievable degree every trait one might desire in a sporting bird or animal. Coupled with his streamlined body and sizzling speed are such attractive matters as accessibility, perfect hunting conditions, and a hardy breeding stock which has successfully met the inroads of gunners and agriculture.

It seems to me that the key word to the whole matter is the one with which Mr. Ashlock began the portion of his article which I have quoted: "*why?*" No writer has ever attempted to answer that question fully. But I am going to attempt it here.

A portion of the answer, of course, is obvious. The mourning dove—our main legal species—breeds over such a wide area, and in such scattered numbers, that in the North he never gives the impression of being tremendously abundant. When fall comes, however, he migrates south, where hundreds of thousands of doves are pressed into smaller areas according to the lack or abundance of good feeding conditions. Throughout shooting history, wherever a bird which was good eating and good sport has been abundantly in evidence, it has always become a local favorite. Thus the mourning dove very early became a top game bird in the South. Meanwhile, in the North, our population, our communication facilities, our publishing business, etc. were becoming more and more concentrated, far ahead of the South. It was therefore inevitable that the doings of sportsmen in the northern portion of the U. S. should receive far more book, magazine, and word-of-mouth publicity than those of the South. In addition, the vacation trend has always been northerly until the recent decades of wintering along the Gulf Coast and so the grouse, the pheasant, etc. received the major applause, while only trickles of publicity came out of the South.

It is logical that a New York State wing shooter, who sees only a few scattered doves during nesting and is unaware of their wintertime southern concentrations, should be surprised and disbelieving when told of the sizzling qualities of the dove before the gun.

Such reasons, however, are but a small part of the real dove story. No other bird—game, domestic, or song—has such a wealth of historic tradition behind it. None even comes close.

As I see the picture, mankind has related himself to the doves and pigeons in three large, distinct, and somewhat overlapping and interrelated historical trails. There is, first of all, the deeply significant religious importance of doves throughout the ages. You will find in many places and especially among Negroes in the Deep South the ancient superstition that it is bad luck to kill a dove, that particularly for the killing of one of the little southern ground doves a lifelong curse will fall upon you. Some people, both Negroes and whites, will tell you soberly that every time you kill a dove a drop of blood will appear upon your gun barrel. Others will inform you with the deepest sincerity that a dove's veins contain a certain proportion of human blood. To the people who believe them, these legends are serious matters.

The second dove-mankind trail through history is also on the nonsporting side, blazed by the ancient marks of the pigeon fanciers, the pigeon racers, the trainers of carrier pigeons, the millions who simply keep pigeons around because they like to watch them. These millions are placed, along with those holding the dove sacred or near-sacred, on the opposite side of the tracks from the place where the sportsman's pigeon was born.

It is in greatest part the sportsman's pigeon which has carved the third trail down through history. Once those three historical trails and their interrelationships have been traced, there need be no further *why* regarding the dove situation of the present day. So let us now follow these three intriguing trails, in order that we may eventually have a clearer picture of this bird and his relationship to sport and conservation.

In almost all parts of the world the dove is a symbol of love, gentleness, and peace. These conceptions stemmed from the symbolic and sacrificial use of the dove in Biblical times, and even much earlier. And so deeply impressed have these conceptions been upon all Christian and many non-Christian peoples that they have become seriously established realities in the mind of man.

The dove of peace bearing its olive branch originated, of course, with what is probably the best-known dove story in the Bible, that of old Noah and his Ark. The Arab version of Noah and the Ark, to which was added some fanciful material not found in the Bible story, appeals to me as being especially interesting. According to the Arab legend, after the dove had brought the olive branch to Noah she was not taken into the Ark but, depositing her message, flew away on another trip. After some time she returned once more, her feet covered with red mud. This proved to Noah that not only were the tree branches above flood height, but also that the bird had found it possible to alight on solid ground. According to the legend, Noah prayed therewith that in honor of this occurrence all doves might have red feet from then on. And oddly nearly all doves of the world *do* have feet of a pink, red, or purplish hue!

Strangely, even in some of the older, non-Christian countries, the dove was anciently, and still is today, held inviolately sacred. It was Mohammed's claim that the counsels of Allah were imparted to him by the dove. Thus, to Mohammedans, all doves and pigeons became sacred, and are still used today in many religious ceremonies. Early in this century, a couple of European youths who were in Bombay killed several pigeons in a city square. When the news got out markets closed, as did the stock exchange, and workers milled around threatening to strike. Before the incident was over a near riot had to be quelled. You can delve back into history thousands of years and still find evidence that the pigeon was sacred.

It is in the Christian Bible, however, that we unearth the strikingly important uses and symbolisms of the dove which have come down to the present day. The dove, even in the dictionary, is understood everywhere to be "in Christian symbolism the emblem of the Holy Spirit."

Chastity, purity, inoffensiveness toward men, beauty, gentleness, all of these qualities and many more were invariably symbolized by the dove. Other references to its habits and characteristics were constantly used in similes: mourning like doves; fleeing like doves; wishing for wings like a dove. The teachings, the similes were constantly repeated. And their effect settled into the gross consciousness of mankind. Yet behind the use of the similes there were some very interesting practical aspects.

There were, as everyone knows, offerings prescribed under Old Testament law for use during cleansing rites, as for lepers, or following childbirth; burnt sacrificial offerings; sin offerings. Since the law applied to all people, it would touch upon both rich and poor alike. A man who must bring an offering to the temple priest might be rich enough to utilize a lamb. But, again, there were many who were so poor they would have been cut off completely from compliance with the religious law if a lamb had been the *only* acceptable offering.

Thus the law was sensibly written so that accessible offerings might be utilized. And, since few birds might be procurable in the desert, and the doves and pigeons were among them, a select few of these common birds were made acceptable. In addition, from very early times pigeons were kept in a state of domestication. Even very poor persons were able to have a dove cote, and thus these domestic pigeons, in addition to the wild turtledoves which were migrant, were among the few birds allowable as offerings under the law. It is interesting to note that the burnt offering and sin offering brought by Mary the mother of Jesus, for the cleansing ceremony after the birth of Christ, consisted of two turtledoves, an indisputable proof of the humble and poverty-stricken condition of the family.

It is of special note that Moses made the law doubly reverent by ordering two turtledoves *or* two pigeons (fowls were always offered in pairs), for a very special reason. Migrant turtledoves appeared in Egypt and Palestine in winter, and were always exceptionally good eating, no matter what their age. But the local pigeons, if old, were often tough and not considered fit eating. Thus, if the season made turtledoves unavailable, local pigeons might be utilized for the offering. But when turtledoves were in season it was necessary that they be used, especially when no young pigeons were available. For Moses had perceived that it would not be proper to offer to God that which would be rejected as unfit by men.

Churches and pigeons have always been found in association. One of the most famous examples is the square in Venice in front of the Cathedral of Saint Mark. Here, decade after decade, great clouds of pigeons feed in the square. The spot is, indeed, almost as famous for its pigeons as for its cathedral. Likewise, Saint Paul's in London, although the hundreds of London pigeons got themselves into trouble some years ago by pecking away at the mortar between the cathedral stones with such persistence that the portico of the building was finally deemed unsafe. After a good deal of discussion the city authorities decided the pigeons would have to go, at least all but a few of them. But, when the time came to destroy them, lo and behold a law turned up which had been on the books in Parliament for ages, rigidly protecting them. A Parliamentary session had to take up the matter before a single pigeon could be touched!

No other bird of any species, and especially no other game bird, has ever had such a deeply religious significance. Yet this purely religious tradition is no more unusual than its general history as it touches human progress. Beside it, the background of the quail, the grouse, the pheasant, the waterfowl, or even of the domestic chicken, pales into completely unromantic oblivion.

Before the dawn of what we know as history, men were already breeding fancy varieties and, it is suspected, also racing varieties. The love of pigeons seems to have been universal, and had no definite starting place geographically. Seldom do archaeologists dig, or historians fit together the jigsaws of ancient human records anywhere without turning up some evidence of the appeal of pigeons to mankind. Although the shroud of ancient history has blotted out the beginnings of domestic pigeon cultivation, there begin to be records of authority somewhere about 4500 B.C. By 3000 B.C. the pigeon was well established as a domesticated bird. And, strangely, all domestic pigeons are fairly well known to have originated from the single ancestral form, the wild rock dove, which still exists in mountainous parts of Europe, Asia, India, and along the rocky coasts of England, and very nearly to type in our city streets today. It was Darwin who first suspected this relationship and who, by breeding and crossing, proved it.

Undoubtedly the original appeal and use of pigeons was for food. In time it was discovered that the birds were rather peculiarly adaptable to selective breeding, and that infinite variety in color and form could be thus obtained—various combinations of colors, unusual feathery adornments such as heavily feathered legs and feet, head decorations, fantails, etc. Such pleasing forms undoubtedly intrigued the breeders so that many birds were saved from the table simply to be admired for their beauty.

It is easy to understand, therefore, since the historical line of pigeon appeal has never been broken even down to the present, that it must certainly have touched billions of people, leaving its undeniably sympathetic impression. It was, therefore, unthinkable—though entirely illogical—in the minds of many people that a man should kill a dove or pigeon for sport.

The use of pigeons for aesthetic purposes was probably the least of the many influences. It was discovered very early that the homing instinct so well developed in this group of birds could be most useful to mankind. Just as correspondents in the last war sometimes had to send their copy out of frontline zones by pigeon, the news of the Olympic Games was delivered to Greek cities in the same manner. When Gaul was successfully conquered, the first official news reached Rome by pigeon. From 43 B.C. onward, history is full of the pigeon's records in warfare.

Peaceful uses were also conceived to which the homing instinct might be put. An actual pigeon post was established as early as 1150 by the Sultan of Bagdad. This operation was repeated many times down through the centuries, until other faster and surer methods replaced it. As late as 1849 a portion of the distance between Berlin and Brussels was without telegraph lines, and so messages were sent to the end of the line where pigeons picked them up and bridged the gap.

About 1878 we in the U. S. began thinking in terms of pigeons and warfare. Birds were tried in the Dakotas, but hawks killed most of them. They were then experimented with along the Mexican border and at Key West, still with little success, although Germany was already building up an excellent pigeon battalion. Finally, in 1917, Pershing insisted that we get something constructive done with carrier pigeons, and the U. S. Army followed his order admirably.

World War Two really brought the carrier pigeon into his own. Carried in tanks, airplanes, jeeps, on the backs of men and of war dogs, pigeons—some 54,000 of them trained by the Signal Corps—were constantly successful in saving thousands of lives. Publicity given to these pigeons and their feats was bound to help build up, quite illogically, a tenderness of attitude in the mind of the general public toward all related species. In such ways has it come about that many persons learn with a kind of shock that the dove is a game bird of unusually excellent qualities. Most of them cannot tell you *why* the idea is hard for them to get used to. It is something left in the consciousness by the long hammering of history.

There are two important attributes of the dove group which we must constantly contact down through all facets of history: streamlined shape and speed of wing. Over and over, these are repeated in practically every one of the manifold uses to which the birds have been put. Parallel with the history of the pigeon as a general carrier and as a specialized war carrier, the streamlined-shape-and-speed-of-wing appeal crops up from earliest times onward in the development of the racing pigeon. For centuries, of course, there was nothing formal about pigeon racing. Its organized inception began in Belgium, which has for many years led the world in development of the sport.

Centuries before, the Chinese had conceived what might, by a far reach of imagination, be considered a variation in that they took great delight in watching the graceful flight of their pigeons. But the tangent they followed was not one of more and more speed. They fashioned, instead, extremely light and ingenious whistles made from bamboo tubes, or of tubes and gourds combined, and these they attached to the tails of their best fliers by means of tiny copper wires. Although such whistles appear terribly clumsy, the Chinese are adept at making them so light that the pigeons have no difficulty in flying with them at top speed. As the wind blows through the bamboo, whistles of varied tones are produced. So fond did the Chinese become of this music in the air—which, they claim, keeps the flocks from becoming scattered and also discourages hawks—that the manufacture of pigeon whistles became a rather excellent business in Peking.

The Belgians went to great lengths to breed birds which could go faster and faster. Soon pigeon racing had spread so swiftly that bird owners came from all over Europe to try their birds against those of the Belgians. In 1818 the first really organized race took place, the course being one hundred miles. Half a century later we in the U. S. began testing the sport, and by this time the European races had been stretched to as much as five hundred miles.

Due to the fact that our railroads were well integrated and widely spread over much of our territory, pigeon racing in the U. S. was given a tremendous boost, for the birds could be easily shipped for long distances and allowed to fly home. At the turn of the century, courses had been lengthened to as much as 700 miles, and birds had made that distance in a single dawn-to-dusk day! Breeders were beginning to discover the unique fact that the homing instinct would respond to careful breeding.

By the early 1900's we were well on our way toward becoming a nation of pigeon racers ourselves. Top enthusiasts had upped the course distance to a thousand miles, which had been covered by the champ in one day, eleven hours. There were records of birds that had flown one hundred miles at an average speed of ninety miles an hour, and of one racing pigeon that had found its way home almost seventeen hundred miles!

The dissension which was bound to exist between sportsmen and others is brought into sharp focus by two old photographs that I came upon recently. One shows a group of pigeon-racing enthusiasts in England releasing five thousand pigeons at one time from several railroad boxcars. The other shows the huge gathering at a sportsman's pigeon shoot at about the same time. Both groups, obviously, had chosen their birds because of the same previously mentioned attributes, yet had representatives of the two groups met at the same pub afterward, undoubtedly reciprocal mutilation would have ensued!

Unquestionably the sportsman's pigeon was born of the ancient necessity for food. By the time Rome had set the pace of civilization people had veritable towns built on city roofs, in which thousands of pigeons were raised and fattened for the table. In later years these dove cotes were extravagantly copied and refined in France, England, and Scotland. Some of the most beautiful of old architectural conceptions have been expressed in them. Many, still standing, are huge, beautiful, and elaborate stone affairs, capable of housing hundreds of birds.

In Rome men were hired for the special purpose of chewing bread until it was a paste, after which it was crammed down the necks of squabs to fatten them quickly. The legs of the squabs were broken so that they could not move, and would therefore waste no energy that could be turned into fat. Breeders soon began to bicker among themselves, and those who broke squab legs began to wrangle with those of more aesthetic taste who went to the open-air theaters carrying their favorite fancy pet birds on their shoulders.

The squab raisers continued their business on down even to our day, but it has finally dwindled into a weak industry due to the fact that little money can be made from it. Meanwhile, however, as more and more efficient weapons began to be developed, wild doves and pigeons were acquired as food, and man began to thrill to the pure sport of hunting with the eating of the game as an added though less important attraction. The streamlined shape of the dove made it appealing to watch in flight, and its swiftness of wing lent a real gamble to the chase. Yet, so common was the meaning of dove and pigeon in the mass mind that these birds were seldom thought of as game birds even then. The grouse, which was *only* a game bird and nothing else, came to be spoken of as such. But the pigeon, which was many things to many men, remained a pigeon.

In England, the same excellent flight of the pigeon made it a natural for the training of hawks for falconry. Putting pigeons to such use, said the racing-pigeon breeders, was a scandalous practice. Simultaneously, in far-off Pacific jungles, plume hunters were taking the filmy crests from the large and beautiful goura pigeons and selling the skins of brilliant fruit pigeons. Or again in England, game keepers were systematically killing wood pigeons and ring doves so that food might be saved for the master's pheasants—while the neighbor who raised his fancy birds or his racers looked on, violently angry.

And then, at last, the gun came entirely into its own and the practice of the live-pigeon shoot drew enthusiasts by thousands, while raising a roar of protest from the protective side of the tracks. Without question much of the protest was justified, yet oddly enough the live-pigeon shoot was instrumental in giving us one of our most popular gun sports of today, clay-pigeon shooting. During the last half of the past century, the live-pigeon shoot in England and Europe rose to amazing popularity. Often thousands of birds were killed at a single shoot, and it is undeniable that the practice founded something of general disrespect for the living target.

During this same period, the great massacre of the passenger pigeons was being carried on in this country. The live-pigeon shoot found its way here, and now for the first time wild pigeons—rather than those raised domestically—were used to a great extent. Meanwhile, in the South, great shoots of mourning doves over baited fields were being held by the wealthy planters and market hunters. The centuries of varied pigeon history had by now begun to congeal, so that the camps of the purist pigeon lovers and the pigeon sportsmen were split and marked off once and for all. History of mankind versus pigeons had made it necessary to choose one's position on one side of the tracks or the other. The wedge was being driven deeper and deeper, the superstitions were taking a firmer grip, the "helpless" dove character, purely imaginary, was being publicized. It was now impossible to be of a neutral opinion. You either sanctioned dove shooting or you didn't. Logic meant little.

Finally live-pigeon shooting was outlawed in the U. S. The passenger pigeon bowed out in extinction. The law stepped in a little way to ease the southern mourning dove situation. The audible dissension subsided into quiet, but the impressions were still left.

Just *why* the idea of shooting a lightning-winged mourning dove was a thought to be forbidden while the shooting of a quail was to be countenanced, no one quite knew for certain. But the stigma was there. The dove of dissension had become a definite reality—one ready to do more harm than good by withholding from the doves the full light of hunting publicity which might eventually turn upon them the brighter light of sound and diligent conservation.

The pigeon has given us even more than something to quarrel about. He has put more words into our language than any other bird or beast. To name a few: pigeonhole, pigeon-toed, pigeonwing (a fancy dance step), dovetail, meaning to fit together neatly, stool pigeon, meaning one who rats on a buddy. In return we have given to the dove a series of personalities, some authentic, some falsely based on weakness. Could it be that the dove is perhaps not the weak, entirely lovable, pitiable character represented by our *romantic* dove of dissension? It certainly could. The conception of the dove personality-of-weakness-and-pity is the greatest hoax ever to find its way down through history.

Weak? Recall that the dove is still with us, almost unaided for centuries, while other species decline. The dove, as we shall see in later chapters, emerges in many ways as one of the toughest characters as to stamina among our game birds, exceptionally rugged in his relations with adverse weather conditions, adaptable to any terrain, temperature, and feeding conditions, with a wonderful endurance in flight and a most flexible adaptability to varied circumstance, and almost completely immune to fatal diseases in the wild. Pitiable? Any dove would secretly chuckle at the idea of pity, for by attracting pity by his general inoffensiveness he has shrewdly made friends who assist him toward continuance. Entirely lovable? Neither more nor less so than any other bird, no more or less placid or quarrelsome than any other. Doves are, in fact, simply sturdy, robust, well-integrated and adjusted citizens of nature, worthy far more of healthy respect than of pity. It is only their seemingly sad voices, added to those two attributes upon which we have so constantly harped—beauty of line and deftness of flight—plus the uses to which these attributes have been put by opposing factions, which have caused mankind to create his own dissension in the doves' behalf.

But here, now, is the point at which we as sportsmen may take a well-deserved bow. For it is not the *sportsman* who has made up out of whole cloth a character to be foisted upon this swift-winged fellow. The legitimate dove gunner has always taken the dove at its true worth, refusing to fool himself into considering it a sad and helpless woodland character. And this straightforward character evaluation by the sportsman is basically what has drawn the sparks from the more formal and romantic side of the tracks where live those fanatics who put words in the mouth of the dove. I do not believe anyone but a fanatic would seriously contend that the religious symbolism of early times should exclude the dove from the game-bird list. To point up the proof; although the dove was used sacrificially and symbolically in Biblical times, it was still hunted for food and raised for food during the same period. Again, surely no one could contend that the pure beauty of doves and pigeons, and their general uses as racers, carriers, etc. should exclude them from the game-bird list, any more than the beauty of a grouse should likewise delete it.

If we were to excuse the dove from putting in an appearance before the gun purely on the old beneficial songbird principle, then we should have to excuse all other game birds too. If we were to excuse him because of his size, we would also have to excuse the quails, which weigh about the same, the rails, the woodcock, and the jacksnipe. If we were to protect him from the gun because of a plea from the sewing-circle type of bird lover, we would be doing him a disservice, for it is well known in this age that those who do most for the birds are the sportsmen. The fanatic type of general bird lover does, and has always done little but talk his way through the centuries, using his hands for wrathful gestures rather than for any really worthwhile conservational work. And last, if the dove should be kept off the list of game birds by certain factions because these factions consider him helpless, either they are not hunters at all—or at least not dove hunters—or entirely confused thinkers. Certain it is that they know less about doves than they should, for the dove, during his migratory season, is just about the least helpless winged creature any gunner ever missed!

Specifically, just what *does* the dove have to offer which makes him so dynamically deserving as a sporting personality? The answer: a mixture of practically every excellent attribute of all other game birds rolled into one. If that sounds like a large statement, I ask you only to keep an open mind while, before leaving this opening chapter, we briefly sift out the ingredients of that mixture. For by that means will we begin to see the dove as a new kind of bird from that which many of us have always considered him, a far more rugged, realistic, and interesting individual than would be suspected from the weak-sister mock-up character with which he is usually burdened. It is the *real* dove character—game-bird character par excellence, if you please—which I would like to have you carry forward into the following chapters.

What is a *game bird?* According to a dictionary at hand, it is "a bird hunted or taken for sport." Another definition I have run across, but the origin of which I've failed to note, is as follows: "a bird which is palatable and which takes to wing at the distant approach of man." Surely our dove fits these definitions very nicely. The truly basic standards by which we judge the relative merits of various game birds are, it seems to me, the relative speed of getaway, and erratic line of flight.

The dove, with his brilliant speed and his dipping, rolling flight, takes the very highest honors here.

Now some comparisons, the better to high-light the dove's truly wonderful and unusual game qualities. First of all, from talking to many sportsmen, especially northerners who have never hunted doves, I find that their surprise at being asked to consider the dove as perhaps our *very best* game bird stems from the fact that they see the bird, in summer during nesting time, as a bird so tame as to be inconceivable before the gun. The thinking here, as can be easily shown, is so completely illogical that it needs clarification. The dove, as it happens, has very cleverly adapted himself to the ways of man. He will nest in orchards, near dwellings, or in village trees in preference to the wilderness because he has learned that food, and very often complete protection may be had in such locations. The dove has studied us, I think, far more than we have studied the dove, and his cunning knowledge has paid off. Yet I can take you to hundreds of farm communities throughout the country and show you quail running in farmyards, pheasants skulking within gunshot of back doors, rails and wild ducks nesting in potholes past which the plow and the reaper run noisily in their seasons. In other words, all game birds except those whose natural habitats are in deep woods commonly consort with man. The only reason the dove appears to be more tame is that being a tree dweller, he is always in greater evidence. The rails you will never see unless you search diligently. The quail and the pheasant you may almost step on, yet they will run through the grass and give no evidence of their presence except their morning and evening calls. But all of them, during the nesting season, are certainly little if any more wary or wild than the dove which makes its constantly cooing presence unescapable. Come hunting season, however, and with all birds, at the first gunshot wariness is immediately instilled. The dove is no different.

As to the qualities the dove has to offer as compared to waterfowl, he matches them, first of all, in speed of wing. He easily betters them in erratic flight. A duck is the most even-coursed bird in existence, and a very large one compared to the target the dove presents. Thus, if we are to assume that the difficult target presented by a game bird is the prime measure of its merit to the true sportsman, then the dove leaves the waterfowl far behind. Yet he offers exactly the *types* of shooting offered by waterfowl: pass shooting, jump shooting, and, at water holes or feeding fields, shooting exactly comparable to gunning over decoys. In fact, he can even be called in to actual decoys! However, while offering all of this miniature waterfowling, he throws in a double bonus of pleasant hunting circumstances that no waterfowl can match: to wit, easy dry terrain, and no prerequisite of nasty weather. In addition, where waterfowl—and almost all other game birds—must be hunted in specific locations, because of their specialized habitat requirements, the dove is so fabulously spread over his territory that in almost all states where he is legal you need take neither long trips nor make expensive and complicated preparations, but simply shoulder your gun and strike out *anywhere* over the fields. In other words, while I would not wish for one moment to do without the particular pleasure of waterfowl shooting, I believe it must be admitted that the dove gives one everything waterfowl can offer plus far greater accessibility, more comfortable hunting, and a much more diffi-- cult, and therefore in theory at least a more exciting, target!

Dove hunting offers one other sporting item exactly like waterfowling. Ducks are difficult for many hunters because they are, in pass shooting at least, always limned high against perfectly open sky. This makes correct range judgment much more difficult than in shooting quail, or grouse, or pheasants. The same is true, exactly, of the dove.

I do not think woodcock shooting and dove shooting can be compared very well. The woodcock is an extremely slow bird, while the dove is one of the swiftest birds at which we point our guns. Actually the only tough problem in woodcock shooting is to avoid the mental confusion of the thick cover in which the birds are flushed. You can get roughly the same with jump shooting doves in standing cornfields, yet, though

I am a woodcock addict, it must be honestly admitted that the woodcock offers only a single kind of shooting thrill, while the dove offers any kind you wish. He does, in fact, offer a greater variety of shooting than *any other American game bird*.

When we begin to compare the dove to the strictly upland game birds, we unearth one more superlative dove point: he is the *only* upland game bird that will come to the gun. Each one of the others must be sought out by the hunter and flushed. The cover, in addition, must often be finely combed for other birds to discover whether or not they are present, while the dove, being a constant flyer, is easily located if he exists in the hunting territory at all.

Of the quail, the grouse, the pheasant, etc., each offers only its one specialized thrill. The dove can be hunted as a substitute for any one of them and still retain his own inimitable personality, his grand and rather miraculous mixture. He is far more difficult to hit than any of the other upland birds, for he presents a speedier, more erratic, and smaller target than pheasant or grouse, while simulating, in either open cover or when taken on a pass in fairly open woods, the habitat of each, or either. Though his size is roughly comparable to that of the quail, bobwhite and his relatives do not come even close to dove speed, and their flight courses are invariably stable as against a dove course quite unpredictable at any given speed.

What more could possibly be asked of a game bird? What more could a game bird possibly have to offer—especially one which is, in this age of swift, economical transport, easily available to a greater mass of hunters than any other, one which can never be monopolized by any special groups divided by geographical circumstance or financial standing? Indeed, if the strange prejudices from out of the history of dove dissension are but put aside, if the hunter will but approach the dove with an open mind, study him, get to know him intimately through a few boxes of shells which draw a startlingly meager number of feathers, he will find one of the greatest, most varied, most highly exciting thrills in the world of gun sports. He will find, too, a game-bird character that is tough, wary, shrewd, so determined he will, amazingly, always run a barrage headlong rather than taking the easy way out, a character wonderfully pleasant to do business with in the field and delicious to do business with at the table—a character wholly and startlingly unlike the one history's inane pampering has embedded in the mass imagination.

Chapter 2

WHISTLING WINGS

I N THE YEAR 1505, a Portuguese navigator named Mascaren-
has sailed his ship eastward around the Cape of Good Hope
at the southern tip of Africa, swung north along the East
African coast, touched at Madagascar, and then headed aim-
lessly out into the great unexplored stretch of the Indian
Ocean. Five hundred miles out in the watery wastes he came
upon an unknown land, a small, irregularly elliptical island
roughly thirty by forty miles in dimensions, a tropical land
of mountains cut by streams which were in the hot, dry season
little more than rivulets, and in the season of rains and violent
hurricanes raging, torrential rivers.

It was a curious island, having no inhabitants, and no sign
of any kind that humans had ever set foot on it previously.
When the explorer and his men began to comb the island
closely, they realized that no mammals whatever dwelt on
it, with the exception of a large fruit-eating bat which was
abundant in the forest. There were, however, a few birds and
among them, on this bleak dot of land that in time was to
become known as Mauritius, was one of the strangest birds
which has ever been known upon the earth.

It was chiefly of interest to its discoverers and to all those
who followed during the next century, because of the unbelievable ridiculousness of its appearance. Here, without question, was the most grotesque bird mankind would ever see. It
was a forest bird, about the size of a swan, but certainly with

nothing swanlike in its structure or demeanor. The Dutch, who came later to Mauritius, called these birds *Walgvögels,* which was to say, nauseous birds, chiefly because no possible way could be found, on this island where food was scarce, of preparing them for the table so that by any stretch of imagination they could be considered palatable to the taste, or tender past a stage comparable to bull hide.

The bird was possessed of a squat, potbellied, dumpy, and hideously awkward body. Its short plumage was dark ash gray and black, the breast more or less splotched white, the wings yellowish white. Its yellow legs, short and stout, were as clumsy as its body. But on either end of this poor victim of nature, in a careless and bungling mood, were its crowning glories of grotesqueness. The bill was a positively huge black monstrosity that terminated with an immense hook of pruning-shears proportions, and the tail was naught but a sparse and tiny tuft of short plumes that added to nature's already grievous insults by curling up cutely and nonfunctionally above a bare backside.

It may be that the first of these birds which the astonished explorers came upon was sitting sedately upon her single large, white egg, laid upon its mat of grass. But, when the men drove the puzzled bird from her nest, she did not run. She waddled, barely making a go of it. And when they chased her, intent now on catching her for closer examination before she could fly away, they discovered that catching her was a simple matter. Amazingly, her wings amounted to little more than a suggestion of those worthy appendages, a few vestigial bones and barely-feathered quills, instruments so tiny and atrophied that they would hardly have lifted a quail from the ground, let alone this ten- to fifteen-pound study in quaintly comical repulsiveness.

Indeed, the bird refused to fly because she could not. Like all her kind, she was flightless, a condition little to be wondered at, since from time immemorial she had had no enemies to cope with. Her grotesqueness was undoubtedly the result of a life lived without knowledge of fear, with nothing to do over the centuries but eat, sleep, and reproduce peacefully. Because of these conditions the old biddy had, as they say, just let herself go.

This strange creature became known to later settlers on Mauritius by a word which in English meant *fool*, or *fool bird*. The dogs of the natives chased the poor dumb creatures about the forests, killing them at will. The hogs, which the settlers had brought with them in some numbers, didn't seem to mind the fool bird's flavor or toughness. They chomped down eggs, young, and adults whenever they came upon them.

At last in the year 1681, on this island whose environment had built them, and the only place in the whole world where they were ever known, the very last specimen of this strange bird was clubbed to death. This creature was given the dubious honor of being one of the very first to be wiped from the face of the earth by civilization. But oddly, in passing into extinction, the fool bird, or as the original settlers had called it in their language, *duodo*, had left behind a phrase destined to pass down through our language to the present day. For it had become, as we so often say of current issues which suddenly lose their importance or appeal, as dead as a *dodo*.

If anything about the dodo was ever more strange than his looks, then it is the unique paradox by which he earns himself a place here in these pages. The story of the dodo didn't quite end, you see, with his extinction. Very nearly two centuries after the dodo had become as dead as, an English scientist named Owen carefully examined some bones that had been dug from a pool of mud on Mauritius. The doves and pigeons had always been described by ornithologists as the most beautiful birds in form and delicate coloring known, yet Owen's meticulous study of the dodo bones from the Mauritius mud pool proved conclusively what other scientists had suspected for years. The world's ugliest bird had been nothing more or less than a ponderous pigeon!

Let us now move out into the Indian Ocean some 350 miles from Mauritius. Here we come upon Rodriguez Island, once the only known range of another very strange bird character, the solitaire. This fellow stood almost three feet high, was quite as flightless as the dodo, to whom, apparently, he was a long lost cousin. The vestigial wings of the male solitaire each bore a bony knob used for defense or for fighting other males. This bird also became extinct, about 1761, soon after men and their dogs had discovered its comparative helplessness. It, too, as has been proved by the study of skeletons found in Rodriguez limestone caves, was a peculiarly specialized member of the pigeon tribe.

The next exhibit necessitates a great leap across to Australia, and far out into the Southwest Pacific to the Samoan Islands. Here we find a bird still very much alive today, the strange tooth-billed pigeon, which occurs only on two small islands in the Samoan group. It is probably the nearest living relative of either the dodo or the solitaire, and has been able to continue its existence because, luckily, it can fly. Anciently it spent most of its time on the ground, even nesting there. But with the coming of the white man, who has always brought wildlife destruction with him, the bird was soon hard pressed and began taking more and more to trees, where it now nests, and through the low branches of which it now flies with extreme swiftness and dexterity.

To look at this bird you'd never guess it was a pigeon. It has a very large and powerful beak of a bright orange color, shaped and curved much like the beak of a parrot. It also sports a crest. In fact, seeing it perched in a tree, one would have difficulty in distinguishing it from a parrot.

Certainly no one of the three birds so far described has the slightest significance for us as American sportsmen. But I have given them the honor of heading this chapter for a very special reason. It has always been somewhat of a pet notion of mine that most of us have an altogether too-scanty background knowledge of our game birds, animals, and fishes. Indeed, most of our specialized sporting books, even in this modern day when a fabulous amount of information has been gathered and recorded here and there about practically every creature on earth, fail to take into consideration the fact that a thorough and mildly scientific account of any sporting subject's family tree gives a certain pleasure and pride to the gunner or angler.

A detailed filling in of numerous background facts gives a definite placement in our minds to the subject with which we deal, a placement in relation to its own close kin, and to the natural scheme of things as a whole the world around. This knowledge, for its own sake, is an enjoyable thing. It lends a far greater aura of magic to participation in outdoor activities. It sets the sportsman up before his cronies as something of an authority, giving him stature—and what human, pray tell, has such sturdy discipline of character as to find the taste of his own ego bitter in his mouth?

All the small facts, the quaint bits and pieces of knowledge, are also often useful equipment to the individual sportsman in his thorough understanding of the sort of wildlife character in direct question. And thus I propose to have you keep in mind the kind of personality we have already discovered in the sportsman's dove while we take a world-wide look at his family. I believe we may thereby turn up some facts of interest, many of which will serve further to clinch our thesis that the dove is not in the least the frail, self-sympathizing weakling of popular legend and tradition.

Just what sort of bird is the dove, from the ornithologist's point of view, and what is his place in the world of birds? Certainly he is so far removed in appearance and habits from the dodo, the solitaire, and the tooth-billed pigeon that they must stand out as gross oddities on the lower branches of his ancestral tree. That is precisely why they appear here, for a list of the doves of the world runs to the surprising total of some 550-odd species, and of this large number there are very few which you would not know at a glance as belonging to the tribe. The great scientific order of the *Columbiformes*, or the suborder *Columbae*, to which the doves and pigeons belong, is outstanding among such classifications as one of the most closely knit groups of birds in existence. But it is not quite the kind of bird group which we in the U. S., who know intimately only the small and conservatively colored mourning dove and a few other species, might suspect. It has some gaudy and exotic surprises for us. And, too, when we begin to delve into the relationships of the *Columbae* to other birds, we turn up some rather startling information. As links in this chain of relationships, the dodo and his odd partner in extinction play rather an important role.

Let us then begin by establishing the exact spot at which this great bird group, the doves and pigeons, takes its place in the family tree in which roost all the birds of the world. Keep in mind that the interrelationship of bird orders and families is a very complicated and not always entirely clear-cut science. However, if we were to begin with only those birds —well known in our own country—which, though highly specialized in adaptation to their own environments, are still closest to primitive bird forms, we would start off with the grebes and loons. If from these basic birds we worked upward in the scale of bird development from lowest forms to highest forms, the list would look very roughly, and with many omissions, as follows:

Lowest	Grebes and Loons
	Gulls and Terns
	Petrels and Albatrosses
	Cormorants and Pelicans
	Ducks and Geese
	Flamingoes
	Herons and Bitterns
	Cranes, Rails, Coots
	Shore Birds (Snipe, Plovers, etc.)
	Quails, Grouses, Pheasants, Turkeys
to	DOVES AND PIGEONS
	Hawks, Owls, Vultures
	Parrots
	Cuckoos and Kingfishers
	Woodpeckers
	Hummingbirds and Swifts
Highest	Thrushes and nearly all songbirds

I have based this list on the classification used in the standard book, *Birds of America*.* Not all classifications entirely agree, of course, but this one will serve our purposes. By

* Prepared under auspices of the University Society, published by Garden City Publishing Co., Garden City, N. Y.

looking at this list we can easily see how the doves and pigeons stand well up in the bird world as regards high development. We also see some other revealing indications. First, they are intimately related to the group just below them, the pheasants, quails, etc., the group to which our common barnyard chicken belongs, or, scientifically, the gallinaceous birds, of the order *Gallinae*. But now look directly above the doves in the development scale and we find our supposedly sad and docile seed-eating fellows also closely allied to our most ferocious bird group, those birds of prey, the hawks, etc.

Going one step further up the scale we discover the parrots. If we now go back to the strange Samoan tooth-billed pigeon (who, remember, is related to the dodo and solitaire), and examine him closely, we find that he, like all true pigeons, secretes in his crop the substance known as pigeon milk upon which the young squabs are first fed. But if we knew our parrots thoroughly, we would also find among them several species which secrete a like substance, which I suppose in their case would have to be called "parrot milk." And so somewhere along this trail, if we were to dig deep enough, we would find a close relationship far back in geological time between doves and parrots. It is exactly as if the bird family tree, as it grew, branched off into various categories whose members became more and more specialized and different from their origins as time plodded slowly onward.

We can also find a great many indications that the doves and pigeons are extremely close to the group two steps lower, the stilt-legged shore birds. In general structure, for example, and especially in the type of bill possessed by each, these two groups show their intimate affiliations out of the past. The link is closest along this line, perhaps, with the plovers, whose digestive organs, and whose bills—in which the nostrils are placed in soft skin at its base—are quite dovelike.

This sort of bird study is intriguing in many ways. Odd it is, indeed, to consider when you see a jacksnipe or a plover flushing from his wet and muddy marsh, that the mourning dove, slashing swiftly across Arizona's high, cactus-studded deserts, is his cousin but slightly removed. And I think, too, that these considerations lead us to visualize dove character as a mixture of several other kinds of game-bird character which we have fixed in our hunters' minds.

If we were therefore to think of the doves and pigeons as being placed in the center of an imaginary circle, the perimeter of which is formed by groups of their nearer relatives we could, this far in our study, then draw a radius leading to the parrots and label it the tooth-billed pigeon. We could draw another line to the shorebirds and label it the plovers.

There would, of course, be many other bloodline possibilities showing relationships with other bird groups either near or far away, but the most important and emphatic ones, for our purposes, would be those lines leading directly and distinctly to the gallinaceous birds—the grouses, quails, etc. Of these lines there are many, some of them joining birds so dovelike and at the same time so grouselike or quail-like that it is difficult for the casual observer to guess to which group the birds in question belong. A look at these strange, beautiful, and exotic creatures gives us a wholly new facet of dove personality to add to that which we have already in mind. Let's examine several of the more conspicuous examples among these arbitrary characters.

First, I think, should come the sand grouse, or, as it is called in India, the rock pigeon. This unique bird stands in a position which we can best visualize as exactly half way between the grouses and the doves. In truth, he is neither strictly grouse nor strictly dove, although the scientists have seen fit as a rule to give him the benefit of the doubt by lumping him in with the whole order to which the grouses belong. Certain scientists, however, have placed him with the pigeons; others have given him the honor of a category all his own.

The sand grouse—of which there are several species—is a dweller on plain and desert in many parts of Europe, Asia, and Africa. It is a bird some fifteen or more inches in overall length, its general shape very dovelike, its feet feathered like those of a grouse, its head and bill much like those of a dove, its tail and wings likewise. Oddly, though it is a ground bird with extremely grouselike habits, its flight is almost identical to dove flight, powerful, sustained, and the bird is migratory. In China, sand grouse which often gather in great flocks, prior to southern migration, are taken in nets just as the passenger pigeon was once taken in America. On the vast Russian Steppes their melodious chuckle as they take flight, a note about midway between the cackle of a grouse and the cooing of a dove, is a common sound. Yet, instead of alighting promptly after being flushed, as is usual with flushed grouse, these birds warily circle a proposed landing place exactly in the fashion of a pigeon.

During a hunting trip to Africa, Walter Wilderding, writer and artist familiar to many an outdoor-magazine reader, was struck by the amazing disappearing act of which the sand grouse is capable. He related how great flocks made up of hundreds of birds could be seen circling along a shoreline where there was little cover. Once they alighted, so protectively colored are they that on open ground one could search in vain to spot a single bird. Then suddenly the birds would be flushing with a roar on every hand, their conservatively colored chestnut and gray underparts set off in blurred contrast against the bright yellow of the throat, and the penciled spangles of yellow and black across back and wings.

If we now move up a step closer to the true doves we can find in many parts of the world, and even in the southern-most fringes of our own territory, birds which are actually doves, but which are so quail-like, or partridgelike, that it is as if they had had a difficult time of it trying to make up their minds which to be. These are the quail doves, the partridge doves, and the crested and plumed doves of such far places as Australia. Most of these fellows have the unmistakable cheek markings of the quail or partridge, a white decoration known to bird students as white malar stripes, running under the eye like that on our bobwhite quail.

To my mind these birds are among the most interesting species hanging around the edges of the game-bird clan. They spend practically their entire time on the ground, usually in dense cover exactly like that loved by quail. They run with striking swiftness through the underbrush, like quail or partridge. Most of them nest on the ground. They flush like quail, and are in fact so quail-like in stance, habit, appearance, and often in markings that were it not for their structural characteristics, and their quaint—and often astoundingly loud—hooting calls, they might as well have been called quail. The Australian plumed dove, for example, bears wing, breast, and eye markings startlingly reminiscent of some of our western quails, and wears a crest quite like that of the western scaled quail (cottontop), except that it is longer.

If we move now from these small doves to the very largest of the pigeons still in existence, we find one more striking evidence that the doves and the gallinaceous birds are extremely close kin. This fellow, the victoria crowned pigeon, is a native of New Guinea and a few other South Pacific islands near New Guinea. Certainly no one would take this bird at first sight for a pigeon. It is as large as a turkey, exceptional specimens running to as much as three and one half feet in overall length! The eye is brilliant red, the breast and back are several shades of beautiful blue. Across the breast there is a diffused half-circle of reddish pink, with more of the same on the upper-wing surface, bordering a large patch of white.

Upon its head this bird wears an immense though delicate, filmy crest, the feathers nearly bare throughout most of their length, which may be as much as eight or ten inches. At the tips they somewhat resemble the feathers of a peacock's tail, except that there are no eye spots, the squarish tips being blue with a border of white. This is one of the dove species which suffered greatly during plume-hunting days. It is a regal-looking bird, one much in evidence in zoos, and much sought after by fancy-pigeon breeders. But it can hardly be visualized through the hunter's eye as a pigeon, for as it struts and skulks on the ground through the jungle growth of its native habitat, it must surely appear much like our native wild turkey in fancy dress.

Those few outstanding examples serve to emphasize an important fact about the pigeon tribe: not only is it very closely related to all those other birds which have for centuries been thought of as game birds, but in the scale of development its members stand *above all other game birds!*

So now, since the relationships are so close, how shall we go about setting the doves apart? That is, what few salient points of physical structure and daily habits bind the doves and pigeons together, making of them the closely knit group previously mentioned?

Perhaps the most infallible rule for identifying a member of the group would be to observe it as it takes a drink of water. Doves and pigeons are unique among the world's birds in that they drink like horses. They simply immerse the bill and suck in draughts of water without removing the bill from the water until they've finished. All other birds scoop up a billfull, then tip back the head to let it run down the throat.

Remember that we are dealing with a very large group of birds (over 550 species as noted), scattered throughout the temperate and tropical portions of the entire world, and you will immediately recognize the fact that the above characteristic, and those which are to follow, set it apart perhaps more definitely than any other bird group. For example, the second important attribute of all *Columbiformes* is the interesting manner in which the newly hatched young are fed. About the time breeding takes place, a change occurs in the cellular structure of the parents' crops. There is a breaking down of the cells that form the crop lining. This degeneration forms a liquid which, when mixed with the light, small seeds and soft material such as berries, eaten by the parents when the squabs are first hatched, is called pigeon milk.

There is an old saying that you can walk up to any bird's nest except that of a dove and the young will open their mouths to be fed. If this is completely true, it is because the young of doves thrust their bills into the bill of the parent, rather than vice versa. The pigeon milk is regurgitated by the parent, accompanied by a jerking of the head and flexing of the wings, and the young, continuing to hold their bills within the parent's bill, take their food. The formation of pigeon milk takes place in the crops of both male and female, and both assist in feeding the squabs.

In nesting habits, the pigeons and doves exhibit traits that are peculiar to the entire world-wide group. The nests are always of the most careless and flimsy construction, usually built of a few twigs so loosely woven together that often the eggs can be seen through the bottom. The number of eggs laid is either one or two, the color white, cream, or in rare cases buff, always clear and without spots. Male and female share the incubation duties, congenially working shifts, so that each may have its opportunity to feed and relax and find water each day. Nestings take place several times each season.

It has always struck me as odd that the doves should never deviate from this habit of laying such a small number of eggs, when other game birds to which they are so closely related always lay large clutches. But perhaps we may see here an evidence of the extremely wise planning of Dame Nature. Surely it would be a tough proposition for a pair of doves to supply pigeon milk to a dozen or more helpless, hungry squabs!

Let's have a look now at the general physical characteristics of the doves. Almost without exception they are birds of unusually streamlined basic contours, the tail generally fairly long, the head and neck small and exceedingly graceful. The bill has a fleshy covering at its upper base, in which the nostrils are placed, and this covering, along with a patch of naked skin surrounding the eye, is often of a gaudy color. The body of the dove is always smoothly molded, compact, plump but never dumpy or fat. The feet and legs are trim, dainty, and it is of interest to note that the toes are so placed as to make it easy for the birds either to perch, or to forage on the ground, where the greatest share of their feeding is done. The feet and legs, if you'll recall the Arab legend from our first chapter, are almost always some shade of red, from carmine to pink to purple. One perverse group of small foreign doves, however, had to break up the quaint pleasantness of both the legend and the rule by having legs and feet that are, of all colors, bright green!

It is when we come to the wings of the doves all over the world that a hunter or a lover of birds can really turn on full admiration. They are always long, graceful, and powerful, pointed, flat, some of the most wonderful mechanisms fashioned for speed and flight dexterity that you can find anywhere among birds. The rapid, quick beats, with a snapping of the flight feathers at the take off, and a whistling sound in full flight or on the turns, have thrilled all mankind for centuries. Yet I like to think that of all dove admirers, we hunters appreciate this snap and whistle of wings, this almost shocking adroitness of flight, to the greatest degree.

In my younger and more studious days, when there was more time for reading and study, I jotted down a verse from Vergil that had been put into English translation by John Dryden, the English poet. Recently I dug it out, and now I set it down here as an example of the universal thrill of dove flight.

As when a dove her rocky hold forsakes,
Rous'd in her fright her sounding wings she shakes;
The cavern rings with clattering:—out she flies,
And leaves her callow care, and cleaves the skies:
At first she flutters:—but at length she springs
To smother flight, and shoots upon her wings.

Perhaps a bit high sounding, but for a hunter, who knows better than any other person what the flash of sizzling wings means, it paints an indelible picture.

One very odd physical requirement of doves is salt. No one seems sure as to just why the doves and pigeons appear unable to do without a large amount of salt in their diets, but it is well known that throughout the world they search constantly for salt springs, and, when their habitats are near ocean beaches, always take at least a portion of their water from the surfline. To the best of my knowledge, no other group of birds shows such a decided evidence of salt requirement.

In general feeding habits, the doves and pigeons are seed and berry eaters, although some species also relish certain kinds of insects, worms, and mollusks such as small snails. Thus, they do a great share of their feeding on the ground, and their bills are soft, horny only at the tip, as opposed to the hard bills of such birds as the parrots. The bills are also very often of a bright color, even gaudy red.

Dove plumage is exceptionally dense, but the feathers come loose very easily and the skin is extremely tender. This is a good point for the hunter to bear in mind, for though doves may pluck easily, if you hurry the job you may wind up with some very mangled-looking birds.

Add to these general attributes the fact that all dove voices are of the cooing variety, and you have a fairly good idea of the *Columbae* of the world. However, there is a great variation in dove calls from species to species, even though the basic *coo* might describe roughly the timbre of them all. The pitch, modulation, and volume of the calls of different species is a study in itself, and an interesting one. Some species hoot like owls. Some give forth explosive bursts of peculiar syllables such as *hoo, prrr-oo, kaaao*, etc., while at the other end of the gamut of sound the softest and most plaintive of cooing is heard. One of the most amazing and comical experiences it is possible to have in listening to dove voices is to get first an auditory and then a visual introduction to the blue ground dove. If you picked up a large bottle and blew in it, you would get a fair representation of this tiny dove's call. But, amazingly, he manages such a loud vocal exhibition that at a distance it sounds exactly like the reverberating bellow of a bull! To hear the sound coming from a thicket or from a cage in a zoo, and then to trace down its source, is to get the surprise and laugh of a lifetime.

At least two further general characteristics of the *Columbiformes* are described by their names: dove and pigeon. The word pigeon comes from Latin *pipio,* which means literally a nestling that pipes. An almost exact translation was often used, and still may be, by English pigeon breeders who called the squabs pipers or squeakers because of the sounds they make when begging to be fed. The word dove, which was once old Anglo-Saxon *duva,* originated from the verb *dufan,* from which came our modern verb *dive.* People had observed the motion of a dove's head as it walks, a forward and backward bobbing peculiar to all the species. *Dufan,* the verb, indicated this particular kind of motion, and thus a dove was a bird that bobbed its head as it walked, as if it might dive at any moment.

To be certain the reader understands one particular point, I want to repeat here something that was touched on in the first chapter—that there is absolutely no distinction to be made between doves and pigeons. Some species have simply been called pigeons, some doves, and those terms have stuck. It is not true that doves are the smaller species and pigeons the larger, as is so often thought. Any of the *Columbiformes* could be either except for the dictates of common usage.

Even the scientific term for the great order of doves and pigeons describes the general *type* when its origin is explained. Anciently, a kind of crypt in which bodies were preserved in Rome was called *Columba*. It was a sepulcher with niches in which cinerary urns were placed. The common rock dove, very similar to our present-day homing pigeons and not to be confused with the "rock pigeon" (sand grouse), was one of the first pigeons raised domestically. It liked to nest and perch in little niches among rocky shoreline cliffs. From observation of this habit, people built dove cotes for their domestic pigeons, but what we call a dove cote they called a *columbarium*, or, literally, a little house with sepulcherlike niches in which the pigeons might roost. From *columbarium*, of course, came the scientific name for the suborder of doves and pigeons, *Columbae*, and the family name of all true pigeons and doves, the *Columbidae*. And if you'd like to carry it further, to see one more instance of the way these birds have wormed their way constantly into our language, note the noun *columbine*, a "dovelike flower," or the same as an adjective meaning dove-like.

Now, leaving generalities behind, we can look upon the world of the doves. Though we are in the habit of thinking of them—because of our knowledge of the mourning dove, the homing pigeon, the western band-tailed pigeon, and the extinct passenger pigeon—as birds of the temperate country-sides, we now discover that the doves are primarily birds of the tropic jungles. Of the hundreds of species, less than twenty (and this includes subspecies and geographical races) occur in the U. S., while all of North America can show no more than one hundred species and most of these, remember, are in hot Mexico and on down to Panama, since the doves are never found in very cold climates or in Arctic regions.

The same situation exists in Europe. The British Isles and the temperate Continent each have their few species, all as conservatively and daintily colored as ours. But if we were to journey into the West Indies, for example, we would begin to be startled by the gaudy flashes of dove's wings in tropic undergrowth, by exotic species numerous and unbelievably varied and brilliant on every hand. On down into South America the same would be true, except more so. And then, if we were to pass on across the world eastward to Africa, to the Indo-Malayan region, to Australia, the South Pacific Islands, and the Malay Peninsula proper, we would find ourselves in the very midst, at last, of the empire of the doves. Here, indeed, is the center of dove population and origin, with infinite variety, hundreds of species, and with the most amazingly gaudy feathered designs and patterns it is possible to find anywhere in the bird world. These prolific doves truly rival the parrots and macaws, and even best them, for though their talkative relatives may have distinctive, clean-cut brilliance of pattern, they lack the many-color combinations, the niceties of design, the daintiness of pastel patternings of the gorgeously variegated tropical doves and pigeons.

As we witness the endless flashing of spectrum hues through the dank jungle, the thorn bushes, the deserts, along the bayous, we realize that here is a true dove paradise, and a hunter's paradise, too. We begin again to question the weakling character which man has foisted upon the dove. It strikes us that we have been unable to find any part of the world, outside the prohibitive Arctic, which does not have its doves and pigeons. Can it be that the "timid" dove—which has made its way from its point of origin in the Pacific tropics clear around the entire temperate world, adapting itself in various phases to mountain, to desert, to plain, to jungle—is perhaps one of the greatest *adventurers* of all wild creatures? Can it be that by abundance and endless variety, adaptability, shrewdness, determination, and downright *toughness*, the dove has plied the crafty trade of continuance on a grand scale, chuckling at those more highly touted species which, declining with the progress of civilization over the whole world, have been the real weaklings? I believe that it can. Living like all other wildlife, under the pitiless, brutal regulations of survival of the fittest, this supposedly pitiable adventurer has slyly wormed his way into our sympathies, while proving himself one of the most fit of all! And nowhere does he point up the proof of it more emphatically than with the eye-music of brilliant colors flashing everywhere in tropic thickets.

It is now easier to see what sort of willful character that gray bullet called the mourning dove carries with him before the gun, what kind of ancestral stamina, stubbornness, and bountiful tradition—glossed over by riotously colored cloaks of feathers which would put his to shame—stretch around a whole world behind him. Look at it like this: the hundreds of brilliantly colored dove species leading to our conservative gray mourning dove are like the flaming tail of a swift comet. And that comet's tail marks the path back across the centuries to that long-ago time when the dove sprang, full winged, sky and distance free, imaginative, and aggressive, from the narrow, earth-bound confines of his *really* pitiable relatives, the grouses, pheasants, and quails, to the limitless skylanes of all continents.

You will recall from our first chapter mention of the fact that the mourning dove will fly through the barrage from a line of guns rather than flaring away or turning back. This is not the act of a timid spirit, or of a stupid personality, but of a game-bird character well aware of his wing prowess, an awareness which he backs perhaps with overconfidence. The fact is, this same trait is the one that has made carrier pigeons useful in wartime. They never went around, they went *through*, paying little attention to the guns. The mourning dove is a chip from the same cool-nerved block. And if you would question whence comes his deliciousness on the table, you can learn—with what envy!—by going back once more to the tropic jungles of his ancient ancestors, what hunters there have known for centuries: that the rainbow-hued fruit pigeons of Malaya and the southern islands are, of all birds in the whole world, authoritatively stated to be the most delectable in taste and texture of the flesh.

Major Dave Harbour, whose writings appear steadily in *Sports Afield,* gives an excellent picture of a hunt for tropic doves in his story "Supplementary Rations," which appeared in that magazine in June, 1945. Harbour was stationed on New Guinea with the Air Corps during the war. Tired of corned beef and K-rations, he managed to get hold of a Japanese .22 rifle and shells. One day, keen both for sport and a change of diet, he left his fighter squadron base and stalked into the jungle, remembering the dove hunting in his home state of Texas. I quote a condensed excerpt from his description of the adventure.

All the New Guinea jungle looks alike. Giant trees reach 200 feet into the sky, their branches supporting a solid mass of vines and plant parasites that stop the sun at the jungle roof. On the jungle floor a tangled mass of giant roots runs crazily in every direction, and over them is thick, clutching green undergrowth. But the jungle is beautiful in its own way. The brilliant colors of its parrots, pigeons and doves, and the breath-taking beauty of its flowers, make it strangely exotic.

My first bag is a giant Torres Strait pigeon, far larger than our domestic pigeons, snow white with a fringe of black on its wings. I creep to within 15 yards of the bird before I can make out its outline in the thick brush. I study the outline of the bird in the moving branches. At last I make out its fine head plucking away at the purple, marble-sized berries which are abundant on the bush. I raise my rifle and wait until I catch the pigeon's head still for a second. I fire, and a fine meal for two fighter pilots falls from the bush. I place the heavy bird by the head on my belt as I once carried ducks in Texas, and with a feeling of real exultation at such early success with my .22 continue on into the unknown jungle.

Parrots of unimaginably beautiful color combinations flutter before me. More than once I have to stop and make sure that parrots are not doves, as the doves of the tropics come in as varied color combinations.

The next hour produces a half-dozen doves, all about the size of mourning doves. Two are identical in color with the mourning dove. Two are chubbier and bluish green, with an almost pure white head. These are the most beautiful doves I encounter. The two others are a deep rust color, their flesh so tender that great care has to be taken in feathering them. These, I find later, are the most delicious of all the doves and pigeons—as a matter of fact, by far the most delicious bird I have ever eaten.

Getting a gun on these birds is not as easily done as might be suggested by the great numbers of them, and by the thickness of the jungle undergrowth. Actually, the thickness of the undergrowth is not to the advantage of the hunter, as almost every bird fired at is screened by twigs and leaves which deflect many shots; and for birds that have never been fired at before these doves are almost unbelievably wary. Every bird has to be detected, often followed from bush to bush, and stalked as warily as an American mourning dove on the last day of the season. It is impossible to use a shotgun for wing shooting, due to the thickness of the bush, but shooting through the jungle brush with a .22 proves to be a sporting proposition and every kill is a real thrill.

The grand climax comes in late afternoon. I am moving hastily down the trail. Suddenly two great feathered forms shoot from beneath my feet straight up and out of sight in the brush above my head. I hear the drumming of their great wings stop almost as suddenly as it began, and know the strange birds have settled in one of the giant trees above the trail.

I cautiously creep down the trail. Almost a hundred feet above I make out the two great forms on a gnarled, vine-draped limb. From that range the birds look like hawks, but the movement of their wings in flight has told me they are game birds. I raise my rifle on the one nearest and fire. I know I have made a kill by the heavy fall of a great body. The other bird circles and comes back to light on the same limb. I draw a bead on him and fire. He falls through the thick vines, hitting the ground not three feet from the first bird. When I pick up these two birds, I feel one of those thrills that come but once in a lifetime.

The birds are great blue pigeons, *half again* as large as the Torres Strait pigeons! Their wings are banded in gold and green. Their breasts are almost white, with mottled black sprinklings. Their bills and feet are a beautiful red, and their bodies are as heavy as those of grown Plymouth Rock chickens. I have to this day been unable to find out what kind of pigeons these majestic birds are, even from Australians who had lived in New Guinea for years. That night the mess table is heaped with platters of steaming brown barbecued pigeon and dove breasts.

Before we leave the faraway foreign doves, I think it might be well worthwhile to glance briefly at a few more of them, particularly since they are so unusual in color and infinite variety, and so strange to U. S. sportsmen. Many of them are dynamic game birds, a fact to be kept in mind by the hunter who may possibly have the opportunity one day to travel in foreign lands, for they are much hunted and highly regarded, and will well repay the effort involved in taking a gun along. There is the big snow pigeon from Central Asia's mountains, an almost entirely white bird. There is the plumed wongawonga of Australia, a very large and curiously marked pigeon whose flesh is so delicious that for many years people have attempted rather unsuccessfully to breed it domestically. There is the Australian crested pigeon with its long, black crest, which it erects, at the same time raising its tail until tail and crest meet in a showy display. And the odd Nicobar pigeon, a strange unpigeonlike bird with a collar of long, lacy black feathers and a stance like a fighting rooster.

In Malaya and the South Pacific Islands, of course, is found the stunningly colored galaxy of dove and pigeon high society. Listen to a few of their names: the crimson-crowned fruit dove; the red-bellied fruit dove; the pink-spotted fruit dove; the rufous-brown pheasant dove; the many-colored fruit dove. Bright greens and yellows, crimson, purple, metallic blues and purples and lavenders all are delicately mixed with whites and grays, with spots and stripes and splotches. The velvet dove, the golden dove, the orange dove. The yellow-bibbed, red-throated, and superb fruit doves; the yellow-legged pigeon, the red-knobbed pigeon—on and on with seeming endlessness.

If these names seem like the exaggerations of an excited ornithologist, look at brief descriptions of a couple of species. Let us pick more or less at random the crimson-crowned fruit dove: wings, back, and tail dark green, with a band of yellow

The common city, or homing, pigeon, a nongame dove that stems ancestrally from the rock dove, found throughout the world. Its liking for building ledges and lofts comes from the habit of its ancestors of nesting along seashore cliffs. It is from this basic type of pigeon that our carrier pigeons, racing pigeons, and fancy varieties have almost all been bred.

John H. Gerard, from National Audubon Society

The ground dove, a small, rather tame, nongame species very common throughout the south, especially in Florida.

Samuel A. Grimes, from National Audubon Society

The large and beautiful white-crowned pigeon. Once abundant in Florida's Everglades, the Keys, and the Caribbean Islands, this nongame dove is now seldom seen in U. S. territory.
U. S. Fish and Wildlife Service, from McDermot, Deputy Warden, Key West, Florida

The Inca Dove. This small southwestern species, a nongame dove, is a bird of the desert, nowadays most numerous around towns, where it becomes very tame. *Pettingill, from National Audubon Society*

One of the few good photographs still in existence of a live passenger pigeon. The species presumably became extinct with the death of the last known specimen in the Cincinnati Zoo in 1914.

Photo from National Audubon Society

The mourning dove, "gray bullet" of the sky lanes.
U. S. Fish and Wildlife Service, by Allen M. Pearson

Mabry Anderson, Mississippi sports writer, illustrates how necessary it is to mark your birds down well. Note the type of cover—wonderful dove-feeding location but very difficult cover in which to find downed birds.

Mabry Anderson, Mississippi

Doves invariably drink at a completely open spot on pond or stream bank, usually, as in this photo, where small gravel is available.

U. S. Fish and Wildlife Service; by Allen M. Pearson

A clean hit for a Georgia dove hunter. This photograph illustrates the amazing stubbornness and determination doves often show before the gun. The hunter stands entirely in the open, yet this bird was one of a flock that ran a barrage of guns, dodging lead all the way but doggedly following their course. This one finally met a gun that judged its pace properly.
Charles Elliott, Georgia

Shooting the evening flight in Arizona. The hunter has just knocked down one of a high-flying pair. On the desert, where distances between feed and water and water and roost may be long, the birds usually fly high and really pour it on. Here pass shooting is at its best. Note that the hunter stands quietly in the shade of a tree, all the concealment necessary for this type of shooting.
Charles C. Niehuis, Phoenix, Arizona

The mourning dove, eastern subspecies. Note the darker color as compared to the western mourning dove. This photo shows a typical southern nesting site in southern long-leaf pine.

U. S. Fish and Wildlife Service, by Allen M. Pearson

The mourning dove, western subspecies, is very pale in color. Note the usual flimsy nest and its location at the top of a hollow stump.

Russell T. Congdon, from National Audubon Society

Mourning dove squab just hatched. Youngsters are covered with yellowish down. The other egg is pipped and will hatch within twenty-four hours.
U. S. Fish and Wildlife Service, by Allen M. Pearson

Six- and seven-day-old squabs. Now the tail feathers of the elder squab begin to show up well. Wing feathers always develop fastest, for it is the wings that will be needed first.
U. S. Fish and Wildlife Service, by Allen M. Pearson

The squabs are fed pigeon milk by thrusting their bills into the bill of the parent. Both parents assist not only in incubation of the eggs but in feeding the young. Often, as in this unusual photograph, both squabs feed simultaneously from the same dish.

U. S. Fish and Wildlife Service, by Allen M. Pearson

Ten- and eleven-day-old squabs. Squabs are almost always of the same sex in each brood and are hatched from eggs laid on consecutive days.

U. S. Fish and Wildlife Service, by Allen M. Pearson

Twenty- and twenty-one-day-old squabs, out of the nest and taking a last look at home. When seasons open in early fall, many immature birds such as these are killed. Such birds are useless for the table, since they are at their thinnest for the first few weeks after leaving the nest. Late seasons give such birds an opportunity to develop, not only in weight but also in agility of flight. This gives them an even break against the gunner and makes them far more sporting targets.

U. S. Fish and Wildlife Service, by Allen M. Pearson

The graduated tail of the mourning dove, its trademark, showing feather color and arrangement. No other American dove has a pointed, graduated tail. *U. S. Fish and Wildlife Service, by Allen M. Pearson*

Band-tailed pigeon on nest in a pine tree, Prescott National Forest,
Arizona.   *Floyd Schroeder, U. S. Forest Service*

An Arizona hunter knocks down a bandtail among the high mountain pines. Note smoke around breech of gun and ejected shell.

Charles C. Niehuis, Phoenix, Arizona

A "burn" in Oregon's coastal mountains. Such spots offer both food and nesting cover for the bandtail and often make good hunting locations, especially in the northwest.

U. S. Fish and Wildlife Service, by A. S. Einarsen

The whitewing, dove of southwestern deserts. The beak is more curved than that of the mourning dove, the tail though quite long is rounded at the tip, and when it is perching, the white of the wing feathers shows. The whitewing is slightly larger than the mourning dove.

U. S. Fish and Wildlife Service, by G. B. Saunders

Group of young whitewings. This photo plainly shows the longer, more steeply curved bill of the whitewing as compared with that of the mourning dove.

Courtesy, Lee Arnold, Arizona Game and Fish Commission

Huge concentration of whitewings on the Arizona Desert.

Arizona Game and Fish Commission

Whitewings gathered at a desert tank. This illustrates what can be done to increase the whitewing population by building watering places near good nesting territory in the southwest. *Arizona Game and Fish Commission*

Most whitewing shooting is pass shooting with the birds flying high from roost to feed and feed to roost. This picture was taken on a rise near the Santa Cruz River just outside Tucson, which is one of the most famous whitewing pass locations in the U. S. Birds flying out from the nearby mesquite forests to the desert and fields for feeding have followed this pass for centuries and been hunted along it since the time of the Spaniards.
Arizona Game and Fish Commission

Close observation of whitewings in flight soon allows the hunter to identify them. Their wing beats appear slower than those of the mourning dove, and the bird sometimes coasts at intervals. The mourning dove has no white in the wing. *Charles C. Niehuis, Phoenix, Arizona*

across the end of the tail; top of the head crimson; throat and breast green and yellow-gray; abdomen with a large purple spot; thigh feathers green; belly and beneath the tail yellow, or red. And again, the pink-spotted fruit dove: head, neck, and breast pale gray-green, the upper part of the throat yellow; wings blue and green; back olive; shoulders with scattered pink spots; tail dark salmon with yellow tip; flanks yellowish green; feet red; bill light green; eye bright orange.

For a good many years bird fanciers in the U. S. have had as one of their greatest hobbies the raising in captivity of such gaudy foreign doves. Some of them cost fabulous prices when imported from their native lands, but it is easy to see how the colors and the varieties have had an effect which pries the fancier loose from his money.

Yet with all this extravagant beauty, we discover once more that doves are not exactly the entirely loving and till-death-do-us-part characters of legend and tradition. Many a dove fancier can tell you of fights between males or between females of the same species, or between different species, that to doves must really be knock-down-drag-out brawls. It is not at all uncommon for battles to continue until the weaker bird is dead. Some species are, in fact, so tough-minded and quarrelsome that they must always be segregated. And when it comes to the true-blue nature of dove romance, especially as regards the males, even though doves are in general monogamous they are certainly not adverse to a little philandering when the little woman isn't looking. Even when the female is incubating, and the male taking his turn in assisting her, he usually grabs at every opportunity, when he is freed from his share of the duties, to make determined passes at any pretty young thing who happens to be momentarily unattached. Wise he is, too, for with his legal wife tied down to the nest until he gets back to relieve her, he can carry on a bit behind her back without her ever knowing it!

If these observations don't clinch the fact that the doves are tough and rakish little *hombres*, it might be added that though they are not birds of the cold-weather zones, those of the moderate climates—such as in our own northern states—

can stand adverse weather conditions about as well as any birds known. As a matter of fact, recent tests conducted by the Army showed that while canaries, when subjected to continued temperatures around thirty-five degrees below zero, survived for very short periods (about 36 minutes), ordinary Army carrier pigeons were by comparison practically immune. Tough barnyard chickens lasted for about 20 hours, but the carriers lasted for as long as 78 hours! Pigeons have also been taken up in planes to 35,000 feet, where the temperature was forty-five below zero. Without oxygen tanks, or special protection from the cold, they shrugged the whole experiment off as all in a day's work, and none of them ever showed any ill effects thereafter. Man himself couldn't tie such a record!

Since it is the English who have always made the most of the doves as sporting birds, and since it is from the English that we originally conceived of them as game birds in our country, we might look very briefly at what the British Isles have to offer in the way of dove-shooting sport. The most popular British species is the ring dove, or wood pigeon, a fairly large bird some seventeen inches long. Its name comes from the large splotches of white that form almost a complete ring around its neck. It is an extremely shy bird, an excellent flyer, and though at times it has been classed, because of its numbers, as a nuisance to farmers, British gunners hold it in high regard.

Another species, the stock dove, is a bit smaller and not quite so well known to sportsmen due to its localized abundance. There is also the turtledove—the *true* turtledove of Europe, and not to be confused with our mourning dove, which is often wrongly called turtledove—a summer migrant. This is a smaller bird, somewhat similar to our mourning dove.

One of the best known of the English doves is the rock dove. This bird is of interest to us also, for it is the *type* pigeon, whose various races are scattered over almost the entire world, from which domestic pigeons were originally bred. This bird is an inhabitant of the rocky coasts of the British Isles. Here it nests among the high cliffs and lives about the beaches, often feeding on small shellfish and never alighting in trees. It is usually an extremely wary bird, and, from its wariness and its habitat, a rather strange kind of shooting was at one time popular in England. Gunners would drift along beneath the cliffs in boats, shooting at the doves when they flushed noisily from above. You can well imagine what a fine art it would be —the boat bobbing in the surf while the gunner tries to swing on such a swift, swerving target.

If we now cross the Atlantic, narrowing down our focus, it is well for the gunner who gets around a bit to keep in mind that some excellent and exotic dove shooting can be had in the islands of the West Indies, a quick plane flight from any point in Florida. Here in the islands, several of our own species overlap. The mourning dove, the white-winged dove, the white-crowned pigeon, and the Key West quail dove are examples. Some of the larger standard species of the island sportsmen are the red-necked pigeon, the plain pigeon, the ring-tailed pigeon, and these taper down in size to the Grenada dove, the white-bellied dove, the zenaida dove, and various smaller ground doves. In our own U. S. Caribbean possessions, the Virgin Islands, there is some very fine dove shooting to be had with several of these birds, and I suggest that travel-minded wing shooters make a note of it toward the time when one of those long-dreamed-of opportunities for an unusual trip comes along. And of course it must not be overlooked that below our borders, in Mexico, besides all of our own legal U. S. species one may find several fine foreign dove targets which never get far enough north to do more than straggle one or two at a time across our southern boundary. Mexico, in fact, has such an abundance of both species and numbers of doves that some of the finest dove shooting in the whole world may be had there, much of it not far below our borders, and often during months when all our shooting seasons are closed.

So now, with all of the material we've covered thus far, we should have in our minds a well-rounded general picture of the doves and their entire history and world background. Let us now get down to immediate focus by beginning to examine those species of our real personal interest, the doves and pigeons of the U. S. Perhaps we should look first, and briefly, at those species that are not legal game. It is of interest in rounding out our dove knowledge to know about these birds, and they are also important to the dove hunter in a somewhat negative way. That is, he must know at least enough about them to be aware of their ranges, so that he can be on the lookout for them when gunning for the legal species. And he must be able to recognize them when he sees them, in order to stay within the law.

The White-fronted Dove. This dove is unlikely to cause trouble or confusion to a hunter for the simple reason that it is seldom seen within our borders. There are several sub-species of the white-fronted dove, the one concerning us being a Mexican bird, progressively more abundant as one moves south from the lower Texas border. At times it may straggle into the very lower edge of Texas, along the Rio Grande. It may possibly come into southern Arizona, although I have never seen it there, nor have I ever heard it mentioned in connection with Arizona.

This bird is a little larger than the mourning dove; in fact, about the same size as the white-winged dove, of which we will hear much more later on. A good way to distinguish between the mourning dove and any other doves that look somewhat similar is to remember that the mourning dove is the only one of our doves with a long, graduated (pointed, or spear-shaped) tail. The tail of the white-fronted dove is fairly long, rather narrow, but squared at the end. It contains some white, but no distinct blotches of white. This fact—and the fact that there are no white patches on the upper wing coverts—easily sets it apart from the white-winged dove, either when it is perching, or in flight. The overall color is gray and brownish. The abdomen is dull white, and the forehead is very light. These are its tags of truce—so if you should ever be shooting either mourning doves or whitewings near the Texas-Mexico border, and should see them, hold your fire.

The Red-billed Pigeon. This is another species seldom seen in the U. S., one that appears only as a straggler in parts of southern Texas. Actually it is a pigeon of Central America, but the fringe of its range is in the lower Rio Grande Valley. It is a fairly large, chunky pigeon that looks, when perched, quite like our homing pigeons, though smaller. In its native haunts it is most secluded in its habits, but an extremely swift and powerful flier when flushed. It is a handsome bird, and looks dark in color when seen from a distance. The red bill from which it takes its name easily identifies it. And, since only the smaller, lighter-colored mourning doves and white-wings are legal game in the vicinity where this pigeon might be seen, it should give no gunner trouble by turning up as an illegal bird in his bag.

The White-crowned Pigeon. It is unfortunate that this fine bird is not today abundant enough to have a place on our list of legal game birds. Basically, it is a tropical pigeon of the West Indies and coastal lower Mexico to Panama. It is a beautiful bird, a chunky, compact pigeon of good size, usually almost as large as our homing pigeons. The entire body is slate blue, with the crown of the head white. There is some red at the base of the yellow bill. The feet are deep red, and there is usually a tinge of yellow along the sides of the neck, with the hind neck bearing a gloss of bronze and green.

This fellow ranges within our borders only on the Florida Keys, and in the Everglades. It nests in colonies, sometimes in trees hanging over the water, and was at one time a very important item of food for the hard-bitten seamen called the Key West Wreckers, who made their living by salvaging wrecks throughout the islands. The squabs were taken in great quantities from their nests, and the old birds killed by hundreds. This uncontrolled slaughter, and the cutting of nesting sites along the Keys and in lower Florida, brought the birds close to extinction, at least in our territory. This is an extremely shy and wary bird, seldom seen nowadays except when nesting flocks are glimpsed in summer flying along the edges of coastal islands, or deep in the solitude of the big Florida swamps.

Since the mourning dove is the only species legal in Florida, there is no danger of confusing the white-crowned pigeon with any legal game species. And, since the bird is somewhat rare in our territory and rigidly protected, purely out of principle no hunter should succumb to the temptation to shoot one should he come upon it. The consequences, also, would very likely be stiff indeed.

The Quail Doves. These birds could not possibly be confused with any of our legal doves. In fact, it's doubtful if in their extremely limited range most of us will ever even see one. I mention them simply for the purpose of rounding out our survey of species which can be considered as appearing within U. S. boundaries, and also because they are interesting birds in their own right.

In his main range, which includes the Bahama Islands, Cuba, etc., the Key West quail dove is called partridge, and indeed the bird acts much like one of the partridge or quail family, spending most of its time on the ground, in thickets or wooded areas, running like a quail, and flushing no more than necessary. Closely related species are also called wood hens in the islands.

The Key West quail dove is slightly larger than the mourning dove, chestnut colored on its upper parts, and with a white belly. The crown of the head, the lower part of the neck, and the upper part of its mantle are all glossy green, and the smaller wing coverts have a sheen of purple. The base of the bill is red, and there is a white quail-like face marking (malar stripe) running across the cheek beneath the eye. This bird was at one time fairly abundant during summer nesting on Key West and some of the other Florida Keys. But cutting of the trees reduced its numbers until today it is rather rare. It is doubtful if this species ever gets as far north as the Florida mainland.

The blue-headed quail dove is an extremely beautiful species, about the same size as his relative above. Whether or not it can be considered a U. S. dove is questionable. Audubon reported it from Key West, and included it among his paintings of American birds, but it is really a Cuban bird of dense lowland woods, where it lives much like a quail. It is possible, and in fact probable, that the bird may turn up now and again as a straggler in the lower Keys. The bird is almost entirely a very dark, rich brown, with pink feet, and with the crown of the head a striking and gaudy blue. There is a splash of black at the throat, outlined by a white border. And the usual white stripe so common among the quail doves runs beneath the eye. A daub of red at the base of the bill dresses this little fellow up most appealingly. Indeed, it will be of interest to hunters who become dove enthusiasts to have a look at these birds in museums or zoos, or in their home ranges if opportunity offers. They're truly strange and intriguing links between the doves and the quails.

The Zenaida Dove. This species has about the same history in U. S. territory as the quail doves. It is somewhat smaller than the mourning dove, with which it might possibly be confused, if a straggler should turn up in dove hunting range in Florida. Properly, this bird belongs to Cuba, the Virgin Islands, and other West Indian islands. At one time, however, it was known on the Florida Keys. The underparts are warm reddish brown, the back and upper wings colored much the same as those of the mourning dove. The wings and the rounded tail are edged with white, and there are several bluish markings on the side of the neck. To the best of my knowledge, it has been many years since this dove has been recorded in Florida. It is much like the smaller ground doves and quail doves, in that it spends most of its time on the ground in dense brush, usually even roosting at night on the ground.

The Ground Dove. This is a very tiny dove, only about six inches in overall length. Perching, it looks quite like a small scale model of a mourning dove, except for its rounded tail. But when it flies a very rich, warm chestnut color shows beneath the wings. As its name implies, the ground dove spends most of its time walking about in thickets. Its flight is seldom sustained, and is of a rather fluttering nature. Though likable little birds to look at, these tiny fellows are most quarrelsome as a rule, among themselves and with other birds. There are two subspecies, the ground dove proper, which ranges from the Carolinas southward throughout Florida, and the Mexican ground dove, commonly seen in gardens and around towns in the Southwest. I have watched these little birds by the hour while fishing in the Florida Everglades, and I'm fairly certain no one could possibly confuse them with the legal mourning dove, first because of their diminutive size, and second because of their tameness and lack of swift or long flight. This is the bird, remember, about which some southerners are so superstitious. If you kill one, it is said, certain evil will befall you.

The Inca Dove. This is a small dove of southern Texas, Arizona, and California. Long before that part of the country was pioneered, this eight-inch bird was a dweller in the cactus and mesquite of the dry Southwest. But, oddly, as the country was settled it began moving into town, so to speak, until today it is seldom seen in what could be called a completely wild state. In Tucson and Phoenix I have seen them many times sitting about in trees at the edge of a lawn, or walking about practically under foot in a yard or along residential streets. Usually they simply move out of your way rather than taking wing.

An inexperienced gunner might easily mistake the Inca dove for a small or immature mourning dove, but since they are as a rule so inordinately tame, it is doubtful if any but the poorest sportsman would shoot them. An easy way to tell the Inca dove from legal game is to keep in mind its small size, its fairly long but double-rounded tail, and the fact that its overall appearance gives a color impression of much more chestnut brown than gray. At close range, however, the Inca dove is unmistakable, for the feathers of its head, neck, shoulders, back, rump, and upper tail coverts are all edged with sooty black, giving the bird a very distinctive scaled effect. The Inca dove is a very pretty little species, but by no stretch of the imagination could it ever be considered a game bird.

Foreign Doves. At present we have two foreign doves on the West Coast, birds introduced by people who had been raising them as a hobby. Just what these species will eventually mean to sport, if anything, it is much too early to say. The birds in question are the Chinese spotted-necked dove and ring-necked dove. Both were first released in the vicinity of Los Angeles. At present they are well established both there and in San Diego. Through a biologist friend of mine now working on the Coast, it is my understanding that these birds have also spread north some distance. And he also informs me that as this is written someone has just released a hundred of the ring-necked species at Bakersfield, where they immediately began nesting. So far both birds seem to nest only in towns, and to appear very little, if at all, as truly wild birds of the country-side at any time of the year.

It will be interesting to keep watch of both species, and to see if they eventually spread out over the whole state of California. Undoubtedly if that happens the conservation people will become interested in them and their relation to possible shooting. Until such time, sportsmen hunting in the above vicinities should simply know their mourning doves and hold their fire on any strange-looking dove of which they're uncertain.

Homing Pigeons. Everyone is of course familiar with the homing pigeons so common in almost every city, and so often seen in small flocks about farms. To the best of my knowledge, it is everywhere illegal to shoot them unless they specifically belong to you as birds that you have raised and released on your property. When I was a kid in Michigan we always had a flock hanging around our barn, some of them from stock we had raised, and some that had joined up from other farms in the neighborhood. I recall that I was always wanting to try them on the table, but they were strictly taboo. I did help clean out a flock for a neighbor one time, however, and I must say that in full flight they were birds to try your skill.

As has been mentioned previously, these birds were introduced to America from European squab-raising or racing stock, and that ancestrally all such pigeons come from the rock dove, the type pigeon of almost world-wide distribution. It is interesting to note that these birds seldom, if ever, alight in trees. The stone buildings of our cities and the barns of the country-sides apparently replace the rocky cliffs upon which, centuries ago, the ancestors of these pigeons perched and nested. What a stubbornly inborn trait this cliff nesting habit must have been in order to have it carried down through thousands of pigeon generations to the present day!

Legal Species. At present we have three legal species in the U. S., all of which we will of course cover in detail in chapters devoted to each. They are the mourning dove, of which there are two subspecies, eastern and western, both of which look almost identical except to scientists; the white-winged dove, technically a Mexican desert species, which crosses our borders in numbers at certain rather definite locations in the Southwest, and of which two subspecies, eastern and western, are recognized; and the band-tailed pigeon of the entire West Coast.

I would like to mention here that among sportsmen the white-winged dove is always known simply as the "white-wing," the band-tailed pigeon as the "bandtail," and invariably when someone speaks of "the dove," or a "dove shoot," the mourning dove is meant. Thus, from here on, we will use the same terms, so that when the dove is mentioned, it will always mean the mourning dove only, thereby excluding the whitewing and the bandtail.

Our survey of the doves and pigeons, their history and general habits, has taken us around the world, brought us back home, and to the present day. But, with the discovery of those species which we can call our own, there is one great link still missing in the chain that has given us the marvelous sport of American dove shooting. That link is an intensely interesting bird character whom none of us will ever see on the wing, or train our guns upon. But because of the great influence of this amazing bird upon the history of the American scene, and upon present-day sport and conservation, his story must be told before we pass on finally to follow the sizzling flights of the mourning dove, the whitewing, and the bandtail over our gun barrels.

Chapter 3

EBB TIDE OF EMPIRE

IT WAS SUCH a day as we would commonly associate with that indefinite, between-seasons period known nowadays as Indian summer. From the scattered and ever present brush burnings, sweet smell of woodsmoke hung pungently on the drowsy air, and in those seaward distances not walled off, inhibited, or broken by the trailless forests standing everywhere inland, sun-touched translucent blue haze foretold with gentle stillness the inexplicable excitement of autumn. It was morning, early morning, with the sun, long slanted, cupping the night-nipped air in warm, bright hands.

For those who had heeded the call to worship, the day had begun properly with prayers beseeching a good future. Here and there men, dressed for hard labor in the scratched-out fields, passed and smiled and paused to speak of the fullness of the yellow-eared corn this season, the verdancy of its stalks; or they stood in small groups easily, implements aslant husky shoulders, drinking in the good feeling relayed to them by the visual evidence of their hard-won winter's security. Indeed, the yellowed patches showing myriadly and without pattern in the ragged forest, patches hacked out with sweat and now ripened full of English grains to tide the long and dangerous winter through, were a pleasure to behold. A man could not be blamed for lingering of a morning to have a last look at it in the stalk before moving upon it with scythe and cradle to lay it low.

From out of the north, slashing in from above the forest,
a swift-winged, streamlined bird came dipping and rolling
down across the settlement. A sun-burnished blue-gray meteor
with whistling wings, it coasted low, circling, skimming the
uneven rows of corn. It swept on, lower now, across a patch
of full-headed grain, trailing a swath of jetted wing-breeze,
leaving a narrow, nodding wake of yellow-ripe stalks behind.
The bird planed upward, circled again. Satisfied at last, it
dropped, let down pink feet, and swung in with a braking
of wings to settle in the patch of grain.

A man with a scythe had paused to watch it, following
its flight with a suggestion of homesickness in his gaze. "What
sort of bird is that?" he said, turning to his partner. "Reminds
me of last year at home. Just about this time, it was, when the
wood pigeons had started to gather."

"We see them often here," said the other, who had been
at Plymouth several seasons. "There's no pigeon in England
like it. Not that large, nor with a long, sharp tail. 'Tis a wild
pigeon, simply. That's what we call 'em. Wonderful they are
on the table, too. Good, gamey dark meat. Their abundance
here is a great blessing, let me tell you."

They passed on, unmindful of another bird rocketing in
over the treetops. And then another, both of which, sharp
eyed, scanned the scattered grain fields and at last slid down,
spread winged, to settle in them.

It was at noon, with all the men at home stowing away
lusty dinners, when the first rustling of far-distant thunder
whispered in through the open doorways of the colony cabins.
Some paused to listen, this fall noon of 1643, wondering that
a rain should come up so suddenly, and on this kind of day.
Some stepped to their doorways, peering out into the bright,
haze-hung sky, and turned back at last, puzzled, seeing no
storm clouds anywhere, yet hearing, still, the strange sound
that lingered on the quiet air, hearing the whispered rustle of
an ever growing, constant thunder.

Louder. More puzzling. Louder still. Not thunder. No trembling reverberations, but an incessant, increasing, swishing
roar. Then the great cloud hurtling from north-inland, rolling

with headlong hurricane speed from over the forest, graying the sun to dimness, battering noon brightness into eerie twilight.

People were running from the houses. Awed, they stood dumbfounded, their wide glances darting over the in-pouring circle of the great cloud that rushed from over the forest, their unbelieving gazes laid against the grain fields and the corn rows upon which the endless gray avalanche descended.

Some were struck dumb with the realization of catastrophe. Some found their voices and the cry went up, not with a sound of simple amazement, but with the timbre of fear ribbing it through:

"Pigeons! Millions of them. Millions of pigeons!"

There was movement now. Running. Frantic grasping of blunderbuss, club, scythe, stick—anything with which to make the charge, any implement with which to defend the precious and already flattened harvest against the in-rolling gray tide, the descending hordes of this awesome feathered empire.

But it was no use. A man might move among them, shooting, clubbing, killing dozens, hundreds, yet those a stone's throw farther on paid utterly no heed. There was an unearthly quality in their determination and aloofness. Though beauty was evident in their appearance, this daintiness of contour and color was belied by the manifestation of the devil which must surely dwell within. What matter if they were driven off today? Tomorrow no doubt they would come again to sweep up what few fallen grains they might have overlooked....

So begins the story of the strange and fabulous empire of the passenger pigeon. It had existed here upon the North American continent for who knows how long before the white man came, forged by ancient habit and delicately balanced prolificacy into an efficient feathered civilization, a communal association ruled by strict mass instinct. Its story is one of the most astounding incidents ever recorded in the natural history of the world. Nowhere else on earth was this particular pigeon species known, nor has there ever been a bird anywhere in the whole world, at any time during the history of mankind, so overwhelmingly abundant.

The most dramatic and classic example of this abundance is furnished by the notes of Alexander Wilson, the ornithologist, who witnessed a passenger-pigeon flight near Shelbyville, Kentucky, at the beginning of the 1800's. The sky was darkened. As far as one could see, pigeons were passing, their dung falling like snow, flock flying above flock in several stratas, and with a front so wide it appeared endless. By estimating the speed of the flight, the width of the column, the number of birds per square yard, and checking the number of hours it took for the flight to pass, he judged this single flock to be about 240 miles long, by several miles wide, with a total of almost two and one-half *billion* birds! Knowing that each pigeon would consume at least a half pint of beechnuts and acorns per day, such a single flock would require over seventeen million bushels of feed each day!

No other bird, and especially no other pigeon was so outstanding in individuality and character, color, form, strength and perfection of flight, nor was any other ever so unique in its communal habits. In addition, the bird was a perfect example of what we think of as the dove *type*. Undoubtedly these attributes have lent much of romance to the passenger pigeon's story.

It was somewhat larger than is generally supposed today. An adult male was about seventeen inches long. Graceful lines and the long, graduated tail gave the bird an exceptionally slender, streamlined appearance. The bill was black, the iris of the eye red, the feet and legs, as described by Audubon, "carmine purple." The sides and crown of the head were blue of a light, grayish tone, with the lower hind neck carrying a glossy sheen that changed in various lights to green, crimson, and gold. The throat and breast were rust-red, shading into white far back toward the legs. The back and upper wings were blue-gray, with the long wing quills bluish and black, and with several black spots on the coverts. The two long, center tail feathers were black, the other graduated ones on either side a very pale blue at the base shading into white down their length. The wing spread was rather startling, being upwards of twenty-five inches. The female bird was a bit smaller, her colors distributed much as in the male, but by no means as brilliant.

You can dig from old history books bits of the beginning of the passenger pigeon's story and how, as we have seen, during the fall of 1643 huge flocks so thoroughly wiped out the crops of the Plymouth Colony that these early Americans lived through the following winter constantly in the shadow of starvation. You can read how the crops failed five years later, in 1648, and how this time the hordes of passenger pigeons saved the same colony from starvation when the settlers killed thousands of them and smoked the meat for winter. You can read how great masses of pigeons so harassed Jesuits of the Gaspé region farther north during those early settlement years, that the priests received orders to exorcise them, that is, to perform the religious rite that cast out the devils by which the birds were supposedly possessed. As early as 1660, the passenger pigeon was being commercialized by market hunters. So common and so easily taken were the birds that they were selling then in Boston at an average price of only three pence per dozen!

Toward the end of the seventeenth century Virginia settlers were still sending back to England constant reports of pigeons "beyond number or imagination." Already they had discovered from the Indians the value of this fabulous natural resource as food. From time immemorial wherever the pigeons gathered to roost, the Indians had gathered, too. In many regions, especially the far north around the foot of Hudson's Bay—the point the pigeons reached in their summer nestings—whole Indian tribes subsisted, after the sturgeon fishing had subsided for the season, mainly on a fare of smoked or dried pigeon breasts. Some tribes, good conservationists, never molested the nesting sites. Others, however, gathered large amounts of squab fat which they used as we use butter. The squabs before leaving the nest were always exceedingly fat, larger by weight, in fact, than the parent birds. These the Indians gathered from the nests, and tried out the fat, storing it for winter. There are records of Indian encampments of no more than two or three families which had stored as much as a hundred gallons of squab oil during one gathering session!

During the 1700's hardy pioneers who began to push farther inland continued to note with awe and astonishment the abundance of the passenger pigeon on every hand. It is difficult in this era to reconstruct in writing the true picture of that abundance so that the words carry any conviction. It is as hard for the writer to conceive as it is to depict it for the reader, for the simple reason that we of this generation have never known wildlife sights even mildly comparable. What do a billion birds look like gathered together in one area? Who can say? To the pioneer clearing land in the Great Lakes region as the eighteenth century drew to a close, it was obvious that there could never be an end to the passenger pigeon.

By 1825 and onward, as more and more land was cleared and planted, though settlers found the pigeon a blessing for their tables they had begun to suspect that the blessing was a mixed one. For in fall, when wheat had been sown, or in spring when the buckwheat fields were planted, no sooner had the seed been broadcast than the land was blue with pigeons. An issue of *Forest & Stream* magazine of nearly half a century ago carried an article by a man named Sullivan Cook, which graphically describes the farmer-pigeon dilemma of the mid-1800's. I quote:

When I was a boy and living in northern Ohio, I often had to go with my gun and drive the pigeons from the newly sown fields of wheat. At that time wheat was sown broadcast, and pigeons would come by the thousands and pick up the wheat before it could be covered with the drag. My father would say, "Get the gun and shoot at every pigeon you see," and often I would see them coming from the woods and alighting on the newly sowed field. They would alight until the ground was fairly blue with these beautiful birds.

I would secrete myself in a fence corner, and as these birds would alight on the ground they would form themselves in a long row, canvassing the field for grain, and as the rear birds raised up and flew over those in front, they reminded me of the little breakers on the ocean beach, and as they came along in this form, they resembled a windrow of hay rolling across the field.

I would wait until the end of this wave was opposite my hiding place and then arise and fire into this windrow of living, animated beauty, and I have picked up as many as twenty-seven dead birds killed at a single shot with the old flintlock smooth bore.

One of the famous passenger-pigeon roosts of that day was along the Green River, in Kentucky. This gathering stretched for some forty miles, and was everywhere at least three miles in width. Bird dung covered the ground everywhere to a depth of several inches. There was not a single living tree or blade of grass anywhere. Trees were killed as though they had been girdled. The weight of thousands of birds roosting in single trees had broken many off high above the ground and often such broken trees were as much as two feet in diameter. Great limbs, snapped by the weight of the roosting birds, were scattered everywhere on the forest floor.

Here it was that Audubon saw hundreds of hunters gathered, waiting for the birds to return from their feeding. One group of farmers had driven a herd of some three hundred hogs over a hundred miles, bringing them to fatten at the roost site on birds which would be slaughtered and overlooked. According to Audubon's account, it was most impressive to be at the deserted roost, gazing about in the utter stillness at this forest that looked as if a tornado had swept through it. Then, toward midafternoon, a shout went up: "Here they come!"

Far off, the whisper of wings could be heard. Soon an immense front of approaching birds appeared in the sky. The sound of wings grew to a roar. A great gust of air swept over the forest as the birds closed in. The shouting of the hunters and the boom of guns was utterly lost in the tumult of the alighting legions. Tremendous concentrations of birds piled onto the stronger limbs in huge masses. Without any sign of diminishing, the birds kept pouring in, on and on until finally the sun went down. But still they came, and so on until well after midnight.

At dawn the roost was empty again, and now all manner

of predatory wildlife could be seen and heard—cougars, wolves, bears, 'possums, raccoons, foxes, and in the sky eagles, vultures, hawks—all of them gathered to make the most of this immense concentration of feathered food.

Another account tells how two youngsters had plainly heard the roar of wings from a roost three miles distant. They took a lantern that night and a big horse pistol loaded with shot, and went pigeon hunting. The birds had roosted in low alder brush at this particular location, and as the lads approached they saw what appeared to be stacks of hay scattered here and there in the brush. But the first haystack dissolved in noisy, confused flight as they came near. At the next stack, they fired the horse pistol. Birds by the dozen crawled off into the brush, wounded, and the lads picked up eighteen dead birds from this single shot.

Here it is interesting to note the effect of the pigeons on other wildlife. At all such points of concentration, predators of many kinds thrived numerously. Hawks, eagles, and buzzards were especially plentiful, for the pigeons were easily taken by them. Yet the pigeon concentrations had a shattering effect on noncarnivorous wildlife. The pigeons swept every bit of food so clean from the land that nothing else, except the predators which trailed them like camp followers, could exist.

They did not, of course, often feed close to their roosting places for the simple reason that a single day would scour the close-in countryside clean. Their system was to fly out before dawn in search of a feeding ground, and so strong of wing were they that great distances meant little. From the best estimates of authorities of the day, their usual speed of flight was about sixty miles per hour. It was said that they were capable of speeds upwards of one hundred miles per hour, but there seems to have been no proof that they habitually traveled at any such rate.

However, the mile-a-minute rate is well established. There are records of pigeons killed in the vicinity of New York City whose crops were bursting with rice. The birds digested their food completely within twelve hours after feeding, and so it was known that they must have fed on the rice during the morning of the day they were killed. It was thus estimated that they must have covered some three or four hundred miles in not more than six hours, for the nearest rice was grown in the Carolinas.

In their long flights in search of feeding grounds the pigeons evidenced an amazing keenness either of vision or of instinct, probably both. If the country over which they happened to be passing had little feed, the birds stayed high in the air, with the front of the flock very wide so that a great amount of territory might be surveyed. Audubon tells of having watched a flock pass over an immense stretch of beech and oak forest. In previous years the birds had fed there, but as it happened this particular year there had been no crop of acorns or beech-nuts. The birds passed on without giving the place a second glance! Yet, in all instances, when a flock came to a territory where feed was abundant, it immediately dropped down, fly-ing low, scanning the countryside intently.

Though they did not fly in any such formation as do water-fowl, the communal habits of the birds showed in strong and interesting ways in their flight patterns. If the birds leading the front altered course slightly, others would follow. Pres-ently there would be a huge curve in the flight, so that as it strung out for miles across the sky it looked like the winding flow of a great gray river. From time to time smaller flocks might come bursting out of the distance, running apparently head on into the main flight. But as they reached the river of birds, they swung and were dissolved by it and into it, smoothly and without causing the slightest commotion in the main ranks. When a hawk or eagle dived out of the sky and made his stoop into some portion of the flight, the birds did not scatter. They simply dived earthward, then immediately upward again as the danger passed, never deterred in the least from keeping their eyes fixed upon those ahead of them. Presently, shooting upward like a tremendous water spout, they would have gained the flight altitude again. But behind them, all following birds now described the diving arc which the attacked ones had made, all of them following this marked path as they reached it, down and then swiftly up, so that the effect from a distance was like a giant roller coaster fashioned from living, moving wings.

These great feeding flights were of course the signal for everyone along the route to seize guns and go after meat for the pot. It was a simple matter, at least when the flocks were over good feeding territory and thus flying low. James Fenimore Cooper, in *The Pioneers*, describes such a scene as follows:

So numerous were the birds, and so low did they take their flight, that even long poles, in the hands of those on the sides of the mountain, were used to strike them to earth. So prodigious was the number of birds, that the scattering fire of the guns, the cries of the boys, had no other effect than to break off small flocks from the immense masses that continued to dart along the valley, as if the whole of the feathered tribe were pouring through that one pass.

Hunters wrote, during that period, of firing into a passing flock and of picking up as many as fifteen pigeons from a single shot. This serves to illustrate how compactly the flights were carried out, and to prove, too, that those who wrote of flights "which obscured the sun, covering the earth with eerie twilight" were by no means exaggerating. If you have ever fired into a flock of birds without taking aim, you know how surprising it can be to see what you thought was an easy collective target fly on with no apparent harm done. Yet I have run on one record of a man who stood beside his field and kept firing without aim into a passing flock, and at the end of only a half hour of shooting picked up 276 birds!

Here is one more strange record. The birds came north very early to seek nesting sites. One such flock was caught in a bad sleet storm, with a high wind, and tried to take refuge in the sugar-maple grove of a settler. Such a grove was a valuable source of food to the pioneer, for each spring it supplied gallons of syrup and many pounds of sugar, which often could be had from no other source. This grove covered some twenty acres. The maple branches were hung thick and heavy with snow and ice. As the flight of pigeons swarmed in, branches cracked and broke. Tree trunks snapped. Within half an hour from the time the birds began alighting, the entire twenty acres was a shambles, every tree stripped and completely ruined!

The passenger pigeon showed an amazing hardiness as regards low temperatures. This is one of the few dove species that ever had a native range into the so-called Far North. It was extremely abundant around the Hudson's Bay district, and habitually stayed on there after nesting until well into December, when the ground was covered with snow. During this season, juniper berries formed the chief item of diet. This apparent immunity to low temperatures was noted as well in spring, for often the nests would be built while there was as much as a foot or more of snow on the ground, and when beech mast and acorns had to be scratched out from beneath six inches or more of snow in the forests. Passenger pigeons kept in captivity seemed to do just as well when the temperature was down to zero as in summer temperatures and showed no ill effects whatever.

If you go back to the previously mentioned feeding flight that Alexander Wilson described, and recall that his estimate amounted to some seventeen million bushels of feed which this single flock would daily require, the feeding problems of the pigeons becomes dramatically emphasized. However, in a virgin country, this prodigious feathered empire had worked out the answers in great detail. By presenting a wide feeding front on the ground, with back legions constantly fluttering over those in front, entire areas could be swept completely clean. In addition, when mast was being taken in the hardwood forest, as was usually the case, there was a constant fluttering, a rising and settling of birds throughout the limbs of the trees. By this means, what with hundreds of thousands of individuals forever restlessly on the wing, moving through the branches, every beechnut or acorn was—perhaps purposely—shaken and beaten from the branches, and fell to the ground to be gobbled up.

Roosting sites could of course be changed as food became scarce, but a nesting site could not, and so the daily flights for food became longer and longer as the nesting continued. It is notable that the parent birds never fed in the immediate vicinity of a nesting. The site was chosen primarily in relation to abundance of food supply, and the mast within the confines of the site and the nearby surrounding territory was left for the squabs to consume during the first days following their ejection from the nests.

Meanwhile, the parent birds swept the country for as much as a hundred miles around. Had it not been for their strong flight, the whole system would have been impossible to maintain. It was a remarkable feat for parent birds to leave at dawn, fly anywhere from twenty-five to one hundred miles, feed, and fly back to attend the squabs. The manner in which this part of the system was worked out was also unique. Since both parents assisted in the incubation and the feeding of the squabs, the flights would at first be either all males, or all females, each group often making *two trips per day!* When the nearby feed gave out, and perhaps a hundred-mile flight was necessary, only one trip per day was made, and thus, on alternate days, so it is said, each parent group fed, the flight being all male one day, all female the next.

The birds apparently realized, too, that they required the very best in feed in order to sustain themselves and to give them strength for the long flights. When a flock had found it necessary to take inferior feed, and then, on the swing homeward, happened to discover a better feeding place, the birds were known to alight, disgorge the contents of their crops, and to fill up again on top-grade material. All of these habits pointedly high-light the fact that here was a really well-integrated and highly specialized wildlife society. It is little wonder observers found a mysterious and unearthly quality about this marvelous communal association.

The name "passenger pigeons," that is, passage birds, hardly describes them as they really were. Passage birds are migratory birds, and though it is true that these pigeons were in a sense migratory in that they nested in the more northern part of their range, and were driven south in winter because their food was buried by snow, they were not actually migratory in the full sense. Their movements seem mostly explainable by lack of abundance of sufficient food. Scientifically, the passenger pigeon was first placed in the group *Columbia*. This is the group meaning *type* pigeons, that is, species most nearly representative of group origins. Later the species was removed from this group, due to certain structural specializations such as wing spread and length of tail. It was placed in the group *Ectopistes*, a word which, translated, means "wandering," or "moving about from place to place." The species name *migratorius* was kept, and thus the full name means migratory birds that wander about from place to place, the wandering in this case being in search of food and nesting sites. But this wandering was not consistently north and south, as it is with all the true climatic migrants such as the ducks and geese. It was just as likely to be east-west, or vice versa, and had very little to do with seasons so long as plentiful and obtainable food could be located.

If there was any one aspect of the communal life of the passenger pigeons which emphasized their extravagant singleness of purpose in adhering to system, it was their nestings. It could not be said that there was anything especially unique about their love-making. They were devoted as mate to mate, and as parent to young. The male, prior to mating, during the courtship period, made circular exhibitionist flights, as do many birds, his specialty as with most pigeons being the habit of striking the tips of the long primary wing quills together with a sharp rap which could be heard at a distance. After the courtship, the usual billing took place, at which time the marital decision was sealed by one bird placing its bill crosswise in the bill of the other. The only unusual portion of the mating display, perhaps, was the way in which the birds, after the billing ceremony, disgorged the contents of their crops. However, this undoubtedly takes place among other dove species also, and without question has some significance, settled over the centuries into the instinct of the species, as regards the future feeding of the young which will soon arrive. But the nesting itself was a vast and well-integrated operation without parallel in nature.

Picture if you can a gigantic flock of birds heading into the north country seemingly without purpose, but flying actually as if directed by compass and prearrangement to a certain stand of oak covering hundreds of acres, a site at which food is abundant. The birds immediately settle down in pairs scattered through the trees, each pair going about the business of love-making and mating with industry and intentness. Let us say that this flock has come from directly south to north, and that it had on its last flight covered a hundred miles. Yet, as the mating gets under way, other flocks begin to appear on the horizon. Some are coming from the east, the west, some have apparently made a circle into the north and so now have a southern course. But each of these flocks, not flying as if in search but with apparently as much compass-directed purpose and prearrangement as the first main flock, comes straight to the chosen site, so that day by day the acreage covered by the nesting spreads out over the forest in every direction. How have these other flocks known where to find their kin? Who can say? Each has come from hundreds of miles distant, exactly as if messages had been sent requesting its presence at this reunion.

If you look now into the pages of history, another startling facet of the system becomes evident. Nesting sites usually remained constant, but, in Michigan, where in the last half of the nineteenth century many of the largest nestings took place, it appears to have been well established that these colossal reproductive reunions occurred in alternate years. To be sure, there were often smaller nestings scattered here and there, and records could not be kept of all of them. But the fact that the main nestings, which drew professional pigeoners from hundreds of miles away and were therefore well recorded, occurred in 1868, '70, '72, '74, '76, and '78 certainly seems significant. And no doubt it was, for available food was certain to be swept clean from hundreds of thousands of surrounding acres during these gatherings. By alternating the years and the general regions chosen, the empire assured a successful squab crop. Food was given an opportunity to replenish itself. The pigeons were, in their way, shrewd conservationists. This system amounted to a crop rotation theory: squabs one year, acorns the next!

To James Fenimore Cooper, again, goes credit for an excellent picture of a nesting site. From *The Chainbearer*, I quote an edited passage:

Every tree was literally covered with nests, many having at least a thousand of these frail tenements. They often touched each other, a wonderful degree of order prevailing among the hundreds of thousands of families that were here assembled. The place had the odor of a fowl-house, and squabs just fledged sufficiently to trust themselves in short flights, were fluttering in all directions, in tens of thousands. Although the woods around us seemed fairly alive with pigeons, our presence produced no general commotion; every one of the feathered throng appearing to be so much occupied with its own concerns, as to take little heed of a party of strangers, though of a race usually so formidable to their own. The effect on us was confounding (as of) a man finding himself suddenly placed in the midst of an excited throng of human beings. The unnatural disregard of our persons manifested by the birds caused me to feel as if some unearthly influence reigned in the place. It was strange, indeed, to be in a mob of the feathered race. The pigeons seemed a world of themselves.

A noise was heard above that of the incessant fluttering which I can only liken to that of the trampling of thousands of horses on a beaten road, at first distant, but it increased rapidly in proximity and power, until it came rolling in upon us, among the tree-tops, like a crash of thunder. The air was suddenly darkened, somber as dusky twilight. All the pigeons that had been on their nests appeared to fall out of them, hitting us with their wings, and at times appearing as if about to bury us in an avalanche of pigeons. All this was the effect produced by the return of the female birds, which had been off some twenty miles to feed on beechnuts, and which now assumed the places of the males on the nests, the latter taking a flight to get their meal in turn. Millions of birds must have come in on that return, and as many departed!

When the parents changed shift on the nest, the returning bird fluttered in from behind and the sitting bird, just as the other's bill touched its tail, raised its wings and departed. Thus no egg was left for a second unattended. It may be that Cooper's estimate of the number of nests per tree was exaggerated. Certain it is that at least several hundred nests were commonly found in a single tree. They were built anywhere from a few feet to seventy or more feet above the ground, and there are many authentic records of even very small trees with as many as one hundred nests. Consider now that a nesting such as the one which occurred at Petosky, Michigan, in 1878, covered at least 150,000 acres, and was strung out for some forty miles, with a depth in spots of at least ten. How could each returning bird possibly have known which nest to fly to! And yet each parent found its own mate unerringly.

Often it was observed by those who kept passenger pigeons in confinement that the males would kill the squabs, but in the wild there seems to have been an unusual solicitude felt by both parents for the youngsters. It was claimed that as the nesting drew to a close, with the majority of fledglings now feeding on the ground but unable to take long flights, a certain number of old birds stayed behind to keep watch over them, while the bulk of the flock went on to a new site where, if the season was not yet too far advanced, another nesting took place. Among those that stayed behind were both males and females, and it was not uncommon to see numerous young birds gathered around a single mature bird coaxing to be fed. It is well substantiated, too, that during the time of the great slaughterings at the nesting sites squabs whose parents had been killed were never left to starve if it was at all possible for other parent birds to feed them. These orphans were carefully attended, as if the old birds knew that the continuance of the species depended on bringing as many as possible to maturity. When a nesting was completed and all the parent birds had left, the fledglings followed within a few days, always departing in the same direction which the parent flight had taken.

The nests, like most dove nests, were flimsy affairs. They were about a foot across, and composed of twigs. As a rule the female actually built the nest, while the male fetched the twigs. In captivity, where the operation could be closely observed, the female would utter a peculiar little sound, at which signal the male would pick up a twig and deliver it. When she was ready for the next one she made the fact known, and the male again delivered material.

There seems to have been some disagreement among bird students as to how many eggs were laid. Some nests contained two, some only one. Most authorities agree that the average nest contained but one. It is certain that several nestings were completed each season, whenever possible. But this still does not show the passenger pigeon as a very prolific species in the strict sense. And yet, so perfect were conditions in virgin forest country that it had risen to excessively extravagant abundance. Audubon was of the opinion that the birds doubled their numbers each season. This I doubt. The really strange aspect of their abundance and communal habits as regards their nestings is that no more *wasteful* nesting system could possibly have been conceived.

First of all, the great concentration of nests broke down trees and shattered limbs with the result that untold numbers of squabs were killed, as well as parent birds. Possibly, when a nest was thus destroyed, the parents built again, but the potential was still diminished. Storms accounted for legions of birds, since the nests were so flimsy. Any storm found a concentration confined to such a relatively small area that excessive damage was bound to result. Had the nests been scattered in the way that mourning doves nest, storms would have killed only occasional birds here and there. In addition, concentrations of birds drew concentrations of predators, with resultant high losses. Further, the long feeding flights which were necessary certainly accounted for hundreds of birds which met accidental death.

All of these wasteful facets of the system, it seems to me, discount Audubon's premise that numbers were annually at least doubled. More likely it is that the pigeon's great abundance had been slowly built up over the centuries, and that this abundance was deceiving. The balance was possibly more delicate than was indicated. This interesting side of the matter becomes plainer when it is noted that, during nesting season, flocks were constantly harassed and broken up by man, with the result that the breeding season was shortened or curtailed. Many birds, in fact, passed entire seasons without finding it possible to breed at all.

The great pigeon slaughter began to get under way in force about 1850. In the light of our present-day conservation thinking, it is of course a shocking spectacle, but it was bound to have happened. There were millions of birds; the birds were good to eat; there was a ready market for them; there was no law to restrict taking them in any way a man saw fit. A man could make a good living at full-time pigeon killing, or some spare-time dollars if he did not care to turn professional. People in the backcountry were poor, they were used to the idea of living off the land, and the marketing of game had been an established business for centuries.

Even in those years of the 1850's, the birds had already become less abundant along the Atlantic Coast. They had, so it was said, moved farther inland to escape the press of civilization. They were essentially forest birds, wilderness creatures. Though some voices were raised to decry the slaughter, most criticism was a matter of principle—revulsion at common methods of taking the birds. Few persons were actually worried about the fate of the species.

In early days, guns were not of course as efficient as ours of today, and though a sportsman might have enjoyment in wing shooting, food, not sport, was paramount. The habits of the pigeons obviously suggested mass methods of capture. When guns were used, as a rule no one cared to waste a charge on a single bird when he could as well have a dozen. And so the various plans for mass slaughter grew in cleverness of conception as the century grew in years.

Along the shores of the Great Lakes, immense flocks of birds habitually flew very low, searching salt springs. For some reason possibly tied up with the manufacture of pigeon milk in the birds' crops, they were frantic for salt during nesting time. And of course they also went in legions to the lake shores to drink. During these low flights, poorly equipped hunters simply concealed themselves and knocked the birds to the ground with clubs. Later, nets similar to the gill nets used by commercial fishermen were strung between poles set atop a rise of ground, a method only mildly successful.

The idea of using nets was developed to its fullest about 1860, when the marketing of pigeons finally flowered as a big industry. Since the pigeons were not especially wary, it was soon discovered that their social habits made them congenial to calls and to decoys. Calls were made by placing together two hollowed blocks of wood and tightly stretching a piece of silk between them, upon which the caller blew in the same manner that youngsters blow upon a blade of grass held between their thumbs. A passing flock in search of feed could be lured to ground by this call, and could be shot into —or trapped.

This led to the idea of making baited beds, to give the birds a substantial reason for alighting. Baited beds immediately suggested live decoys, which it was soon discovered worked much better than a call. And, since gunfire frightened birds in the neighborhood and collected but a dozen or so per shot, it was inevitable that the baited bed and the clap net were to be used in conjunction as the standard method of taking adult birds.

The beds finally emerged as extremely refined and cunning devices. Some were called mud beds, and consisted of a moist area of cleared space frequently watered down and heavily baited with anise seed and saltpeter. On such a bed the birds could get both food and the much-needed salt. The other type of bed was called a dry bed, and consisted merely of a scrupulously cleared space upon which grain was scattered. However, the pigeons were often rather selective in their feeding, and would not come to field grains if they happened to be feeding on beechnuts. In such instances, beech mast had to be used, and, since this was troublesome to acquire, the mud bed with its salt supply seems to have been most popular.

A professional pigeoner would select sites for several beds, far removed from each other, but all near the nesting site. He would carefully prepare the beds, then set up his net and make several strikes one day, move on to the next bed while giving the struck bed a rest to alleviate the pigeons' fears, and so on.

The pigeoner constructed a blind near the bed, and beside the bed he placed his net, so affixed to springy saplings that by pulling a rope he could release it, at which time it would come flying up and over the great mass of birds gathered on the bed, and clap down tightly, capturing hundreds. A method called penning was a variation, and was used as a rule for the less wary young birds which were just beginning to fly. A large pen of slats was built near the nesting site, and in it a group of adult birds was secured. The pen was then baited with grain, and when enough of the gullible youngsters had walked inside to feed, a net was whisked across the entrance. You can easily judge the effectiveness of this method by looking at a single penning record: almost five thousand birds at one throw of the net!

It was during the years of the great pigeon slaughter that the name stool pigeon came into common usage. The stool pigeon was a decoy. In early days, four or five live birds were captured, and, after sewing their eyelids shut the hunter would tie them to a pole near the bait bed. Then he secreted himself in his evergreen blind some yards away. By running a string to the pole, he could jiggle the perch and cause the birds to flutter. They, being blinded, never tried to fly off, but only to keep their balance, and of course this fluttering called the attention of passing flocks.

Later on, the stool pigeon most commonly used was not blinded. It was simply a live bird that was placed upon a little box or stool, and secured there, after which the stool was placed on the baited bed. Strings were so attached that the box, or the bird, could be moved up and down, at which times it would flutter its wings. Passing birds were attracted, and dropped down to feed. Some pigeoners had the stool pigeon tied to the end of a long, limber pole, which was raised and lowered above the bed. As a rule, the first group which alighted with the stool pigeon was not netted. Hundreds of others would be sitting curiously in the trees, undecided. If the stool pigeon was made to flutter, this would startle those already on the bed. They would fly up into the trees, but presently, when they dropped down again, the entire flock would usually follow, and then the rich strike was made.

It was difficult to keep the stool pigeon in place, and when a pigeoner finally got himself a good one, which would stay put, he took good care not to lose it, although very often a hawk would come diving in and grab the stool pigeon before the owner could snatch it away. Some pigeoners lost several decoys in this manner each season, a fairly large loss, for a good, trained stool pigeon brought as high as twenty-five dollars.

The flier was a bird used in conjunction with the stool pigeon. Some professional market hunters always utilized several fliers at their beds. These were the birds that did the long-range decoying of passing flocks. A string was attached to the leg of the bird, and, when a flock was sighted, the flier was tossed from the hunter's blind into the air. It flew to the end of the string, and was then of course drawn slowly and gently down. From a distance it looked as if it was just alighting to feed. The flock would turn and come wheeling back for a closer look; the flier would be dragged into hiding; the stool pigeons on the bed would take over.

Some of the nets were as much as thirty or forty feet long, and there are records of pens as large as a hundred feet long by twenty feet wide by five feet deep, with huge nets which could be sprung over the top. As a lot of the pigeon traffic was in live birds—which were used for live-pigeon shoots, or fatted and sent alive to market—some of these huge pens had auxiliary feeding pens built along their sides. The trapped birds could thus be shunted into the feeding pens, and confined there until they could be shipped. One of these mammoth pens, copiously baited, would often attract such a gathering that the birds would be piled atop one another in several layers, all trying to get at the feed, when the net was sprung. One record of such a large pen tells how the pigeoner packed his feeding pens full after the first strike, and how disappointed he was because a few minutes later he could have captured a like amount, but had no place to put them.

When birds trapped beneath a net on a bed were to be killed, the pigeoner had to use extreme care not to splatter blood about on the bed. The pigeons seemed to know what the blood of their own kind meant, and to shy away in great alarm from any bed so marked. Thus it became the practice to kill trapped birds by simply pinching their necks with a small pair of pliers, the nippers of which had been bent so that they did not quite meet.

Though there was always ready market for adult birds, these were often inclined to be tough, and the meat dry. Even immature birds just learning to fly weren't wholly satisfactory, for they lost weight very quickly after leaving the nest, and took some time gaining it back. It was the squabs that were the most avidly sought. They were a mass of fat. The meat was tender, and since they were completely helpless until they left the nest, they were easily though brutally taken. Squab gatherers would climb trees and punch the young out of the nests with long poles. Or they would take heavy sledges and hammer upon the trunks of the smaller trees, with the result that the squabs were jarred from the nests. Many were so fat that they burst open when they struck the ground. It was common, too, to go through the nesting site selecting trees which had an abundance of nests, and to cut these down. In falling, they brought other smaller trees down with them. Squabs by the dozen would then be picked up. Some especially unscrupulous hunters set fire to trees containing numerous nests. The squabs squirmed from the nests and fell to the ground. It is easy to imagine what shocking waste went hand in hand with all these methods.

At that, such methods were hardly more wasteful or unsporting than certain of those used for taking adult birds. It was common practice in some places to bring pots of sulphur into a nesting or roosting site after dark, and to set them afire. Overcome by the smoke, birds by hundreds toppled from the trees. There is one particularly unusual record of a shiftless old pigeoner who didn't want to bother with a net and other equipment. He soaked bushels of corn in whisky, and spread it on a bait bed. After feeding, hundreds of birds would topple over, dead drunk. He had only to approach and gather in his catch.

Naturally, the prices which the birds brought urged the slaughter along. During the 1870's pigeoners in the field were receiving from twenty-five to sixty cents per dozen, and at certain times during the season much more than that. The New York marketers claimed at that period that an extra hundred barrels of pigeons could be handled and sold every day without causing the prices to fluctuate in the least. Pigeons were then retailing at from two dollars to six dollars a dozen, and there were instances where pigeoners working the nesting sites received as much as five dollars and fifty cents per dozen wholesale when the take was poor. It was not unusual for the more clever pigeoners to make from ten to forty dollars per day with their nets. One old-timer at Petoskey, Michigan, was alleged to have banked a fortune of some sixty thousand dollars made entirely from pigeon trapping over a few years.

Look at a few of these pigeoners' records. Here is a man who took five hundred dozens—6,000 birds—in a single day's catch. Here is one, in Ohio, who caught 1,285 birds with one spring of the trap. Here are five trappers working together who took 5,200 birds in two days. Here is a single operator who caught 3,500 with one spring of the trap. Such records could be quoted for pages. Though some voices of caution and anger were raised at this time, there was no really serious question in the average mind but that the passenger pigeon, at least in reasonable numbers, was here to stay forever.

Naturally there were thousands of spare-time trappers, settlers who just happened to find a nesting in their neighborhood. One of these might ship a couple of barrels a season, or perhaps a dozen or so barrels. But there were in addition, it is estimated, as high as five thousand full-time professional pigeoners who did nothing else the year round except follow the nestings and the roostings. There might be as many as five hundred such professionals gathered at a single nesting during the later years, in addition to the local people who were taking birds to sell and to eat.

The better professionals studied the pigeon's habits intently. They took note of the direction of every sizable flight. They learned to tell almost exactly where a nesting would take place, and were thus enabled to be on hand the moment it began. News was sent by letter or wire all over the eastern U. S. as soon as a site had been determined, and the pigeoners came on the run. If the nesting was so harassed as to be broken up, the trappers simply watched the flight direction and trailed it down, enlisting the services of operators in various states to advise them of the new location of the birds. Sometimes the new site meant a thousand-mile trip for the trapper. But what of that? Money was literally growing in trees at the end of the journey.

The famous nesting of '78 at Petoskey, Michigan, wrote some astounding statistics into history. The first birds were shipped out during the later part of March, and the last birds about the middle of August. That's almost five months. During the peak weeks, the shipments ran roughly as follows: the railroads carried away an average of fifty barrels of birds per day, which meant forty dozen adult birds or fifty dozen squabs per barrel, or an average of about 27,000 birds daily. Thousands, yes, tens of thousands of live birds were being shipped at the same time. Steamer cargoes, in addition to the rail shipments, were sailing away from five or six nearby ports. There were also hundreds of boxes leaving by express, and wagonloads hauled away by people who wanted them for their own consumption.

Remember, now, that untold numbers of squabs were dying in the nests for lack of food, after the parents were caught. The average was fifty per cent. Remember too, that literally tons of squabs and adult birds lay rotting in the forest, lost in underbrush and overlooked. Undoubtedly well over 50,000 birds per day at a conservative average were being slaughtered, and still the nesting was so large that the activity failed to break it up, until this carnival of killing had gone on for nearly five months!

One spring in the early '80's the first big nesting was discovered in Missouri. The horde of slaughterers immediately gathered. Practically every squab was killed. The nesting broke up, and the birds set a northeast course. Wire facilities were good at that time, and the flight was followed by watchers, the news being relayed back to the waiting trappers. The word finally came that the birds had again settled down to nest, this time in Michigan. Again the pigeoners rushed to the scene, many having left Missouri before the nests were built. A repeat performance was staged, with all the new squabs cleaned out, and of course many of the parent birds taken. The nesting broke again, and headed east. Soon the word came over the wires. The birds were trying again, this time in the Catskills. The squabs were bringing the highest prices then, and so once more the legion of hunters descended. Every squab was cleaned out. A local ice house did a land-office business, furnishing some fifteen tons of ice to get the birds the short distance to the New York market. You can well imagine how many birds that meant. The result, obviously, was that this entire flight, millions of birds, not only failed to breed at all that year, but lost hundreds of thousands of their own numbers as well.

Let us try to reconstruct out of various bits of history what the scene was like at one of the big nestings during the peak of the pigeon-trapping industry. Let us visit this fantastic gathering of men and birds. The village to which we travel by train lies near the shore of Lake Michigan, in the northern part of the Lower Peninsula. It is a very small village, its few standard businesses—blacksmith shop, hardware and dry-goods store, general store, etc.—dependent upon the settlers who have torn mediocre farms from the clutch of the surrounding forest. Ordinarily, it is a sleepy village which seldom knows hurry or excitement. But it has boomed suddenly into a community of several thousands. As we get off the train, we see men hurrying everywhere. The streets are full of wagons. There is no room to be had at the small hotel. There are no rooms available anywhere in the houses of the villagers. Every house has rented all extra space to accommodate the influx of outsiders.

Children and dogs are noisily romping in the streets. Everywhere there are groups of people—on the streets, in the stores, the hotel lobby, the depot—discussing pigeons, comparing notes on prices, waiting for wires from the New York markets which will mean a rise or drop in prices. We pause to talk here and there with strangers, and we discover that we've soon met men from as far away as Texas and New England, all of whom have come to seek their fortunes from the nesting which stretches for miles along the lake shore some distance from town. There is a frantic bedlam reigning on every hand.

Down at the freight office at the depot there is evidence everywhere of pigeoners. Many more have come on our train. The freight office is bulging with their equipment. Nearby there is a packing house. Wagons are drawn up before it. They are heaped high with dead birds, which are being unloaded. The unloaded wagons move on to make way for others which are constantly pulling in behind them. Inside the packing house everything is confusion. Dozens of hired hands are busy icing and packing dead birds, getting them ready to ship as quickly as possible. Not far off there are several large, apparently hastily built poultry houses, with dozens of slat crates piled nearby. Most of these are full of live birds. Several hundred bushels of grain are also in evidence, to be used for feeding the birds until they can be shipped.

We hitch a ride with a wagon driver and head out toward the scene of operations. The streets are full of feathers. The smell of birds is everywhere. The mere track of a road over which we travel has deep mudholes, but these have been filled solidly with the wings and tails of pigeons—miles of them. We pass encampments constantly, whole families who have come either to gather meat for themselves, or to work for the pigeon buyers or trappers. Our driver, whose wagon is drawn by oxen, tells us he gets five dollars per wagonload for what he hauls. He is forever turning out into the forest to let loaded wagons pass on their way to the packing house. We count a dozen wagons and estimate that there must be fifty or more in the vicinity. And here, strung out for some distance through the woods, is a whole tribe of Indians. They have brought all their belongings, and will stay until the nesting is over, gathering squab fat, smoking pigeon breasts, working for the trappers. We pass several settlers' cabins in clearings some distance outside the village. Strings of pigeon breasts are strung everywhere between trees. They have been pickled for several days in brine, and are now drying, after which they will be stored. They'll taste much like dried beef, and will see this family through the long, cold winter.

There are so many people in evidence that we know everyone for at least a hundred miles must have converged on this site. Camps are scattered everywhere as we approach the nesting. And now we can hear the sound of axes, the shouts of men and boys. It is impossible to look anywhere above without seeing pigeons on the wing by hundreds, thousands.

As we penetrate farther into the actual nesting site, there is a stench of rotting birds. Tens of thousands have been overlooked, or have been crippled and have crawled off to die. Ahead of us several workmen swing axes, cutting down trees which have an unusually large number of nests. To either side numerous boys have climbed trees and are punching squabs from the nests with poles. On the ground others are scurrying about through the underbrush, picking up squabs. As each one is picked up, the finder simply yanks off its head without ceremony and tosses it onto an evergrowing pile. The clothes, the hands, the faces of everyone we see are blood spattered. Feathers fairly carpet the floor of the forest. The confusion, the noise of birds and men and guns and falling trees is overwhelming. We question a squab gatherer. He tells us he is hired at one cent per squab for all he can find. On the outskirts of this nesting site, we know, net trappers by the hundreds are sitting in their evergreen-bough blinds, watching their bait beds, waiting to make the next strike. How, we wonder, can there possibly be any pigeons left when this open-air slaughterhouse finally closes shop for the season. What a strange war this is, men seeking to build an empire, and in the process ruthlessly determined to destroy an ancient empire of birds. What a strange war, indeed, the birds frantically attempting to aim their single powerful defensive weapon, reproduction, and the men just as frantically trying to eliminate that weapon from the combat. . . .

Here and there, of course, there were sportsmen in America scattered throughout the empire of the pigeons. Men who took delight in watching for the flights, who shouldered their guns and tried their aim on the swift wings of single birds out of the passing multitudes. The pigeon, they instructed history to tell us, was one of the grandest game birds man ever knew.

Here and there, too, there was a different kind of sportsman, the kind who tried his skill at the live pigeon shoots. It seems strange, today, to note that a group that called itself the New York Association for the Protection of Fish and Game held a great pigeon shoot at Coney Island in 1881, a shoot at which *twenty thousand* live-trapped passenger pigeons were killed! But perhaps this practice had its useful purpose, too, for the shoot in question so highly incensed everyone who heard of it that public pressure was brought to bear for a law against using live pigeons as targets. A bill was soon afterward introduced outlawing the use of either wild or domestic pigeons for such purpose, and it passed.

There were, too, many angry voices raised against the scandalous practices at the nesting sites. Michigan finally passed a law making it illegal to net pigeons within two miles of a nesting site. Arrests for violation were even attempted, but to little avail. The conservationists were a weak voice pitted against an industry that brought thousands of dollars each season into various poor farming communities.

And anyway, it was too late for laws. People the country over now waited and watched each spring, wondering and puzzling as to why no large pigeon flights materialized. By the early 1890's, Wisconsin pigeons had practically disappeared. In the East they had completely disappeared years before. But, it was said on every hand, they would be back. They've simply been bothered too much. They couldn't possibly be gone for good.

By 1895 the game dealers had hardly seen a barrel of pigeons for several years. In 1896, a dozen-odd birds were discovered nesting along the Ausable River, in Michigan. In 1897, a bill came into the Michigan Legislature asking for a ten-year closed season on passenger pigeons. But what difference did such a bill make now?

One of the most touching records left us of this period of the pigeon's decline is an incident that occurred this same year at Sault Ste. Marie, Michigan. Here, where the endless flights of pigeons had poured spring and fall across the St. Mary's River, on into Canada for nesting, or south following the sun, there had not been for years so much as a feather to remember them by. And then one day, residents of this tiny frontier village stood to watch a flock of homing pigeons circling round and round the town. There was something strange about this flock. One bird, a male, had a long, wedge-shaped tail, unlike the square fan of the homers. It was a passenger pigeon, a lone, lost, lonely remnant out of the past, trying to make friends with these tame birds of the village. It was the last of its kind ever reported from the vicinity.

Oddly, though the birds were easily kept in captivity, few persons had tried to raise them. Why bother when they were so plentiful? There were a few here and there, but inbreeding soon destroyed these, and when crosses were made with domestic pigeons, they invariably proved infertile. Again just as oddly, every person who now saw a wild passenger pigeon secured it if at all possible, which is to say, killed it. These were the so-called bird lovers who doted on their collections of mounted birds and eggs. Apparently it never occurred to anyone to secure these stray birds alive. There are hundreds of records of single birds shot for collections.

By the early 1900's, with only sight records of a few birds here and there, everyone was determined to find a theory to explain the phenomenon of the disappearance. One common explanation was that the birds had moved en masse to the interior of Canada. Another was that they had moved to the far western Rocky Mountains. This explanation gained many adherents from time to time, for there were many reports of huge flights of pigeons seen in the West. What the originators of these reports had seen were great flights of band-tailed pigeons, a strictly western-mountain species.

The passenger pigeon, we know now, never did get very far west, no farther than the Dakotas. It was a bird of the mixed hardwood forests of the eastern U. S. and Canada. In the beginning it was undoubtedly most numerous along the eastern seaboard. As civilization began crowding, it diminished generally in the East and moved inland, concentrating throughout Kentucky, Ohio, Indiana, Illinois, Michigan, and on south. The range of the pigeon did not extend beyond the southern limits of the U. S. There was one record of a straggler in Cuba, but Mexico had none, although some naturalists insisted that the birds had disappeared into the interior of Mexico. The fact was, they never did occur except as stragglers even as far south as the Gulf Coast. The uplands of Alabama and the other Deep South states seem to have been the southern limit of their range.

One strange extinction theory which gained ground was that a mammoth flight of the remaining pigeons, intent on leaving the U. S. and their persecutors, had been caught in a storm over the Gulf of Mexico, and had been drowned. Several ship captains on the Gulf were alleged to have said they sailed through miles and miles of dead, floating pigeons. Immediately even some ornithologists snapped up the chance to blame the pigeon disappearance on some cataclysmic agent.

There was precedent for such a theory. In Massachusetts, near Gloucester, there is a place called Pigeon Cove, named for a large flight of pigeons that had been driven into the sea there by a storm and destroyed. Dead birds were said to have washed up on shore in great windrows. Often it occurred, in summer during the great northern nestings, that flights were overwhelmed by storm while attempting to cross one of the Great Lakes. There are several records of thousands of dead pigeons washed ashore along Lake Michigan. In addition, ship captains on the Great Lakes often told how the birds would alight on their ships during a storm, or at night, tired out from battling the elements, and how at such times the sailors would sneak along the rail and catch them in their bare hands. Thus was the stage set for the Gulf of Mexico disappearance theory. No one ever came even close to proving the contention, however, although at the time there was plenty of opportunity. And it is entirely discounted today. It is interesting to note in connection with the accounts of flights drowning during storms, that those responsible observers who actually examined birds so destroyed along the Great Lakes invariably found them to be birds of the year. When caught over water in fog or wind, a flight of old birds would rise above it and fly very high, but often a flight of young birds became confused and was dashed into the waves.

In 1905, six birds were seen near Vanderbilt, Michigan, and this was big news—and it came from a section where less than twenty years earlier the big news had been millions of birds preparing a nesting site! Rumors were now being frantically investigated all over the nation, and even as far away as the Caribbean Islands, of a bird or two seen here and there. In 1906 there was a great flurry of excitement in New York State. A fair-sized flock had actually been seen passing on north. The birds were back! But the flock was never heard from again.

Rumors continued. They still continue today. In 1948, one such rumor was passed on to me: a pair of passenger pigeons had been sighted in the west. Over the years each of these rumors has been investigated as thoroughly as possible, and each has proved false. The only one which ever proved otherwise originated in Cincinnati, in 1914. It was to the effect that the last passenger pigeon in existence had just died at the Cincinnati Zoo. The ebb tide of this vast feathered empire, which had begun several centuries earlier with the coming of the white man to America, had at last subsided completely, lost irretrievably in the glass-smooth sea of extinction.

Since that day, most writing about the passenger pigeon has been of the wailing-wall variety. I do not see the extinction of the bird in that light at all, and I believe we should be mature enough today in our conservation thinking to see this page of wildlife history in its true perspective. Some of the scenes during the years of the pigeon decline are not pretty to witness in print. Yet from these very scenes some of our first yearnings and determinations toward wise conservation were born. Therefore, I am sure, the bird and its extinction played a valuable and vital part in the conservation history we are making today. It was an elementary lesson that we have been a long time beginning to learn: that superabundance of wildlife, when pitted against civilization, has *always* an unknown survival factor. The extinction of the pigeon was one of the facts repeatedly pointed to when the need for migratory-bird laws began to be emphasized. It later played a part in the actual passage and the final strengthening of those laws. Thus, in its way, the wiping out of the pigeon assisted in saving our waterfowl and other wildlife.

There is a further aspect of this bird debacle seldom touched upon. It is this. Deny it as much as we may, were any species to rise in such abundance today, the same thing would happen. Greed would be a part of the reason. But only a small part. The vital issue would be that the progress of civilization will never allow itself to be balked in the slightest by any overpopulous wildlife species. The story of the buffalo is a prime example. The *way* in which it was controlled may not be pleasant reading, but the fact remains that there was not room for white civilization and the buffalo. The same was identically true of the passenger pigeon.

The pigeon required two basic necessities: fabulous amounts of food, and an opportunity to continue its communal habits. Once the forests were beginning to be cut, the food supply diminished. At first this did not matter greatly. The forests dwindled slowly then, cut for the most part to make way for fields of grain. The pigeon was highly adaptable. Where once he had gorged himself beneath the beech trees, he now gorged himself in a field of wheat. Had there been but a few scattered pigeons, no one would have objected. But were the passenger pigeon still existent today in his former numbers, he would be the scourge of our part of the world, violently hated, and with a bounty upon his head!

It was therefore extremely lucky for us that the pigeon's habits were as they were. Thereby was his necessary containment made easy, instead of a troublesome problem to be dealt with in our agricultural century. As the forests diminished, the pigeon found the huge nesting sites he required fewer and fewer. As the commercial slaughter progressed, he found his immense flocks constantly harried and broken up. For him, existence in small bands was impossible. His empire had been built upon mass tactics, and where some wildlife species found it possible to adapt themselves quickly to the coming of civilization, to spread themselves thinly, to study the white man and discover how to get along with him, the pigeon could not. Its empire, like many other highly specialized civilizations both of men and of beasts which have passed from the earth, was simply *too* perfect and inflexible.

It is said that our ancestors, by slaughtering the birds, robbed us of grand sport today. I do not believe it. In reality, the debacle was one of the simplest cause-and-effect occurrences that has ever taken place. The elimination of the forests would have done in the pigeon, had none ever been killed by man. The slaughter simply hurried the process.

It may well be, as the chronic bemoaners have claimed and still claim, that the stage sets of extinction were being erected in the New York market places and among the gatherings of pigeoners from the 1850's onward. But unquestionably the main theme of this tragedy in nature was played by the woodsman's ax. Today that conclusion is evident everywhere, in the spread of the clean, furrowed land where hemlock, pine, maple, beech, and oak once stood.

Chapter 4

THE GRAY BULLET

I F YOU HAVE never had a hog for a hunting partner, then you have missed an experience! The hog I see in memory and chuckle about as I write that line is a huge old yellow and black spotted boar, a Kansan by birth, a dictator by inclination, and the most efficient mourning dove hunter I have ever known.

This hog was strictly a meat hunter. But then, what's sport to a hog? If I hadn't been schooled in the irascibility of Kansas farmers, I'm sure a lot of potential little pigs would have lost themselves a sire!

I had been around Wichita, Kansas, for some days, waiting for September first and the opening of mourning-dove season. Bill Walker had told me, "You stay around and we'll have us a real shoot." And that we did. Early in the morning, when it was cool. It was some of the toughest shooting I ever did, or rather, tried to do. I poured two boxes of shells through my gun, and came up with eight birds and forty-two excuses. Bill was having a worse day than I. Not that we didn't enjoy it, but we were determined on opening day to get our limits. And so, come afternoon, we left the Arkansas River and wandered off into a big farm to try a field of kaffir corn.

This kaffir cornfield lay along a small creek, the banks of which were a tangle of brush and scrub trees. On the far side of the kaffir corn there was a big meadow, and here the yellow and black spotted boar held forth. This kind of a setup is a perfect one for doves. The hog, naturally, isn't necessary. But the meadow, the kaffir cornfield (always a favorite feeding spot), the creek to furnish water, the dead scrubs for midday roosting, couldn't be improved upon. In addition, roadside hedges of osage orange, a lot of wild sunflowers growing along the fence rows, open-ground patches where the birds could pick gravel, the big river (the Arkansas) with towering trees along its banks, just a quarter-mile away, all made this spot a natural. No dove could, or does, ask more, and these didn't. They were there in abundance. The walking was easy for a hunter, and as always in dove hunting you weren't loaded down with a million hunks of equipment, nor with heavy boots or clothing. If you didn't want to walk in the heat of the day, you could simply sit and wait for a dove that had decided to change his siesta perch to come winging over completely in the open.

The only thing I would have removed from the setup would have been that hog. And if I had been smart I would also have removed the string of doves from Bill's belt. Being low man, he was forced as per agreement to carry birds for both of us.

The old boar lifted his head from whatever business a boar hog has in a meadow and looked at me. He grunted and chomped his teeth. I said, "Now, Bill, this whole stretch is yours. I don't aim to have truck with that boar, doves or no doves. We once had a boar ..."

"With your caution," Bill said, "you'll live forever." He headed for the kaffir corn. "This time of day," he said, "we'll have to move the birds if we want shooting." I stayed where I was, watching the hog. Finally I skirted him wide, going out into the meadow and along the roadside fence.

As to moving the birds, Bill was right. A dove's day is a very well-regulated affair. That's one of the first things you have to learn about dove shooting. Weather, of course, will make a great change in their actions. That is, rain, or high winds, especially cold winds. But during good average weather, with the sun bright and hot, as it usually is wherever and whenever you hunt doves, you have to get up early to get the first run of really fast shooting.

The birds leave their roosts just after sunup. If you are in areas where the feed is concentrated in small regions, you usually find that the birds have banded together to form fairly large roosting sites. For example, I recall a small patch of mesquite near Tucson, Arizona, where the ground was littered with feathers, and where at my best guess at least several hundred doves were compactly roosting night after night. These flocks are always very loose in formation. The dove is gregarious after nesting season is over and migration has started, but he is not what might be called colonial. His banding together is a matter of convenience for the most part, and when a flock flies out from a roost, it is seldom noticeable as what you would ordinarily think of as a flock of birds. They go two, three, six, ten at a time, following a fairly definite flight lane toward their chosen feeding ground, but without any special order or formation. In such a location as we were in, in Kansas, however, the feed and water is so abundant and so spread around over wide territory that doves may be flying at dawn from every direction, each small roosting of a few birds heading toward its favorite breakfast spot, the total effect being a crisscrossing of flight lanes in such a maze that no system emerges at all as viewed through the hunter's eyes.

After the morning flight, the birds settle down to their feeding. Until 9:00 A.M., the weather being normal, there will continue to be a certain amount of trading around from field to field, of flying from feed to perch and perch to feed. If there is shooting of any amount in the vicinity, this of course keeps the birds on the move. And, since it interrupts their feeding, naturally the feeding period lasts longer, for doves are prodigious eaters, and have a lot of determination about not quitting, no matter what, until their crops are stuffed full.

Until around 9:00 A.M., if you've picked a stand correctly, you will hardly need to move from your tracks. From then on the shooting slows down and the hunter must move around progressively more and more until well on toward noon. By noon, the dove knocks off work and decides to rest and digest his cropful of feed. He'll sit about on telephone wires or dead stubs, or gang up in leafless or lightly foliated trees. Or he'll putter about on the ground here and there in safe places.

During this siesta time he is exceedingly wary, especially if he has been in a shooting area. It is difficult to get close to him as he perches, and he does almost no flying at all unless forced. These lazy hours will last, depending upon how hot the weather, until well on toward late afternoon. Then feeding will begin again, but since the birds are usually perching as close as they can get to their feed, their activity doesn't start as a rule with any big flight. They simply drop down and begin to feed, trading here and there a certain amount, the activity growing as the afternoon wanes.

Toward evening, however, if there is some especially concentrated food supply, they come zooming in by tens and hundreds, and the fast shooting starts once more. From here they fly to water, and then to roost, with the shooting getting better and faster right up until time to quit. The evening flights, indeed, are if anything better than the morning, for when the birds come in to water, hurrying to get their drink and to roost before dark, they leave no molecule of air unturned beneath their wings and they keep you busy till your gun barrel is burning.

But to get back to that hog. By the time I had circled in toward the creek, both Bill and the boar were out of sight. A dove came swinging across the field, flying lazily, a typical dove habit during the heat of the day when there's no real reason for going anywhere. Just loafing along, he looked easy. Of course he saw me, but on he came. Then suddenly he banked and shied and turned on the steam. You could fairly see him set his wings for a deeper bite. This habit they have at midday of puttering along, then bearing down so quickly at sign of danger, upsets the subconscious calculation you've already made. I tried to make my swing catch up with his sudden new rate of speed. Therefore, when I fired my barrel was straight up and I was hurrying so fast I almost lost a tooth to the buck of the gun. But I saw the bird fold cleanly, and I estimated the shot at thirty yards and felt proud of myself after my unhandy shooting of the morning.

I realized just then that I'd heard another shot. A moment later there was another. I picked up my bird and trotted up a little rise that looked down on the field. At that instant there was a wild yelling from down in the corn, and though I couldn't see Bill I could make out an awful floundering around. The next thing I made out was a blur of motion near the brushy creek bank, and suddenly there was Bill up in one of those scrub trees, yelling his head off. Even at that distance the most cloistered individual would have recognized the sound as a long string of Kansas cuss words.

After some time, I saw Bill clamber down. Presently he came out of the corn into the meadow and I went to meet him. "That damn hog," he said. "Of all the lousy . . ."

"Hey, now," I said, "where are our birds?"

His face was livid. "Listen. I killed two birds in that corn. Flushed 'em like quail and knocked them down clean. I hear someone coming through the stuff, and I think it's you. I go to meet you—only I meet that hog head-on. He just let out one squeal and took after me."

"And you made it to the tree."

"Yeah," he said. "Just. Why—he might of killed me! And you know what? I dropped our doves when I shinnied up that tree. And you know what else? That damn hog stood right there and ate every last bird!"

Up to then I was laughing. "Why didn't you shoot the so-and-so?"

Bill fairly roared at me. "Shoot him, hell! Right then I didn't want my mind cluttered up with any thinking except how to get to that tree by the shortest route!"

Well, it had been a good shoot, anyway. But you can be sure on the next day we stayed clear of that farm. Anyhow, it was no trick to find birds. That facet of dove hunting has excellent advantages for the gunner. You don't have to waste a lot of time and energy looking for game and not finding it.

For example, if you're after woodcock, or grouse, or pheasants, or quail, you go where you *think* there are or should be birds, and you start out hunting. Maybe the birds are there and maybe they aren't. In a strange state or locality you can do a lot of scouting around before season and still not be sure what kind of shooting you'll have on opening day. But, all other things being equal, you can take a quick whirl around the countryside in your car the day before dove season, or any day thereafter for that matter, and know without question when you come to the place where the birds are. For birds that spend much time flying and perching, as opposed to the ground dwellers that fly for the most part only for escape, are always easy to locate. The dove is like a miniature waterfowl, and like the waterfowl, doesn't have to be laboriously chased down after his hangout is located. Place yourself correctly and he will come to you. As noted earlier, he is the only upland bird who will.

The dove is a blessing to a lazy man when it comes to locating a hunting ground. For example, when I am hunting doves in the South or Southwest, especially when I am not headed for some definite location, I simply get in my car and start driving around. In sections such as the Southwest where concentrated feed and water holes are comparatively few and far between, you find either and generally you'll find the doves. In such places you can look either for the feed and water, or for the birds. You'll see them flying, or perching on telephone wires and dead trees. Later on, after you get the lay of the land, so that you know the flight lanes and directions, you can work out the best stands. In states like Florida or Georgia, where water is plentiful nearly everywhere but favorite feed is usually concentrated in certain counties, naturally you have to find the wide general locations of the dove flocks first. You can drive many miles in Florida and never see a dove. And you can also, in the counties where feeding conditions are right, see literally thousands ganging up at a roost or a feeding field. But the whole point is, you actually *see* the birds so that you know what kind of shooting territory you've picked without a lot of blind plowing around and aimless guessing.

While it seems to me that feeding locations are the most important leads to good dove territory in the Deep South where water is usually plentiful, the same is not quite so true in the Southwest. There water is at a premium, and you may be certain if you first locate a water hole, or tank, as the natives say, you'll find birds, assuming, of course, that there is good enough feed within reasonable flying distance to make it worth a dove's time to stay around. In the midwestern shooting territory, such as Kansas, both feed and water are pretty generally spread over the countryside, and so are the doves. Which brings up a companion point to the ease of locating the game: seldom do you have to go far from home base to have good shooting.

At the time of my Wichita hunt, I was staying right in the center of town. Walker picked me up and we were shooting within twenty minutes. And we had had no special location in mind. This convenience, to my way of thinking, makes dove shooting the greatest of wing-shooting sports, for over a vast portion of the U.S. it assures the *average* hunter the trickiest shooting it is possible to partake of right in his back yard. The fellow who doesn't get much time for shooting, or who is unable to keep in physical shape good enough to stand tough hunting, just takes a quick few minutes' drive from his doorstep, gets out for a stroll over the easiest of terrain, and gets real shooting. If he doesn't have even enough "git" to walk, he can sit.

As to methods, here again the mourning dove fits any man's needs and opportunities, inclinations and shooting abilities, depending upon how you approach him. You will recall that earlier in the book I stated that a greater variety of shooting might be had with the dove than with any other game bird. In quail, grouse, woodcock, or pheasant shooting, you simply flush your birds and take your chances. Technically there is little difference in the actual *shooting*—range, angles, speeds—whether you use a dog or walk up your birds. In waterfowling, you get two main kinds of shooting: over decoys, or on a pass. A third sort, jump shooting, may be had with waterfowl under special conditions. And you can further divide pass shooting, under very special conditions, into two varieties: shooting on an open pass where you have no obstructions; and shooting in tree-studded swamps, such as in Arkansas backwaters, where flying ducks must be sorted out from among confusing obstacles. But unfortunately, in waterfowling, seldom does it occur that all three or four types of shooting can be had in the same location.

With the doves, however, you can usually find a good stand for almost every kind of shooting right within the particular bailiwick where you happen to be hunting. And the possible varieties are greater even than those for waterfowl. You can change your methods from day to day, thereby adding immeasurably to your enjoyment. So now, let's get these various mourning-dove methods and approaches down and have a look at what each is like.

The advantage of open-pass shooting, in terms of pure sport, is that it invariably pits the gunner against his bird when that target is performing at its best. A typical example of this variety of dove shoot would be on a flyway between roost and feed, or between feed and water, on the Arizona desert. You would, let us say, locate such a flyway, then take a stand in mesquite or cactus which partially conceals you, so that the birds, during the hour or so their flight lasts, continually pass over you or at least within gun range to right or left, flying at top speed and limned against the open sky.

One of the best such locations I can recall out of experience is one I found some few miles from Tucson, not too far distant from the almost dry Santa Cruz River. In this particular case, the shooting was somewhat unusual because it always occurred at the least-expected time of day. By scouting around, I had discovered a cut-over grainfield out in the open on a small ranch, where the birds had found some especially good feed. As there were no scrub trees or dead stubs where they might hang around during their afternoon period of inactivity, I simply stumbled by accident onto the fact that when the feeding eased off, birds by twos to dozens would lift from the field and head in the direction of the Indian reservation some distance away. Thus I was able to avail myself of something unusual in dove hunting, a heavy midday flight. Obviously, they were heading for brush where they might rest until time to feed and go to water again. I simply parked my car by the highway, toted a small box filled with shells, and a jug of water off into the desert far enough to be within the law as far as shooting too close to the road was concerned. Settled with reasonable comfort in a small patch of cholla cactus, I waited for the birds to start flying, and then I took them—or tried to.

I was far enough from the feeding ground so that the doves, full and hot and in a hurry to get to perch, really were steamed up as they passed my cholla patch. Here would come a single, and when the time was ripe I'd rise up, swing, and shoot. Never would the angle be the same. Sometimes to right, sometimes to left, sometimes straight over. Ten yards, twenty, thirty, forty, never a constant range. Talk about fast guessing and burning up a gun barrel! And just about the time you feel you're beginning to click, here comes a fooler, a bird flying low to the ground and rising, as you rose, just skimming the vegetation, maybe ten feet off the ground, turning, twisting, rolling. But he seems so close you simply have to take a chance, and as you swing you find you can't swing *that* fast, not on a bird so close. Naturally, you miss—I do, anyway—and you promise yourself that the next one like that will be a snap shot, or no more than a half-snap at the most. But just then one zooms by at twenty-five yards, his wings whistling so it brings you up swinging—and hell, you begin to think you can't shoot anyway, a fact borne out by the light weight of your ammunition box as you finally head back to the car with your few birds.

Of course, this was an unusual circumstance, and the intense heat was—I like to believe—a drawback to straight shooting. But it is a good example of what this kind of pass shooting is like. In California, I got another somewhat similar dose, except much faster. This was an instance where doves were feeding some distance up on a mountainside north of Los Angeles, and, toward late afternoon, coming down to a tank in the valley. Now if you have never seen a dove fall down a mountain, you don't know what a fast-moving target is like. They start out a thousand or so feet above you. You are located about the same distance from the tank, so they are not beginning to break speed for a landing when they pass over. These doves start out with a few wing strokes as they head down the mountain. From there on, gravity plus more powerful wing beats send them hurtling down till their leading edges simply burn.

Many, way up over you, will play out an air current, riding it high, rolling and dipping, and some will be so close to the prickly-pear tops that you'd swear they'd crack up. And all of them traveling with an audible *swish* and *whistle*, like high-velocity shells passing over. I won't quote you any shooting records of mine on this kind of pass, but I will say it's the fastest swinging my gun ever did. And I will tell you it's an experience no gunner who wants to have seen everything should miss.

The average southwestern pass, in California, Arizona, New Mexico, or Texas, is usually an early morning or late afternoon shoot on reasonably level ground, with the heat not too bad. And the reason I note open-pass shooting in the Southwest in particular is that the more arid portions of legal dove range usually furnish the best such pass shooting. The reason is obvious: roost, feed, and water are likely to be separated by distances which force the doves to make longer trips than in less-arid regions, or in more heavily forested locations. However, if you look for the flyways, you'll find them in any good dove territory, though they may not be quite as definitely defined, or as long, as in the Southwest.

One example of an excellent stand for a pass in the Midwest and South is a cornfield over which the birds must fly to feed or water. When corn is standing the birds won't feed in it to any extent, for they can't get at the grain, and there will usually be few weed seeds on the ground between the rows. However for some reason, in passing over a cornfield, especially if there is a pond or feeding patch nearby, the doves will pass low, often ducking and twisting just below the corn tassels and between the rows. They will do this in other types of cover, too, but a cornfield is an especially good blind for a hunter, and the shooting you get can easily be arranged to give you either a preponderance of head-on and straightaway shots, or of crossing shots. With the birds low, it is very pretty shooting, indeed.

It might be well to add that you don't require as much of a blind for doves as you do for waterfowl. It is important, however, that you wear clothing to match your surroundings to a reasonable degree. A dove is a sharp-eyed little critter, and he sees a white shirt just as quickly as does a duck. If he happens to have been shot at, he'll shy in a hurry. But, with proper clothing, all you need is a minimum of concealment. On opening day, sometimes you may not even need that. I have stood right in the center of an open pasture field and shot doves winging over within easy range on the first day of season.

A wary dove has a most exasperating habit of heading right at you; then, often without your being aware of how he does it, he will angle just barely enough to keep him out of range. You have to keep in mind that a dove on the wing is probably the most maneuverable bird known over a gun. He can be hitting a sizzling fifty miles per hour and change direction with hardly a noticeable movement of wing or body. Just a slight dip or roll does it. Which means, of course, that you have to be prepared for this, for a bird that has not seen you and then suddenly sees you rise from concealment and swing up your gun when he's close in will twist in a split second. Where you expected he'd be, he isn't. He's higher, or lower, or farther away. And the disconcerting side of it is that he doesn't change general direction. He stubbornly keeps going. Needless to say, if you hunt with several others, and each of you takes his stand along the flyway a hundred yards or more from the next, those down-flight from the first gun get the wildest shooting. And, as a dove continues on down the line, flying through the barrage, he's getting wilder and faster with each wing beat. The end man, indeed, had better be an outstanding wingshot, or else use caution on how he places any bets regarding high bag for the shoot!

I realize that anyone who goes hunting does so for the purpose of bringing home game. But I do not think that the *amount* of game brought to bag is necessarily a measurement of the amount of sport chalked up. In theory at least, it should be just as exciting to miss as to hit. The *trying* is the sport. If you then go one step further, you would have to arrange your shooting so that the bird definitely has a chance, and this, obviously, you would have to consider in direct relation to your own ability as a wing shot. For example, the man who is so ineffectual that he has difficulty hitting the trunk of a tree at twenty yards could probably have good sport and still call it fair to the birds—especially if those birds are doves—by trying to pot them from telephone wires. But the man who is an expert skeet shot is taking unfair advantage unless he so places himself that the bird is performing at its best, and with maybe a few obstacles thrown in. If he does otherwise, he'll make a good kill, but he'll be patting himself on the back for shooting under his capacity rather than straining to pit the best of his abilities against those of the game.

What I am leading up to is that there is a second kind of pass shooting quite unlike the open pass. It is pass shooting in open woods and it is no shoot for an inexpert gunner, unless he's the right sort of sport. Then he'll have the time of his life trying. For doves passing through a stand of tall elms or cottonwoods on their way to feed, water, or roost offer shooting as difficult as a wing shooter can find anywhere. It is one of the most exciting endeavors known to man.

Typical of it would be the shooting along the Arkansas River near Wichita during the dawn flight before the afternoon of the hog. Here as it happened the birds were flying from roosts to feeding grounds and water on the far side of the river. And some of them were coming from the far side of the river to search feed on the far side of the woods. The stretch of timber was mostly big elm trees, fairly widely spaced. As they were very tall, and with most of the foliage at or near their tops, this left many openings through which a dove could pass, if he was willing to take a chance on knocking his brains out. And, doves being doves, none of them so much as slowed down, but bored right through, high up toward the foliage, dodging and twisting between the tree trunks so that at this thousandth of a second you saw a bird and during the next he was blotted from sight momentarily. Some birds, of course, went over the treetops, and might be seen momentarily crossing a patch of sky. The stand of timber was possibly as wide as two city blocks, and ran along the high bank of the big river for some distance.

We took up positions on the riverbank. If a shot was made at a bird coming from across the river, you had to wait till he had made land, since he couldn't very well be retrieved if he fell in the water. And, birds coming through *toward* the river were usually heard before they were seen, and then the shot had to be made before they had sizzled along far enough to clear the trees and be over the water.

That, in my opinion, was the best woods pass I have ever been on. I defy even the best of shots to take more than ten birds for twenty-five shells under such conditions. The reason I go into detail about this particular shoot is to show you a way to get really tough shooting, if you like tough shooting.

I think Walker and I were both probably somewhat over-anxious that morning beside the Arkansas. I would spot a dove going over the woods, and just as I pulled up to take him as he crossed a patch of open sky there'd be a whistle of wings to my right, low, in the woods. Like a tyro, I'd change my mind and start looking for the whistler. Meanwhile I'd lose sight of my sky bird, and here would come, or rather there would go, the whistler twenty yards from my nose and at head height. Consequently I shot elm trees most of the morning. But when I did manage to throw a curve around a tree trunk and nail one fair, it was a thrill. One of the biggest hurdles in this kind of shoot, to my mind, is proper leading. For example, you spot a bird and begin your swing. There are several trees in the way. Big trees. Thus, if the shot is long, and as you know the birds are traveling at a rate that will require a big lead, you're shooting at open air in front of one tree trunk while the bird has just been blotted from sight two trunks back!

The high point of that shoot I'll never forget. I thought Walker was far away from me, and apparently at the moment he thought vice versa. My gun had been quiet for a few minutes, and I was standing motionless beside a tree. Presently I noticed a movement some distance away in the woods. There was Walker, stalking a bird that had for some reason alighted in a small dead scrub. For laughs, I began stalking the same bird. When I felt I had a reasonable chance to reach it, I pulled up and let drive, beating him to the shot. Imagine my consternation when the bird flew away without losing a feather! And to make matters worse, Walker quickly threw his gun under his arm, nonchalant as anything.

"So that's what you're up to," he said with a sneer. "Good Lord, I didn't know you were a pot hunter."

I protested profanely, but to no avail. He swore he had merely been walking through the woods when my shot so close to him startled him practically witless and only then had he seen the bird dive from its perch. You may be sure, too, that he let the story get about as much as possible when we got back to town, and that he swore my birds had all been shot sitting. Indeed, if it had not been for the hog episode, which I used for a little political pressure, whatever reputation I might have had among his friends would have been entirely ruined. So much for the woods pass.

I won't deny that the third type of pass shooting, which I choose to call the slot pass, is a more or less manufactured sport, a means to the end of putting drastic obstacles in the way of a full bag. I never think of this kind of shooting without chuckling at a trumped-up instance of it which did everybody a lot of good who knew of it.

The incident took place in the southwestern part of Georgia. This is probably one of the finest hunting locations in the country. There are a lot of big plantations and commercial shooting preserves which have been stocked and developed persistently to make top-notch quail and turkey hunting. This in turn has had a very definite effect upon the mourning doves. They always did gather in winter in southwest Georgia, anyway, both local and flight birds, but the quail and turkey developments have made what were excellent feeding conditions for them even better, and in the winter flocks of thousands upon thousands of mourners swarm over the territory. Most of the shooting here is habitually done at feeding fields, of which more later.

The man so sadly involved in this slot-pass shoot was a New Englander by birth, inclination, and recalcitrant determination. Everything there was better and finer than anywhere else. To hear him carry on about his grouse and woodcock, you would wonder why the rest of the country even bothered to patronize the sporting-goods stores. All this, of course, led him to believe that when you'd shot grouse and woodcock you'd had the only worthwhile shooting thrills extant. Naturally, such a man was bound to be unhappy over getting dragged into a dove shoot.

On the trip down, he extolled endlessly the virtues of his home birds, and spoke with the most bitter derisiveness regarding the dove. Now no one objected to listening to grouse and woodcock talk, or to agreeing that they're pretty fine fellows. But since this lad had never seen a dove in a legal location, nor shot at one, his condescending attitude toward the bird called for drastic measures. And so, by friendly collusion, he was placed that first Georgia evening on what had come to be known as the slot.

Let me describe the setup. It should be near a feeding field, roost, or watering place. But not too near. In other words, it should catch the birds coming in, after they have begun to lower in flight, so that the bulk of them pass the gun between the treetops and the ground, but before they have started to break speed for a landing. The slot itself may consist of a fire lane or road through pine trees, or any such stand so arranged that the doves fly across a small, perfectly clear shooting space with trees on either side. In this case there was a large, bare field backing up against a pine woods, into which a road ran. If you stood ten or fifteen yards up the road and looked out over the bare field, you had the feeding field farther down on your right, but out of sight. Also, as the birds came in along the edge of the woods, flying from left to right, they crossed in front of the hunter, who could not see them until such time as they were almost to the opening made by the road into the woods. Thus at the most, standing ten yards back in, the gunner had perhaps a thirty-yard flight to follow. If he came out into the open, the doves, which were wild and wary, would see him and shy out of range.

I would say that many of these birds were traveling forty

and fifty miles an hour, because they were really in a hurry and knew where they were going, and the eating competition was going to be stiff once they got there. It hardly needs to be added that a dove traveling that fast, one you don't see coming, doesn't take long to go thirty yards and pass again from view. In addition, in this particular instance, there were few quartering shots. Most of them were higher or lower, but straight broadsides, which meant the utmost in fast reaction to a sighted bird, and fast swinging to get on him and make the proper lead in time to get off a shot. And the real obstacle in this kind of shooting is that you hurry to swing ahead for a lead, then the small range of your angle of vision begins to inhibit you so that you squeeze off the shot too quickly, trying to beat the bird before he passes from view, and consequently shoot behind him. Also, when a lot of birds are flying, it's extremely confusing to try to pick one so quickly from the passing horde.

So this is what we've called the slot pass, and you can find a lot of places to try it out, some harder, some easier than the stand described. It's the sort of thing a team of highly competitive expert shots can have a lot of fun with. The best places to look for such a setup will be in the wooded South— the Carolinas, Georgia, Florida, Alabama, and so on. To digress from my tale momentarily, I know of such a place in Florida that will give you an idea of the possibilities. This is another instance of a road running through a pine woods. Another road crosses it, and a little way down this one there is a dove roost, used year after year.

Toward dusk the birds come in here literally by thousands, flying down the road, lowering down into the slot itself as they near the roost. It is truly an awesome sight to stand on that road toward evening and watch the flight, whether or not you do any shooting. You'd swear every dove in the country had decided to stop over here. And the speed at which they let down into that slot of a road, the whistle of many wings a constant blur of sound, is an exceptional hunter's thrill.

Across the intersection of these two roads there is a telephone wire. And nearby there lives a Florida pine-woods

family. To show you what sort of display the doves put on
there every evening during the big winter concentration, you
have only to talk to these people. Doves for the table? Sure,
they have doves as often as they want them. Until they get
sick of them, in fact, and without the expenditure of a single
shell. Soon as it's dark they go out with a lantern and pick up
all they can eat from the ground beneath that wire. The late
flyers hit it by the dozen in their rush to get to roost!

But back to my New Englander. He was placed in the pines
on the Georgia road stand looking out over the bare field, and
another member of the party was put there with him, so he
couldn't sneak away. When the doves started flying and the
guns started firing, the big grouse man grew red in the face,
and more red, and then a mild purple. He shot and shot without touching a feather, and without daring to look around at
his partner, who, incidentally, was for the most part holding
his own fire and trying to hold in his laughter.

At last the grouse man was so furious he barked abruptly,
"Let's get out of here—to a place where a man's got a *chance*,
at least."

"Why," said his partner, all sweetness and light, "it's just
like shooting those streak-o'-lightning grouse, except the shots
are all wide open."

After that it was thought best by all concerned not to press
the point. The New Englander was taken down to the feeding
field, where the shooting was at least somewhat easier. The
only remark he was heard to make that evening was when he
knocked down his first bird. "There, damn you. . . ," he mum-
bled to himself. He didn't finish whatever it was he had in
mind, but now he goes to Georgia every winter—for the quail
shooting, so he tells his New England friends and those of us
who know the slot-pass story.

And so we come to the feeding-field shoot. All things considered, probably the average sportsman who knows anything
at all about dove hunting thinks of a dove shoot as taking
place at a feeding field. Undoubtedly this method is the most
popular. It is also easier as regards finding a good location,
for once the birds have gathered at their favorite seed bin they

are conspicuously in evidence and not confined to any sky lane so restricted as a flyway. They very often, in fact, come in to a feeding field from every direction, and the whole nature and success of the shoot will depend upon the size of the feeding location and the number of hunters either at the site or in the general vicinity.

For example, I have shot at locations in Arizona where the site was only a small patch of ground no more than a city block in size. One or two hunters on this kind of stand will do all right over a period of several hours, as the doves trade around here and there, or as doves that have been frightened off by shooting come back determined to make another try. But a tiny feed patch, especially one that is isolated, means that every dove will leave and fly some distance at the first barrage. Perhaps you hold your fire until a few birds have come in and settled. These, acting as decoys, will draw down others who pass by. But that first shot drives them all away, and then you must wait once more, unless of course there is a tremendous concentration in the vicinity, in which case doves not yet shot at or near will be constantly coming in.

A New York stockbroker friend of mine, who was born in Texas and always goes back there for the hunting, will never shoot at the first dove that comes in to a feeding field. The gospel in his part of Texas says that the first bird comes as a scout. If you shoot him, no others come in. If everything seems on the up and up, the others follow in a few minutes. Of course I don't believe this. The first dove in may merely act as a decoy to others flying over, showing them that the location is a safe one.

The point to be made, however, about letting a few doves alight is that doves *can* be decoyed. In a heavily shot area you can draw doves down to a new location by making cut-out decoys and placing them around on the ground. This practice is followed to some extent in England with the wood pigeon. In my opinion, however, the use of decoys is a lot of nonsense, for the mourning dove at least, because you can invariably get just as good shooting without them.

A large feeding area is the best bet, and all the better if it is somewhat isolated. Here birds shot at on one side of the field will fly on and still alight on the far side. When the shooting slows up at your stand, you can change locations and still do all right. But of course in a large feeding area several hunters working together and spread out around the area can do better. Shooting from these various locations keeps the birds moving, and also somewhat confused. It doesn't take a flock of doves who are determined to feed in a patch very long to spot exactly where the firing is coming from, if one lone hunter stays in the same spot firing away. Even when two hunters are present, it is a good idea to keep changing positions from time to time, for two guns won't confuse the birds. They'll quickly begin to avoid the locations. However by shifting positions, some birds will always be brought within gun range, for some will constantly be letting down into the center of the area, out of range, and others, seeing them, will attempt to let down away from the x-marked spots, and will bring themselves within range of the new positions.

The perfect hunt of this type occurs when a big concentration of hunters and a big concentration of both birds and feed are found at the same time in the same locality. The barrage, with perhaps twenty hunters spread out around a large feeding site, sounds like real warfare, and the birds fly crazily. The more birds there are, the wilder their flight from gun to gun, and, I might add, the greater the waste of powder. You'd think of course that every last bird would be driven away at the first round. But strangely doves are stubborn little devils. They will keep circling and crisscrossing the area at every angle, really bearing down, but more often than not they'll refuse to get out. The shoot gets to such a pitch, when many hunters are present, that you don't care much whether you hit or miss. Everything is simply moving too fast and too noisily. If your limit is ten birds, you know very well you can get that number eventually, and your firing gets like the old Indian story—you shoot at the bird just to make him wilder so the next fellow can't hit him.

Now it may seem to some readers that a great many birds would fly away wounded on such a shoot. Fortunately, this is not the case. I have heard enthusiastic dove hunters speak of doves as tough, as far as carrying away shot is concerned. This is definitely not true. In the first place, a dove is an exceedingly trim creature, built for high speed and maneuverability in the air. He is therefore built along very dainty lines. His long wings cannot stand the hit of a stray pellet. Even a tipped wing will bring him down. Dove bones are small and the breast, though it makes a delicious piece of meat in the pot, is not hard to pierce. Invariably one or two pellets hitting anywhere will bring the bird to earth.

This brings up another item which applies to all kinds of dove shooting, and which should be kept in mind by every hunter. The mourning dove is gray and pinkish brown. The only white on him is on his tail feathers, and when he falls these will seldom be spread so that the white shows. Thus, a dove blends perfectly with almost every kind of cover into which he may fall, especially during the time of year when the shooting is done. And so you must mark your birds down very carefully, in cover, or even on bare ground. I recall one particular dove that I killed in the South one year, and for which I searched an hour. The bird fell not an inch over twenty yards from me, and it was definitely a dead bird in the air. It fell in short, dead grass, and I walked right to it—or so I thought. There should have been no difficulty at all, except that the hour was late and the light bad. There was nothing to hide the bird. But I never did find it. That will give you an idea.

You can often get a choice stand, whether on a pass or at a feeding field or tank, which will assure you of dropping your birds on fairly open ground. Of course, if a field is surrounded, say, by sedge, which makes a perfect place for concealment, you have to take it as it comes. One surrounded by trees is a different matter. On such a location, you should pick your stand not only in regard to where your birds will fall, but to your best advantage in another respect.

Remember that a dove likes whenever it is at all possible to have clear vision. They will even roost on the ground when tree roosts are scarce, but when this occurs they choose a spot in the open, not in brush. The only times I know of when you can catch doves unaware in spots from which they have poor visibility is when especially good feeding conditions occur in places from where their vision is obstructed, such as deep grain stubble, tall weeds, hogged-down corn, etc. In these places, however, I suspect the birds feel secure because they know they cannot be seen readily by an enemy.

When they perch, it is always in trees or bushes with very light foliage, or else on dead or leafless trees. Especially when any shooting is going on, a dove will never make for a heavily foliated tree. But he will very often, at the first barrage, rise in confusion and circle around, heading finally straight for his favorite type of perch.

When I was a kid, in Michigan, we had a big apple orchard near our house, and on the far side were several tall old walnut trees. If a dove was frightened from its feeding in the garden, or from a nest in an apple tree, or, come fall, from the hayfield where it was picking up seeds, it flew always to the walnut trees. These of course have light foliage and to a dove are appealing because they afford a good view. Thus, when you pick a stand at a feeding field, whenever possible it should be near such a favorite-type perch to assure you the best shooting.

In certain sections where feed is too plentiful over a great area, the feeding-field shoot now and then runs into trouble. For example, in Kansas I found that true, and the same thing is true in some of the peanut- and pea-growing sections of the South. In such places a dove doesn't need to have any *special* feeding ground. He can come down almost anywhere and fill up his crop. And so, unless there is a large and well-scattered number of hunters working the countryside, you have to keep chasing down your birds, a none too easy task when a dove can rise and fly a mile if he likes in about the time it takes you to load your gun and light a cigarette. I have heard South Carolina hunters complain about this. And in Georgia, in the peanut-growing section, there is the same difficulty. One dove-hunting friend of mine who lives in Georgia told me, "Our season opens at the wrong time. Here we have a tremendous acreage in peanuts, and doves love peanuts. There are plenty of birds, but when you start shooting they simply get up and fly to the next field. If they're shot at there, they move on to the next one, and so on. Eventually they'll find a place where there are no hunters. Later on, when the peanuts are harvested and the farmers start plowing up the fields, food becomes scarce. That's the time when a hunter would have a good chance at the birds. But by then the season is over."

The situation is quite different, however, in certain states. In the vast rice fields of southern Louisiana, for instance, the birds get pretty well bunched in certain counties, while other counties may have very few. The same is true in Florida and Alabama. When you get a big concentration in a Louisiana rice-growing district—sometimes actually millions of birds— let me tell you, there's shooting to be had! The feed may be abundant, but so are the birds—everywhere. Your shots may flush and drive off a great number, but others, trading from field to vast field, will be right on their tails, and you can simply stand in waist-deep cover with doves flying crazily and burn powder to your heart's content, always shooting on open shots with no obstacles.

I have seen fellows take a shell container and a jug of water, use the box for a stool and just sit, sweat, and shoot until they either had shot a limit or had emptied the shell box. Maybe that sounds too easy—physically, that is. Well, I don't think so. I have walked fifteen miles a day along the Lake Superior shore after prairie chickens, sharp-tailed grouse, or ruffed grouse, and though I think it's wonderful hunting, it certainly is a disappointing way to wear yourself out on those days when you happen not to have shooting to speak of. But just ease yourself down beside a southern rice field, or conceal yourself in some thin bushes in a southeastern pea or peanut field, and when the birds start flying if you don't find yourself busy and full of enjoyment then you shouldn't hunt doves in the first place.

The old southern-gentleman idea of course was to have a boy or two to keep flocks of birds stirred up, and to pick up the birds you shot. It's still done on some plantations. That's going a little far for my money. I'm willing to retrieve my own birds if I don't have a dog who'll do it. But the point I want to make in relation to the so-called ease of this sport is that I'd rather take my exercise shooting than walking. I go hunting to shoot my gun. *At* something. And the oftener the better. I have shot over a feeding field with a light pump gun when the birds were abundant and on the wing constantly. You couldn't drive them off, and I've emptied the gun, jammed new loads in, emptied it again, until it was literally too hot to handle. That, to my notion, is excitement.

One of the most appealing facets of a feeding-field session with the mourning doves is that the angles of shots are so extremely varied. Here is a bird coming in high and fast. Here is one barely skimming the ground. Another shooting up, rising swiftly, another head-on and burning his feathers, all of them rolling and dipping and swerving as is the habit of these gray bullets. You have to be in the midst of it to know what it's like. All I can tell you is that on a good stand the shooting is as crazy and intense as anything American gunning has to offer.

And that brings us directly to an important caution. A gunner who thinks anything of his hide will make sure he knows where his shooting buddies are, where everyone else known or unknown is, and that he himself is at least a hundred yards away from the nearest gun. Indeed, two hundred yards is better! The extremely varied angles in this kind of dove shooting, and the excitement and pitch of it when things are looking up, make gunners careless. You get swinging on birds above, behind, in front, right, left, and low, all of it happening so quickly that when a lot of guns are ganged up in a small area you and your neighbor have better chances of bagging each other than birds.

To give you an idea, late one afternoon I stood beside a big mesquite tree in Arizona watching a hawk and waiting for doves to come in to a feed patch. Two hunters came sauntering along a railroad track nearby. They took a shot at the hawk. Just to be sure they didn't get me mixed up with the hawk, since he was soaring low over my mesquite tree, I took a careless shot. Presently we had got together and stood around talking near my car. Then, suddenly, doves started coming in, some of them so close they could have been bagged with a net. I downed a bird and ran forward to pick it up. But my new-found partners were so busy with the doves that they didn't even appear to see me. They were suddenly hammering away right over my head and practically at me, with shot cutting the bushes ominously. Luckily there was a ditch beside the railroad track. Into it I went, forgetting the possibility of a stray rattlesnake. And I stayed there, flat and still, until the flight was over.

Afterward I reprimanded these two in pretty sharp terms for their carelessness. "Why," said the one, "I thought you were right there beside us all the time." Careless? Sure. Careless on both sides, probably. But if you have never hunted doves and think the same excitement and close calls couldn't possibly happen to you—or worse—then take my advice and don't try to prove it. Keep a safe distance between yourself and every other hunter, your own partner included.

It is almost impossible to put down concisely what types of feeding fields will be the best gunning bets. The range of the mourning dove is so large, including all of the U.S. portions of southern Canada, and hundreds of miles south of our borders, that all manner of farm crops and wild feed is available, yet certain types of feed will be absent from certain locations because of climatic and altitude limitations. In addition, the mourner is not an especially choosey eater. A tremendous variety of grains and seeds appeals to him. Obviously, if no open water is available over a large area, good feeding conditions won't hold doves. They are willing to fly surprising distances to water if feed is especially good, but will choose an inferior feeding location in order to be within reasonable distance of water.

Agricultural sections where wheat, rye, buckwheat, or corn is raised will draw the doves, rather than submarginal or wilderness land areas. Soybeans, cowpeas, peanuts, sorghum, Lespedeza, mungo beans, rice—all these are a dove's delight. Kaffir, black-eyed peas, and millet also are good. Burned-over areas, where many seeds may be picked up often entice a dove concentration, and so will good stands of foxtail, mullein, milkweeds, sunflowers, and in the West what is known as dove weed. But abundant weed seeds won't hold the birds as well as cut-over grain fields, or fields from which beans, etc., have been harvested. This is because a dove neither eats from a head of grain, nor scratches for food. He picks up fallen seeds and waste grains, and thus the places where the larger grains may be had will be his favorites. One of the best bets used to be cornfields which had been, as farmers say, "hogged down." Nowadays, however, few farmers turn hogs loose in a field of ripened corn, and so it is seldom that such a location can be found.

I would suggest that no good feeding locations be permanently written off if you intend to do a whole season of dove shooting, even though for some time you may not see doves near them. The dove is a creature of meticulous habit in some ways, and in some others completely unpredictable. For example, at times of bad drought in the wheat belt, when few ponds are available for drinking, you will see doves pass over from feed to water day after day, the long flights not varying either in time of day or exact direction. But such an observation can lead you to believe that the same thing will *always* happen in some other location. You have to remember that the first is a case of fitting special conditions to convenience. In a large area in the Deep South where both food and water are abundant, the birds may feed for several weeks within certain confines and then, without having been disturbed and for no discernible reason, all leave. Oddly, they may switch to a location which, as far as a hunter can see, is an area of far less congenial conditions. Or you may go out for a morning shoot in a huge rice field, find thousands of doves, and, even though there is little shooting, discover in the afternoon that every bird has pulled out. They will move from a certain field, or a whole section, or even an entire county—like that—with no change in the weather, or any especially large concentration of hunters to blame. Why, only a dove knows.

It is a good idea to keep in mind, too, that you can never

predict how much shooting a concentration of doves will put up with. On one day—or for a week or more—you may find that it is absolutely impossible to frighten them away from a feeding location, no matter how many gunners are present. The next day they may be so wild that no gun will get near them. The old custom in waterfowl shooting of resting a good marsh, shooting it only every other day, or only a couple of days each week, may be applied advantageously to dove fields, too. However, quite often you can watch the general flight direction of the birds which retreat from your field, and with not too great an effort you can move with the birds.

No matter how you find doves in relation to their feeding grounds, it is best never to plan on permanency. No feed patch remains constant for very long. As soon as it begins to get worked down, the birds look for something better. So study your locality and study the birds. No matter where they go, they're never very hard to find again.

In very hot weather, when you are sure doves have been feeding regularly at the place you've chosen, don't give up too early in the afternoon even though you fail to see a single bird. Many of the very best flights, when it is extremely hot, do not begin until almost dusk. This, of course, is helpful to know when pass shooting also. Or when tank shooting. In some states there is a time limit, which may mean you'll have to quit too early. You shouldn't shoot, anyway, when it is too late in order to be sure of finding your downed birds. But up until such time, the near-dusk hot-weather flights will always be tremendously fast and concentrated, which makes for some most exciting shooting.

Now it might be that some gunners will make little distinction between feeding-field shooting and water-hole, or tank, shooting. However there is a very definite difference, an exceedingly sharp contrast in the types of shots you get, depending entirely upon your approach to this method. For that reason I want to point out the contrast.

In the first place, water-hole shooting brings doves within a precise range. There are exceptions, but in almost all cases the action of the birds is far more predictable here than elsewhere. Doves seldom choose a watering place that has dense cover. That is, the particular *portion* of a pond or stream bank which they pick out is invariably a flat, open sand bar or gravel bank. A pond may have trees all around it except in this small spot, and thus a gunner can take a position to give him the exact shooting angle that is easiest for him. For this reason, tank shooting is perfect for the wing shot who is not altogether an expert and who has difficulty on passes and at the feeding field.

While the birds may pick an open, sandy spot, they are very whimsical in regard to the particular one they choose, and which pond, stream, or lake they choose, in areas where watering places are abundant. One perfectly situated water hole that appears to a hunter as if it could not be resisted by doves will constantly go unattended, while another that looks far less congenial will have every dove in the territory drinking from it. Just why, no one seems to know, although it may be that the popular spot has gravel available of a size especially desired by the birds. Even in arid regions doves will often pass up one of the few really good watering places to flock by hundreds to some tiny seepage. No small puddle should be put down as unsatisfactory when you're looking around in desert country for a dove tank.

I recall an irrigation pond of possibly three acres extent around which I hunted all one season in the desert. There were doves literally by thousands in the vicinity. They utilized the brush and mesquite trees around this pond for roosting and perching places, and a few doves came each day to drink at the open side of the pond and to putter about on its sandy bank. About a half mile away there was a culvert running under a main highway. A tiny puddle of stagnant water was always at one end of the culvert. It was no more than five feet square. But that was the place where the majority of the doves that roosted and perched by the big irrigation pond came to do their drinking. They would sometimes be piled around that tiny seepage until it was a moving mass of hundreds of fluttering and shimmering gray wings. In this case it is just possible that some minerals—salts, perhaps—were present in this seepage water in greater abundance than in the pond. In fact, salt and mineral springs of various kinds will often draw doves, appealing to them far more than perfectly clear, sweet water. Generally, however, in arid regions almost every bit of water, large or small, will have its quota of doves which come for their daily drink, a fact that makes finding a location for good tank shooting far simpler in the Southwest than in the South and Midwest.

You can make of tank shooting what you choose, depending upon how close you place your stand to the spot where the doves alight. You can peg the general range, the shooting angles, and the speed at which the birds will be moving almost perfectly. For example, let's say birds have to fly a mile to drink at a certain pond. There is a small, open sand bar on one side of the pond, and you know this is their favorite spot. Now then, doves have a habit of coming in, circling a pond, and then dropping down to alight. Bird after bird will follow this exact routine. Thus, if you choose a place of concealment directly behind, or to left or right of the drinking bar, you will know precisely how the majority of birds will pass before you. You can set up to take your birds as they come in, or as they circle. They will have broken speed toward the end of the circle, and you can drop bird after bird by holding in almost exactly the same way.

If you want your birds to be really easy, you can plan your setup just as you would plan a decoy setup for ducks. Each bird, as it swings in and flutters down to alight, will be practically stationary, hanging for a split second just above the ground, wings spread and feet letting down. Certainly there is nothing difficult about such shooting. Personally, I'm not in favor of it. I have done my share of duck shooting over decoys, and I know it is exciting. So also is this dove shooting which is so similar. But I don't think hitting a spread-winged duck at fifteen yards as he hangs above the decoys is either very difficult or very sporting. Likewise doves.

As a matter of fact, I cannot say that I am totally in favor of water-hole shooting. Some old-time dove hunters get furious with people who shoot at the tanks, while some feel that the method is legitimate. It seems to me that a stand forcing you to take the birds as they circle makes for good, and legitimate, shooting, if a man is willing to stop at that and not be tempted to shoot birds alighting on the bar itself, or, as some do, shoot directly and blindly into a whole compactly bunched flock on the ground.

The real sport to be had with water-hole shooting, in my opinion, is to place yourself some little distance away from some very small seepage or cattle tank. At such a place the birds won't circle before landing, for there's nothing to circle. And if they have come from a mile away, they come in at a clip that fairly fries the fat off them. One fall I shot at such a place for several evenings, well on toward dusk. The birds all came from the same general direction, and by placing yourself so you faced either with the birds crossing from your right to left or vice versa, you could make the swing of your gun which was best adapted to your shooting style. And believe me you really had to swing.

I stood about fifty yards from this tiny watering place. That meant that every bird crossed me at anywhere from a little above head height to barely skimming the ground. With some of them it was like shooting at ground game such as rabbits, only these rabbits were traveling at rocket speed. Their astounding maneuverability allows them to keep up maximum speed until just before alighting, especially when no circling is done. The hot desert had kept them in siesta until almost dusk and so now they were rushing to drink and get to roost. You couldn't have asked for prettier shooting, or for a more drastic change of consistent angles from the ones you get the most of at a pass or a feeding field. The more you crowd the hole, however, the less difficult and sporting this approach becomes, a blessing perhaps to the poor wing shot, but I'm afraid we still have among us too many meat hunters to put a stamp of hearty approval on water-hole shooting in general.

The fellow who needs a bit of a break from his game to make up for his gun-lining deficiencies should think of another approach to the doves which is simply wonderful sport, but probably the least difficult of all that the dove offers. This is jump shooting. It comes the closest to quail and woodcock hunting, especially the former, of anything I know, yet in all fairness it must be said that it is easier, as to dropping a high percentage of your flushed birds, than either.

It must also be said that jump shooting of doves is one of those kinds of hunting that you don't get every day and just anywhere. Some years ago when almost all grain was cut by a binder the heavy stubble which was left was usually quite high. After the cutting, the fields often lay throughout the whole winter without being plowed. There was lots of waste grain lying down in the stubble, and in such fields doves would feed by hundreds. The stubble concealed them, and cut off clear vision for them. If you walked into the wind, you could usually get within twenty yards before the birds would fly. The result was that beautiful, quail-like shooting might be had in such fields.

Nowadays, however, the fields are usually quickly plowed up, or the grain stalks cut too short to afford cover for any great amount of such gunning. However, there are many places where it still may be had, and if not in stubble then in some other cover that is comparable. Hogged-down cornfields, previously mentioned, make excellent locations. And one of the beauties of jump shooting in a large stubble or hogged-over cornfield is that a couple of hunters easing slowly along keep flushing birds and taking their shots, but birds not hit meanwhile circle back and alight behind. Thus the field can be worked back and forth, if it's large enough, sometimes for a whole morning. As long as there's not too much shooting, the birds will stay put—a definite advantage the dove offers as compared to the quail or pheasant for this approach.

The quail, being a ground bird with short wings, gets off the ground faster and reaches the maximum speed of his buzzing flight very quickly. The dove, with his long wings, rises more slowly, and though he would leave the quail behind in a walk once he got under way, the beginning of his flight pattern is much more labored. In addition, a jumped dove will invariably drive straight away, at least for a few seconds directly following the flush, while the quail may fly sharp right or left, or back over your head. Thus the jumped dove is not a difficult target, but there's something about the *idea* of jump shooting this long-winged sky-lane game bird that makes the sport exciting and unique.

I well remember one time when I was in North Dakota on a fall fishing trip and ran into what would have been wonderful jump shooting, if the doves had been legal there. Hundreds of them were feeding in the cut-over wheat fields, and in weed patches here and there. We had to walk across a big field grown up to weeds that were waist high, and every few feet several doves would go up, some of them waiting until we were practically on them. What I would have given, right then, for an open season! I did, however, have this disappointment made up to me a little later on, in Arizona, and I stumbled upon the location entirely by accident.

Just at the edge of a well-irrigated ranch there was a long, narrow stand of tall weeds. They were dead and dropping seeds, and apparently the doves found them to their liking. As I came onto the ranch looking for a place to shoot, a dove suddenly raised from the weeds. I shot and dropped it. Going in to pick it up from this stuff which was almost head high, another got up not ten feet from me. That one surprised me so I didn't even shoot, but I did turn and work down through that weed row. And I took my limit of birds before I had reached the end!

Foxtail or mullein patches, or fields grown up to wild sunflowers or milkweeds are good bets for jump shooting. You have to search these feeding places out and get to know which ones will produce, for doves feeding in such locations can't be seen and will often stick very tight during a whole feeding session. Unless you have seen doves let down into such places, you never know whether or not they're there until you give the place a trial. If there is dead grass or other ground cover deep enough to hide a dove, and taller growth abundant enough to scatter seeds, in good dove territory the spot is almost certain to get a play from the birds at some time. Your shooting will mostly be done at around twenty-five or thirty yards, for the birds won't lie, like a quail. As soon as they hear you and get alarmed, they'll flush. But their comparatively slow getaway should allow you to make a good score. I would say ten birds to every fifteen shells should be average for a reasonably efficient wing shooter, something that no average shot will be able to do consistently on full-flight birds.

Anyone who has ever tried to stalk and jump-shoot doves in a small feed patch, or in sparse ground cover, knows by now that it's a waste of time. For those who've never tried it, it should be mentioned that in a small feeding location every bird will get up and leave at the first shot, and in a location with thin ground cover you simply cannot get close enough to the birds. However, if you know your hunting territory thoroughly, there's almost certain to be some spot where fairly good jump shooting may be had. And these spots can be important. For example, if you start early in the morning on a pass and find the birds all flying too high, you may have a very light kill. So from there you go on to a feeding field, and if you still aren't filled, you look for a jump-shooting location. This will for the most part be an activity that takes place in midmorning, or in midafternoon before the late flights start.

There is one more interesting type of shooting you can get with the doves, which comes during their siesta time when other methods are either not paying off at all, or are very slow. It's what a southwestern friend of mine calls drop shooting, and is as good practice with a shotgun as you can get.

When you know that the birds are through feeding and have taken to their perches for their lazy session of digesting their breakfast, you stalk them in the dead stubs and the lightly foliated trees in which they're resting. A dove sitting in a dead tree keeps an eye on everything and is difficult to bring within range. You can try for him, but he'll usually get away before you can reach him. But in trees with leaves on, you have at least an even chance of coming within range. The dove habit that makes this stalking good sport is the way they leave a tree. Almost always their midday perches will be fairly high up, and when they take off they don't do so with a clatter of wings, but with wings folded and a straight drop. They simply fall from a perch, utilizing gravity to give them momentum. As they reach to within a few feet of the ground, their wings unfold and they plane upward with a quick sweep and begin to fly.

It's a very pretty sight to watch this maneuver, and it makes for very satisfactory shooting. Seldom will you be quick enough to get off a shot as they drop, but you can try for a shot just as they break the drop by spreading their wings, or as they make the upward plane, or as they break away in full flight. It doesn't sound difficult, but it is really quite a trick to know just where to hold, success on each shot depending of course on how quickly you are able to prepare for the shot.

You have to pick the perching places which will be advantageous to this kind of shooting. If the birds happen to be in low brush, of course there's no place to fall. They then make a noisy take-off and a straighter getaway. Once, on a hunt in Kansas, I missed the morning flight entirely, not getting out until just after noon. There was a row of tall trees running in back of a lane beside a farm pasture field, and in those trees there were dozens of doves taking it easy during the heat of the day. They were wary, having found out a lot about guns that morning. Almost every tree held several birds, which would all fall out at once when I was possibly twenty yards distant. I worked quietly—except for my shooting—straight down the row, rested for a time to let the birds come back, then retraced my steps. I found the shooting somewhat difficult, especially since you never knew which tree held birds. But presently I caught on a little better as to where to hold. I wound up with ten birds before the late flights got started, and had as nice shooting as any doves have ever given me. It's a very good trick for the fellow who is forced to do his hunting when the doves aren't flying, and for the beginner at doves it teaches a great deal about their flight and how to hold on them.

Of course, after we get all through saying exactly what a dove will do and what he won't do, our neat theories can all be destroyed in an inkling by the weather, which has a very definite influence on how well the birds keep their minds on their feeding and on danger, and a striking influence upon their manner of flight. One time I was up in the San Joaquin Valley, north of Bakersfield, California, when the air was warm and still, and the sun shining brightly. Out in the flat country doves were flying with no apparent intent, their laziness and lethargy indicated by the way they hung about with slow wingbeats, and the way they took little notice of any possible danger. Most of them flew low. A man walking across their domain might as well have been a fence post for all the attention they paid.

Presently the sky clouded a little. The air quickly became chilly, and a high wind had soon come up. In a very few minutes there was not a single dove aloft. An inexperienced dove hunter would have sworn this was doveless territory. Then, as suddenly as the flying had stopped, a new flight began. The birds came down the wind, riding it as if it were a bronco, ruddering with tails and wings, traveling at awesome speed. Almost every bird was now far up out of gun range, and so suddenly gone wild and wary that even with many safe yards between them and man-danger the sight of a human being would cause them to swerve and pile on steam. A few birds were down within perhaps thirty-five yards, and a few of them were dropped. But entirely by luck, I'd say, and their momentum carried them as much as fifty to seventy yards even when they were crumpled cleanly, stone dead in the air!

A fine rain or sleet with a high wind can have the same effect on doves. Or again, they will rush to a roost at the first drop of cold rain, and sit facing into it, huddled and looking depressed, though never trying to get under any really good protective cover from heavy foliage.

I have seen them huddle on the ground in a mullein patch during a chilly drizzle or a misty rain, and let you come up almost upon them before they would flush. When you are out on such a day and find no doves flying, and few perching, it is a very good idea to prospect the jump-shooting covers. You never can tell. About the best prediction that can be made is to say that doves will always fly wild and high and be extremely wary when the wind is high or chill, and that on hot, still days they will fly lazily until frightened. However, any sudden change of weather invariably alters the mood of the birds, and so when such a change catches you afield with the shooting slowing down, a variation in your approach and method may pay off. Usually the doves themselves will change it for you.

To my mind, all of these unpredictable whimsicalities of the mourning dove make it a really thrilling game bird, but one on which a single day's shoot for a beginner is not always a fair trial. Though meticulously systematic and punctual in the general routine of each day, the dove is exasperating in his manner of particular choices and actions. He follows absolutely no true or stereotyped flight pattern. Even when doves are plentiful, each day is a new equation in approach. Yet perhaps the most intriguing of all facets of dove hunting is that because of this lack of flight pattern no matter what the method or approach, every bird that comes within gun range is always an entirely new and most uncertain shooting problem.

Chapter 5

SHOOTING THE BREEZE

THE PROPORTION OF DOVES shot *at* to doves shot undoubtedly forms one of the most widely divergent statistics in the gunning world. But it certainly is possible to bring those figures into closer acquaintance by a thorough knowledge of and proper balance among the ingredients that go to make up dove shooting, which is to say, the bird, the gun, the shell, and the man who proposes to do the shooting. I do not intend, however, to put the discussion on any higher-mathematics plane.

The theorists who get everything down to pat science would have us believe that we have only to recognize the truth of their ballistic gospels in order to put them into practice and become never-miss geniuses. It is true that there are good guns and bad guns, proper and improper shot sizes. But the man pointing the gun, and the bird at which he points it are such variable entities that in the last analysis the facts and figures remain just that. *Any* gun plus *any* load will invariably be prepared to do a better job at the ranges for which the combination was intended than will the man who stands behind it and points it.

Don't misunderstand me. I have nothing against gun bugs. I simply suspect that hunters and gun bugs often go disguised as one and the same thing, when they're not at all. The real hunter is interested primarily in the game. He gets himself a well-made gun adequately fitted to himself and to the job he wants it to do, fills it with a reasonable load, learns to shoot it with fair accuracy, then goes out into the field, keeps constantly trying to shoot more accurately, and just has himself one hell of a good time, hit and miss as they come. The gun bug is interested primarily in his tools. He gets himself a gun and then begins worrying and puttering, figuring and theorizing, rebuilding and refurbishing. He intently peruses ballistics tables, chooses the exact load that makes what he talks himself into believing is consistently the perfect pattern for his gun at the desired ranges. He then goes into the field and, although he worries and frets and fidgets while the hunter is having plain old ordinary fun, he actually does have one very valuable advantage over the hunter. To wit, he can at any given time and without a moment's hesitation pull out of his red cap the perfect excuse to fit the precise situation relative to each of his misses. The strange thing about these two types is that they each wind up, give or take a miss here or a bird there, with practically the same amount of game.

All of which leads me to the point that if you are waiting for me to tell you what is the perfect gun for dove shooting you are going to be disappointed, because there just isn't any such gun. The dove, as perhaps no other game bird, high-lights the fact that the man is far more important, and for that reason, in order to become a successful dove shot, you have to get used to the idea that shooting doves cannot be compared to shooting any other game bird.

The *why* may be illustrated by comparison. The buzzing, straight-line, moderate-speed flight of quail flushed from under the nose of a pointing dog calls for a fairly constant set of computations by the hunter, and a fairly constant type of routine and performance. The same may be said of grouse and woodcock. Either of these birds calls for simple enough shooting theories and tactics, except for the confusion caused by their brush habitats. The pheasant, though faster, performs quite consistently, has a straight, low flight, and forms a large target. Waterfowl come closest to doves in calling for the same computations and judgments on the part of the hunter, but the duck, regardless of range, takes up a large space in the sky as compared to the dove, and his flight is always of a perfectly orthodox pattern and pace, while that of the dove is anything but. Thus, if in your mind's eye you project the picture of a dodging, rolling, swerving dove storming down the sky, at any moment high, or low, far off, or close in, with always changing *pace*—all of this particular performance a very *tiny* picture in relation to any other bird at which you have pointed a gun—if you consider these items you come quickly to the conclusion that many matters seemingly important with other game birds lose stature when the dove-shooting chips are down. This bird calls primarily for good *shooting*, and for constantly and radically different hunter computations rapidly following one after the other.

I do not deny, of course, that giving ourselves every possible mechanical break toward making a good score is worthwhile, *if* we keep the relative importance of each portion of the equation in its proper place and balance. Therewith, let us discuss first the simplest item in the bird-gun-shell-man combination as related to doves, shot sizes, and loads.

Fortunately, in dove hunting there is no room except in a very minor way for the ancient argument of the duck hunter as to which is best, small shot or large shot. By its small size and dainty build, the dove precludes the use of large shot sizes. A charge of numbers 4, 5, or 6 at average range would tear a mourning dove to bits whenever a solid hit was scored. Some years ago, number 7 shot was often called pigeon shot, but this was because it had been used a great deal for passenger pigeons and for live-pigeon shoots. Those birds, being larger, required in general something a little heavier than the shot called for with the mourning dove.

Remember now that we are talking strictly about shot sizes and not gauges of guns. I have heard some hunters make the claim that, shooting a double, a load of number 7½ chilled, standard powder load for the first barrel, plus a heavy base charge of number 6's in the second barrel to take the high birds was just the ticket. There is probably nothing wrong with that idea. The main objection I make is that a double so loaded —if you're on a good stand—means you're going to be lambasting a lot of close-in birds with high base 6's, and cutting them to pieces. Regardless of the gauge of your gun, it is true that the larger the shot, the better the velocity holds up at extreme ranges. For example, the charge from a number 6 shell loaded 3¾-1¼, 12 gauge, leaves the gun muzzle at somewhere around 1,440 feet per second. By the time the charge has traveled sixty yards, it is moving only 650 feet per second. The same load of number 4's would be going roughly 720 feet per second. Now the point is, anything over forty yards is a long shot, and as we will see later, no gunner is going to kill doves consistently at much over that, and surely not at sixty yards. Number 7½ shot would be traveling slower than number 6's when they reached sixty yards. But still fast enough to kill the bird, *if* any of the shot hit him. One large-size pellet will certainly do more damage than one small one, no matter how fast or slow it is traveling, but since past the forty-yard mark all patterns disintegrate thoroughly, there is no way to be sure you're going to get *any* pellets into the bird, no matter what the size. The long-range pattern of small shot will be better for the simple reason that there will be more pellets in any given space and thus, since either load, regardless of drop in velocity, still has enough punch to kill the bird if it hits him, I see no sound reason for the larger size. In other words, bad holding and deterioration of pattern at extra-long range are to a far greater degree responsible for the lack of kills than is small-size shot.

Here is a good example of how the large-shot theory breaks down in practice. I was shooting with two partners on a pass where most of the birds were traveling too high and too fast for effective shooting. Both my partners were shooting twelve-gauge guns, the one with number 7½ standard loads, the other with high-base number 6's. The lad with the 7½'s was doing no good. The fellow with the high-base number 6's was dropping a bird for every five or six tries. He asserted, and indeed got number 7½ to believing, that the heavy load of 6's was responsible. So I suggested that since their guns were identical, they trade guns for a few shots. The result was that original number 7½, now shooting heavy 6's, continued to draw a blank, while original number 6's high base, now shooting standard 7½'s, continued to score in almost exactly his previous proportion. The answer, obviously, was in distance judgment, lead, and swing. It seems to me that standard dove loads should begin at nothing larger than number 7½ and work on toward smaller sizes. A practical load matched to the bird, plus any given gun, still leaves the man pointing it the most important part of the equation.

For several falls, I used number 7½ skeet loads for my dove shooting, and had entirely satisfactory results. With the gun I used, and my particular degree of expertness in pointing it, I found that this load would do whatever I was capable of doing. I am not convinced, however, that this is the *perfect* dove load, and in a moment I will tell you why. But the light-powder load, plus a not-too-large shot size, does keep you from tearing up birds at close ranges, and the load will do a lot better than one is inclined to imagine when it comes to reaching out for a dove—if you hold properly. Obviously, choke and gauge both figure in the equation, and we'll get to them presently.

Some years ago, when jacksnipe were still legal game in my home state, I became sold on them. You cannot, of course, compare a jacksnipe to a dove in speed. But the two birds are in the same general category as regards size, and it seems to me that it takes about the same amount of punch to kill either.

Since I had never hunted jacksnipe up to that time, I looked around and discovered that number 9 shot was generally considered the ticket for them. As it happened, the very first batch of shells I bought were loaded with a heavy-powder charge. After I got so I could hit the little devils, I began to change my opinion about the killing power of very small shot. Later on I tried low-charge number 8's on ducks, and didn't think much of them, but later still I discovered that high-base 8's would do a stone-dead job on ducks or prairie chickens at reasonable ranges. Thus I began to use the slogan: never underestimate the power of small shot at surprising distances.

When later I became a dove hunter, I began to think again in terms of that slogan. I tried number 9's with a heavy-powder charge, and I decided you couldn't find a better dove load for average shooting conditions. Skeet loaded, I didn't favor number 9's for the simple reason that I felt they lost velocity too swiftly when you got out toward forty yards. The only drawback to getting too stuck on heavy-loaded number 9's is that very often you can't get them in the stores. However, you can always drop back one size, to number 8's, and use them either heavy or light loaded, and do a fine job. With these small shot sizes, it is simply a matter of having confidence in them and not blaming the shell when you fail to connect. Start blaming your loads and you'll harm your shooting, because nine times out of ten something else will be at fault and you'll never discover it. Hold right, and you'll kill doves with small shot. Today I use whichever one of the several loads so far mentioned is the easiest to get where and when I'm hunting: number 7½ loaded heavy or light; number 8 either way; number 9 loaded heavy. All these are perfectly adequate and legitimate and practical mourning-dove shells. Nothing larger is in the least necessary.

It is obviously impossible to discuss loads without speaking of patterns. And my main reason for going into some small detail about these matters is that we sportsmen as a group are rather mediocre wing shots. By pointing out a few of the fallacies in our pat theories, we begin to destroy the potential upon which our excuses are based. Once we lack excuses, we immediately begin to train ourselves to become better shots, because we relate a poor performance to the really vital reason for its occurrence: the lack of expertness with which we point our guns.

My point is not that by becoming more and more expert we may bring home larger kills, but that in any art—and wing shooting is most certainly an art—proficiency begets greater enjoyment. A man who misses too often learns to miss more and more often, and a man who hits more than he misses learns slowly to hit *much* more than he misses.

Everything I have to say about patterns I want to restrict to ranges not above forty-five yards at the most, for neither pattern nor gun pointer is an effective enemy of the dove with consistency past that point. A man in Mississippi once told me he had not the slightest doubt that more powder was burned on doves in his state, with a lighter lethal effect, than for all other game. I believe this holds true in every state where doves are legal. It is well known that many top-notch skeet shots, and exhibition shots in the employ of the arms companies, have made miserable showings when contacting doves for the first time. Any one of them will state that by and large and over a long period of hunting time, the dove tries the skill of a wing shooter more than any other game bird. Thus the dove backs the argument that the importance of patterns as well as shot sizes is grossly overestimated in our search for a place to lay the blame. Few hunters actually are aware of the sort of pattern they are getting with any particular explosion of a shell, but almost all hunters profess to believe that they know.

First of all, if you have killing velocity for doves at any specified shooting range, then the finer the shot, the more surely lethal your pattern should be. More pellets will strike within the target area. Many a reader will be ready to argue that point by saying that it all depends upon how well your barrel handles any particular size of shot. And that is exactly what I am hoping readers *will* say, because it is one of the most misleading facts in the shooting world. It is true that any given barrel will handle certain shot sizes somewhat differently from the way it handles others, but in any decently made barrel the difference is so very slight when really thoroughly and expertly computed—regardless of how unalterably you may believe the contrary—that by itself it can make utterly no difference in your final score on birds at legitimate ranges. In addition, I have yet to see even the worst of guns that threw a pattern of any size shot with a big hole at exactly the same place each time it was shot. And the reason is this: any barrel, no matter how well made, will never throw any two charges exactly the same. There are too many variables, even down to how perfectly each individual pellet in the shell is made. In addition, a great many barrels will rather consistently throw a bit high, or a bit low. But this, luckily, *is* something the pointer can control. He has only to know what his gun does—and this he should know thoroughly—and then to get used to compensating for it with the angle of his swing.

Now suppose that you are setting out to pattern a gun. You hang up the usual square of white paper, measure off maybe thirty yards, and let fly. You do not get a true picture of what is happening with a pattern, if you want to be technical about it. You don't know, to the split second, when each of those pellets arrived at the desired spot. The only way you could ever know would be to have the shot charge photographed on its way to the target. Imperfect pellets, pellets smashed out of round as they leave the gun, wadding that got in the way may slow down certain pellets or force them off course, so that only half of the entire charge hits simultaneously while the rest strings out some distance behind. Regardless of controlled shot strings, any individual charge is a whimsical entity. At the precise moment when the foremost pellets in the charge reach the bird, there may be gaps in the pattern that you cannot possibly know about. The smaller the shot, and thus the more of them, the better *chance* for a simultaneously saturated pattern, assuming a reasonably well-made tube, and enough killing power per pellet for the particular bird when the charge reaches it.

Let's say now that you are shooting a 12-gauge gun, full choke, at a thirty-inch patterning circle forty yards away. Even if you shot a load as large as 1¼ number 6's, you'd have upwards of two hundred pellets within the thirty-inch circle, regardless of the exact thousandth-second of each individual arrival. Now leave them there for a moment and watch a dove fly. Let us suppose the bird has been shot at and has really turned on the steam, and he has a tail wind behind him. He is traveling sixty miles per hour. We'll talk later about how fast doves fly, in case you don't believe they're capable of such speed.

At sixty miles per hour, this dove moves eighty-eight feet

per second. His widespread wings stretch across at least twelve inches of our thirty-inch pattern. His head, neck, and vital body parts stretch at least six inches the opposite way. One or two pellets hitting wing bones, head, neck, or vital body parts will drop him. If the dove stood perfectly still, thus stretched out, and was anywhere within that thirty-inch circle which contains almost two hundred pellets, there would have to be a terribly big hole almost completely free of pellets, or else the shot string would have to be strung out over a very great distance, to avoid having at least one or two of them hit him. But he isn't standing still. He moves a little more than four whole inches during 1/250 of a second, better than two inches in 1/500 of a second, over one inch during 1/1000 of a second. If you had used number 7½ or number 8 or number 9 shot, there would be progressively far more than the roughly two hundred pellets plastering him. When you are trying to swing your gun at top speed and judge the proper lead for a bird of this small size, forty yards away from you and moving four inches through a shot pattern in less time than it takes you to squeeze the trigger—do you suppose, given any reasonably good gun and small shot, that your pattern, regardless of how poor, is going to be consistently responsible for your misses? It might, possibly, on this shot, or the next, or the hundredth next. But not consistently.

I do not mean to imply that I think certain shells do not give better pattern and shot string and power performances than others. Indeed not. The way shells became good was by constant and costly experimentation by the arms manufacturers, and certainly this has not been in vain. For example, probably the greatest single stride made in years in the manufacture of shotgun shells which will give the utmost in possible performance as to pattern and power was brought about as the result of some ten years of research and experiment by the Western-Winchester people. And because of the peculiar problems involved in dove shooting, shells made on the basis of those research results surely give the gunner one more excellent break toward mechanical perfection when used for this sport.

The great manufacturer problem in trying to get good patterns from shells has always been control of the burned powder gases which send the shot on their way. In a rifle shell, all gases are sealed *behind* the single bullet as it travels through the barrel, and therefore give their maximum power. The lack of a sealed chamber of any kind in a shotgun shell, plus the fact that many pellets travel through the barrel simultaneously, has always posed the problem of gas leakage, which cuts down maximum power, and of pellets melted, deformed, or fused together by being surrounded by the very hot gases. This leakage thus has always been mainly responsible for what we ordinarily call bad patterns.

To contain the entire amount of expanding gases completely behind the charge of pellets all the way through the barrel would keep all the push where it belonged, and would eliminate the possibility of ragged patterns due to fusing or deformation of pellets. This was finally and successfully accomplished recently by Western-Winchester, by placing two cup wads in the shell, above the powder and under the shot, wads with flanges that expand as the charge leaves the shell case and enters the barrel. Thus all of the potent gases are kept where they belong, all the way down the barrel. This is an excellent example of the sort of thing which really can make some difference in final dove scores over a period of time. But we should let the manufacturers do the worrying. All we have to do is learn where and how to throw our patterns most effectively.

Chokes are an altogether different matter. They are something we can actually pin down to constant performance within close tolerances. How important they are is simply a matter of how important you choose to make them. Of course the most advantageous choke, or lack of it, in a tube must be related to the kind of bird you intend to shoot, and the type of shooting you intend to do. The so-called brush gun, open bore and short tube, so often effective on woodcock, and for the first barrel on grouse or quail—if you use a double—can be much more deadly than close-choke enthusiasts would have you think. This is just as true on doves.

And yet, I would not say that an open gun is a good dove gun for the simple reason that during any one session of dove shooting you get altogether too many kinds of shots, from birds trying to fly down the barrel—on which the open bore is perfect—to birds sizzling over or past at thirty-five to forty-five yards. At long ranges, though the open bore throws a pattern so wide that it helps compensate for lack of correct holding, this large pattern is likely to be too thin for consistently good effect.

On the other end of the scale, I have a 20-gauge gun choked down close. I won't claim that my pointing is of the never-miss quality, but I will say that I do a good job of getting a shot off in a hurry. It is a bad fault. When a bird flushes close in, one of two things may happen. I either miss completely because I shoot too quickly and therefore hold badly in relation to a pattern that may be not much over six inches across, or else I make a square hit and have little left but feathers and pulverized bone.

If I were going to shoot doves on a pass, or at some point along a pass where the birds were all moving about thirty-five yards from the gun, this gun would be called perfect by most hunters. It would also be—and has often been—perfect for tank shooting on birds that circle and break speed one after the other at almost the identical spot. In other words, where you can pick your range, and know you'll be shooting at nothing closer than thirty yards and from there on to forty or forty-five, a full-choke gun would generally be considered a fine implement. But on mourning doves in particular that is seldom the case. If you have several guns, and want to bother to carry the close-choked weapon in your car for those times when the birds are flying high, well and good. But notice that I said *you*. I cannot ever be entirely convinced that it is worthwhile even to own more than one gun, regardless of the kind of shooting I intend to do. If you can learn to judge distance correctly, and to point a gun correctly, you soon come to know which shots you can make, which ones you can make, *maybe*, and which ones are definitely out. No one forces you to try those. Getting completely used to one gun is a much overlooked side of good shooting. Intimate knowledge of one gun, habit so instilled in using it that you transcend technique and work automatically, plus sensible limitation of your shooting to the actual known limits of the gun, cut more ice than forty guns. And so I cannot but conclude that for the one-gun man a conservative, middle-of-the-road approach to chokes—the importance of which is probably highly overestimated anyway, and one more excuse to fall back upon for missing—will give the best overall performance for general dove shooting. A modified, or improved cylinder barrel will give you enough spread on the close shots, and not too much on the long shots so that, give and take here and there, you'll neither batter your birds to pulp nor thin your pattern past the point of effectiveness. Again, where and how you hold will be far more important than choke, anyway.

The foregoing brings up the question of the several excellent gadgets now in common use, of which Poly Choke and Cutts Compensator are examples, for giving you several guns in one as far as boring is concerned. I have nothing against them in principle, and I would say that one of these choke modifiers is a very good idea to replace the extra gun spoken of a moment ago. But I would also say that for the man who just can't let well enough alone they are the damnedest nuisances imaginable when dove hunting. Let us say that you equip your gun with some one of these choke modifiers. You go out at dawn and stand on a pass where the birds are moving high. You tighten down. Later in the day, you get into variable shooting and so you change to a more conservative opening. That is entirely sensible. But dove shooting, you have to remember, is usually a fast and furious affair. You are almost always doing more shooting per hour, and at a far greater variety of ranges, than with other game birds. If you get in a dove field and set your choke for a wisp of high-moving birds, then switch again to take a scattering of birds moving in low and close, then medium again for a middle-range loafer, and so on and on, you waste your time, confuse yourself, and get generally muddle thumbed for no better reason than to ruin otherwise good shooting.

So we come to that big, big question: What is the best gun, as to gauge and model, for dove shooting? And my answer, as I stated in the beginning of this chapter, remains the same: There just isn't any such thing. You can call one kind of gun a duck gun and another a grouse and woodcock gun and a third a quail gun, but you cannot do that with doves. There is neither a gun too large, nor a gun too small for these fellows, because of their varied and unorthodox flight patterns. The whole matter simmers down to setting advantages on the large-gun side against advantages on the small-gun side and making your choice as to which advantages you'd rather have.

The double has two disadvantages, to my mind, for dove shooting. It requires too much reloading, and it means extra weight in the wrong place, which is to say the far end of the gun, for swift swinging. To illustrate the point, the double when used on grouse gives you just exactly the number of shots you need. One for the rise with the open barrel, one for the straightaway at longer range in case you miss. Seldom will you get a chance for the third shot. And few long, fast swings are needed. But on a dove pass or field you could often use a feed belt pouring shells through and still never have too many. And you'll constantly be required to follow a bird, swing far past, and fire all in a split second. Thus I would say that the pump or automatic should be the starting point at which to begin choosing your dove gun. They give you extra shells, and are light in the front end.

When we get down to gun gauges, we get into such an argumentative and complicated problem that it is difficult to convince any man of anything unless he wishes to be convinced. There is certainly nothing wrong with using a 12-gauge gun on doves, as far as the size of the hole in the barrel is concerned. My main objections to it are that I do not think such a large gun is necessary, I do not think it can be handled as well as a smaller gun for this kind of work, and it will take a lot to convince me that large guns are not basically responsible for much of the poor shooting of which all of us are more or less guilty. Let me digress a moment in order to show you what I mean.

Years ago, nobody thought in terms of small gauges for shotguns. When finally the twenty-gauge appeared, no old-line wing shooter would get even close enough to it to have a good look, let alone pick it up and shoot it. In the day of the old-timer there was much more game, and far fewer game laws. Consequently, the old-timer had much more practice with his gun, and I don't mean skeet practice. Skeet is a good pastime, and it will teach you many general theories toward betterment of your shooting, but it will definitely not teach you how to hit a live bird. It will only get you used to shooting your gun and knowing something of how to hold for any particular kind of shot presented.

The old-timer became proficient with his large-bore gun, and he passed down to the next generation the idea that with a large gun you couldn't very well miss. Young fellows got in the habit of saying a small bore meant you had to hold too keenly, but with a large bore they felt perfectly confident, and so they never tried very hard to learn *how* to shoot, or to get better. Smaller gauges force a man either to learn the how of wing shooting, and to try to improve, or to go home empty-handed. This is especially true of the average fellow who doesn't get to do a lot of shooting.

There is another side to this matter. It is commonly and surprisingly believed by even fairly experienced gunners and particularly by beginning wing shots, that shotgun shooting is a simple matter, while rifle shooting is extremely difficult. Actually, just the opposite is true. But the belief exists so commonly among persons not experienced with both arms for the simple reason that the rifle, with its single bullet, requires that we *learn* to shoot it before we can do any good at all, while the shotgun, with its numerous pellets can—we think—just be thrown up and shot and we can't very well miss. Thus we find very few good wing shots, but quite a number of good big-game shots. We find very few wing shooters who really know their guns, or what those guns can do. Because a rifle is *aimed* and a shotgun *pointed,* it would seem the shotgun should be far simpler. But with the rifle you take your time, and you have your sighting equations all doped out for you beforehand.

Shotgun shooting, on the other hand, is a complicated mental and physical procedure, and nowhere does this become more solidly emphasized or evident than in dove shooting, where the target is small, swift, and the shots greatly varied, a setup that requires great speed of calculation, decision, and swing, and perfect rhythm.

By and large, most shotgun men like to brag of their long shots, and the feeling is altogether too general that success on a long shot is the measure of a good gun pointer. Nothing could be farther from the truth. The 12-gauge gun, for example, will give you an extra few yards of killing range over the 16. The 16 gives you a few over the 20, and so on. But the gun strainer calls on his gun to do something it was never intended to do. At the extreme maximum of its killing power—a figure seldom even correctly known by the man who owns the gun—few if any gunners have the ability to hold properly to be sure of consistently killing birds. They kill one, cripple four, and clean-miss twenty. They have completely unpredictable and thoroughly disintegrated patterns at such ranges, they don't know where they're shooting, and just what they find to be proud of in such a garbled situation when they do score more or less lucky hits, I have never been able to figure out.

If the only reason for using a 12 gauge on doves is to give you more killing-power range, I see utterly no point in it. To the man who tells me he dropped three doves at sixty yards with his 12, and therefore cites it as the perfect gun for this sport, I say, "So what?" But I would try to learn something from the man who told me he made a straight run on a whole limit of doves at thirty yards, no matter what size gun he used. The really good shot is the one who picks his targets within the limits for which his gun was intended, the man who, if you please, can judge range well enough always to *know* that the bird is within those limits. And, since in dove hunting the shots on any given day are almost never consistently outside reasonable range limits, I see no point in using a 12 just to get a little extra, unnecessary yardage, and a pattern a little bigger so you can be mentally lazy and not point more keenly.

So much for my own pet theories. But there are also very definite disadvantages in the large gun for general dove shooting. As I've said, it's rather often a hot-weather sport, and, though you may not do a great deal of walking, a 12 is a lot of weight to tote for no sound reason. Yet comfort is but a minor issue. I know a crack wing shot who for years used 12-gauge guns and scoffed at anything smaller. One day he took a 20 belonging to a friend and went out into the desert for a dove shoot, and surprised himself so greatly by his much-bettered score that he was converted overnight. The answer was simple. The 20 was much easier and faster to swing than the 12 because it was less gun weight. The less the range, obviously, the faster the swing must be made, and when you're trying for birds at full-flight speed within, say, thirty yards, you have to work any gun mighty handily. It has been proved numerous times among expert shots who do a lot of quail and dove shooting that they will miss more birds with their 12's than with smaller bores. Smoother, faster handling is the answer.

I think a 16 is better for doves, for this reason, than a 12. And I think a 20, likewise, is better for the purpose than a 16. A lot depends, of course, on the physical size, strength, and co-ordination of the individual shooter, a fact too often overlooked generally. A 200-pound man who is quick and alert and has extra-good muscular co-ordination can toss a heavier gun around with better results than can a 125-pound man who has the same attributes. Yet, the same 200 pounder, if he can do well with a heavy gun, obviously should be able to do better with a lighter one, in a sport where speed is essential.

It might seem, therefore, that according to my theories the .410 should be a better dove gun than the 20. But at this point I call a halt. In the hands of an expert shot, who knows the limits of his gun and can judge when he is surpassing those limits, the .410 can be a deadly instrument. There are a lot of gunners, in fact, who use the .410 for doves and who do very well with it. But the .410 shell is unsound ballistically, with a long shot string and often a spotty pattern. For the average hunter it simply does not have enough shot in the right place, or enough punch behind them to carry a general stamp of approval.

This brings up the peculiar situation existing regarding the 28 gauge. Some years ago it became popular with trap and skeet shots, and gained some field popularity, which, oddly, didn't hold. Apparently the gun appeared at the wrong time, before we knew enough about the effectiveness of small gauges. Consequently, few 28's appeared, most of them were hung on 20-gauge frames, or were extremely expensive. We have never so far had a really good 28 at a popular price.

Now then, the 28 shell is a sound one. It contains the same amount of shot as the .410, but it has more powder and better shot distribution and spacing, thus more power, range, and punch. The 28 gun—not on a 20-gauge frame, but a real 28 all through—is lighter than the 20, handles as fast as the .410, and for some odd reason has less recoil proportionate to loading than any shotgun made. If I were going to be put down and quoted as to what comes closest to being the perfect dove gun for use by a crack shot for general shooting, this is the one I would choose. Unfortunately, neither the gun nor the shells have so far become available in quantity and within the average sportsman's price range. If they ever do, this will be the dove gun you'll want—but you'll have to learn to *shoot*.

All in all, then, it would seem to me that at this time, in lieu of a 28, the 20 should be an entirely reasonable and sound choice for dove shooting. It is light to carry, handles swiftly, has all the range any gunner could possibly want, and packs a real punch. I have used mine on almost every kind of game bird in the U.S., and successfully. What inconsequential disadvantages it may have in maximum range as against the 12 and 16 are compensated for by the speed with which it may be handled. The many times I have dropped ducks stone dead with it at average ranges certainly prove to me that it has all the wallop needed for the much smaller dove.

There is but one more item to be emphasized in relation to choosing a dove gun, and that is to think in terms of a stock with very little drop. You want a gun that not only handles well, but one that can be swiftly pointed. A straight-stocked gun brings your eye where it ought to be, as the gun is thrown up, more quickly than one with a lot of drop. This eliminates one more adjustment, or operation, for the hunter, and every one counts.

So now, let's suppose that we have chosen a proper gun and load—for the sake of illustration let it be a light 20-gauge pump action, conservatively choked, loaded with high-base number 9's—and we are going after doves for the first time. It takes but a few minutes of watching them in full flight for us to realize that here is a tough and touchy target. How fast *do* they fly? This we are going to have to know something about before we can possibly compute what our leads should be, and, if we are used to quail, which fly at speeds of from twenty-five to roughly forty-five miles per hour, the dove is going to fool us. The quail gets off the ground and comes rather quickly into full flight because of his short, powerful wings. Once he reaches getaway speed, however, he stays at it as a rule, and certainly he cannot turn on any more steam. The dove, on the other hand, is flying when we spot him—unless we happen to get a chance at jump shooting him—and thus he may be lazing along unperturbed, or frightened and going places. Limned against open sky, his small size further adds to the difficulty of guessing his pace, as also does the fact that a dove flies with supreme effortlessness, whether he is just pottering, or bent on burning his flight feathers.

I will probably be criticized roundly by the scientists when I say that doves often fly upwards of seventy miles per hour. So I'll beat the scientists to the draw by criticizing them first. Most of them agree that the mourning dove is a thirty-five to forty mile-per-hour bird. That may be true as far as it goes. The trouble is, those same scientists probably weren't shooting at the doves they clocked, and they were probably figuring basic general flight speeds, without the assistance of tail winds.

I would say that a dove on his own, flying in calm weather, going nowhere in particular, probably has a customary flight speed of around thirty-five miles per hour. I don't believe he will ever fly a great deal slower. He has a basic speed habit, just as we do in walking or in driving a car. Put a wind behind him, however, and his speed will increase at least as much as the speed of the breeze he's riding. Take a shot at him, and you'll see him set his wings deeper, work them faster, and fairly leap ahead in the air. Let him come down a mountain with a tail wind and a shot charge chasing him, and you'll see some flying that is about as far above thirty-five miles per hour as that figure is from standing still.

I have never measured dove flight speed as precisely as it should be measured to become official, but I have many times seen them fly along beside my car when my speedometer said sixty, and watched them swing out in front, stay there for what would be a few city blocks, then with a burst of speed slash across into a field, whirl, and alight while I was still passing. A bird couldn't turn that trick at thirty-five miles per hour, no matter how far off my speedometer was, and his sensational maneuverability in turning aside, cutting speed, and alighting so quickly is something else to reckon with.

I have shot at doves flying downwind and running a gun barrage when the shooting was at only moderate ranges, and wondered why I couldn't hit them no matter how much lead I used. Then, trying what I considered a perfectly foolish idea, I have upped the lead to ten feet or more and suddenly scored a lucky hit. Obviously the birds were passing at a great deal more than the basic thirty-five miles per hour to make such leads necessary, and since leading such an erratic and tiny target such distances is something no hunter can do with consistent success, a kind of shooting no one can possibly know or learn very much about, I simply gave it up and picked the easier shots. Undoubtedly, doves do not fly any mile-a-minute speed, or over, for great distances. But they don't need to. A thirty-five to forty-five mile-per-hour speed is fast enough to make tricky shooting, and if a bird does turn up his speedometer to sixty for only ten seconds, and it happens to be during that ten when you're swinging your gun on him, then he's a sixty-mile bird as far as you're concerned, and you'll have to lead him accordingly.

Thus, any kind of dove shooting is going to call for at least a good basic knowledge of how a shotgun should be handled, and it might therefore be a good idea for us to review a few of the elementals. I think it is safe to say that fundamentally there are only three ways to get off a shot, assuming of course that the gunner doesn't just shoot blindly and hope for a lucky hit. The general terminology for these is snap shooting, half-snap, and swing.

Snap shooting is the fastest method, and is a perfect style for brush shooting when the targets are quail, grouse, or woodcock. Snap shooting also has its place in working the doves, but if you can do nothing successfully *but* snap shooting, then you will definitely have to enlarge your repertoire of styles if you want to be able to call yourself a good dove shot. In ordinary field work, for example, on quail or woodcock, pheasants or grouse, the greatest share of the shots is at birds rising and going away either at an angle or tail-to. In addition, the gunner is usually within fairly close range. He swiftly throws up his gun, aims either directly at the bird, or with very little lead at a point where he knows the bird will be when the shot gets there, and slams off the shot. For jump shooting of doves, the snap is proper. For doves passing close, it is a *must*.

For example, here is a dove passing within, say, ten yards of you traveling at forty miles per hour. You cannot possibly throw your gun to your shoulder, follow this bird with it, swing the muzzle ahead of him, and shoot. In order to do so you would have to swing the gun almost as fast as the bird is flying. Thus you must either snap shoot with extreme speed, or wait the bird out, letting him put distance between himself and the gun, after which you can swing on him. Contrarily, however, it is senseless to try to snap shoot on doves at general ranges. You may make a few lucky hits, but you'll never know how you did it, and most of the time you will shoot far behind for the simple reason that their speed, added to the equation of the greatly lengthened arc of shooting, means that while you may point and shoot at a perfect leading distance the bird is meanwhile closing the gap at a swift pace.

The half-snap style of shooting, as practiced by most wing shots, is primarily for use when the range is in between. For dove shooting at ranges around twenty yards it can be very deadly, since it is a combination of snap shooting and swinging. You know at this short range that you cannot point behind, and swing fast enough on a full-flight bird to catch up with him, pass him, and gain proper lead. You feel also that you may very well miss if you attempt to snap shoot at him. And so, you bring the gun up swiftly *below* him, swinging upward at about a forty-five degree angle to the point which you consider the proper lead point. When the muzzle reaches that point, you snap off the shot. There are variations, of course, but basically the half-snap motion is from below, moving up and ahead swiftly, with the muzzle actually stopping at the predetermined point as the shot is squeezed off. It is the perfect shooting style for medium-short ranges, but unless the gunner is an expert it is just as worthless as full-snap shooting at thirty to forty-five yards.

I doubt if any other game bird calls for correct swing shooting to such a degree as the dove. Primarily, of course, learning to swing correctly is the most important part of learning to shoot a shotgun at flying targets. But a very great many hunters fail to learn the art simply because they can't get the hang or the habit of continuing to move the gun muzzle as the shot is fired and *after* it is fired. By and large, at least seventy per cent of your shots at doves will call for swing shooting, which—assuming the proper requirements in coordination and speed on the part of the hunter—means at birds anywhere from twenty-five to forty-five yards.

In principle, of course, this style of wing shooting means that you spot the bird, throw the gun up with the muzzle bearing behind the bird, then swing the gun along the exact angle and line of flight of the bird. You swing swiftly, passing the bird, keeping the muzzle traveling along the angle and flight line. When the muzzle has reached a point that you consider the proper lead for a killing shot, you squeeze the trigger. But you do not halt the motion of the gun. The muzzle must continue traveling at the same speed during the time when the shot is being fired, and to assure that you do not halt or even slow up or pause or hesitate, the muzzle should be kept in motion even *after* the shot is fired. A great many otherwise good wing shots ruin their performance by failing to follow through in this manner. If you get in the habit of stopping the swing immediately as you fire, you discover that you are actually hesitating during that split second of firing. And such a habit, obviously, completely disrupts the most perfect computation of lead, for the bird closes the gap and the shot becomes actually a snap shot at the end of a long swing. Successful swinging takes rhythm and practice and the ability to do two things at once. If you master swing shooting, then snap and half-snap will be a cinch, and since for dove shooting—because of the constant variety of ranges and angles during any one session of shooting—you will need to utilize all three styles, it is best to go after proper swinging first and let the other two take care of themselves. Snap and half-snap styles are fast, but neither is by any means as precise as the slower method of swinging. Once you learn to swing correctly, you have only to be able to judge the range of your birds, their speed, and then to successfully compute proper leads, to become a dove shot as good as they come. And if you can become a crack dove shot, you won't have to worry about your score on other game birds!

In judgment of range and flight speed, the two main items upon which the amount of lead to use must be based, you have first to come to know your bird, so that you can judge immediately whether it is a loafer, a bird moving with purpose, as to feeding ground or water, but not frightened, or a bird which for some reason—perhaps because it has been shot at or has a tail wind behind it—is moving at its fastest pace. If you get so you think in terms of these three speeds for doves, you won't go too far wrong. Your lead will simply be progressively a little more for each one, depending of course on the range. Exactly what those leads should be cannot very well be put down on paper. They will depend on several complicated individual equations: perfection of your muscular co-ordination; speed of your reactions; the firing time of the gun you are using; the speed with which you swing the gun. In other words, a good dove shot can tell you only what works for *him*.

Starting from scratch, a bird passing at a perfect right angle to the gun will need the greatest amount of lead of any bird at any given range. As the angle sharpens, the lead will decrease. These are mere fundamentals, but in dove shooting the fundamentals, so often generally overlooked or forgotten, are your most important tools. If a right-angle bird is passing you at thirty yards, and you use a lead of two feet and make a kill, then you might figure roughly that, for you, a bird passing at forty yards will need a lead of four feet and one at fifty yards would require at least eight feet.

I can give you in very rough figures the leads that work for me on doves flying at what might be called medium-fast dove speed, in other words, about what you'll find during a feeding-field shoot on a calm day. Passing at right angles, twenty yards out: about 1½ feet, but you cannot use the swing method on him, unless you are tremendously fast. As a matter of fact, a twenty-yard dove, no matter what his angle, is one of the toughest of wing-shooting problems. It is my opinion that doves in full flight below that range are very seldom hit except by chance. Thus, if you set twenty yards as the lowest reasonable range, and begin at that range using the snap method of shooting, or the half-snap if you're fast enough, you can work out from there to find your perfect individual killing range.

At twenty-five yards, in my book, you can also use about 1½ feet of lead on crossing birds, and do very nicely. But this, of course, now becomes a swinging shot. For me it is one of the best ranges for passing birds, for with a conservatively choked gun you'll get your shot all within no more than a twenty-inch pattern. You have to shoot keenly, but you invariably kill cleanly or miss completely. At thirty yards, for me, lead on this shot will jump to 2 to 2½ feet; thirty-five yards will call for 3 feet; forty yards for 4 feet. At forty-five yards you will need at least 5 or 6 feet, but I would not attempt to tell anyone how to hold on birds at or over this range. It is chance work. If you have the gun for it, say a 12 gauge, choked down, loaded with high-base shells, you may get the hang of it, or there may be times when the birds are flying high that you'll suddenly catch on and start dropping them at fifty yards. Well and good. I must warn you, however, that the next time you try it you'll probably realize you've forgotten how.

Let me emphasize once more that in dove shooting you should not become discouraged too quickly. The habits of a gun remain constant. Those of a man shooting it do not. After a series of misses that get you rattled, if you'll just think about a hypothetical dove which is sitting on a bare limb thirty-five yards away from you, you'll soon get yourself straightened out. You know darned well you could hit that sitting bird ten times out of ten, and so it isn't the gun or the shells. It's you. It's bad holding. Think of it this way, and you'll quickly be able to pin down the fault, which is probably in your speed of swing, or your computation of necessary lead.

Just how you can go about learning to estimate range properly is something else you have to work out for yourself. One way is to mark off known target ranges and shoot at them until you get distances fixed in your mind. Another that works very well in actual dove shooting is to place your stand at known distances from several trees or bushes close by. Birds passing near them will be expertly measured for you. But such measures, in my opinion, should be used only for practice. Don't get dependent upon them.

There will always be certain shots that are easy for any individual hunter, and some that are difficult. Crossing shots, especially perfect right-angle shots, should be easy for everyone, because close attention to lead will so consistently drop these birds. The simplest of computations can be made where there is no strange angle to judge. An incoming bird, overhead, will also be an easy bird for you if you snap shoot at it when it is at twenty yards, and possibly forty or forty-five feet in the air. Simply throw the gun up till the muzzle blots out the bird, so that he is behind it, squeeze off the shot, and he's yours. If the range is doubled to forty yards, for me at least, a lead of three feet in front will turn the trick on these overhead incomers. The really tough birds are those coming in from whatever angle and dropping down, sideslipping, swerving, so that you never know exactly where to hold at any given instant, especially if there's a wind. I doubt if any wing shot, regardless of experience and expertness, can tell you how to hold on these. It's something you have to learn by trial and error.

As I have said repeatedly, the dove has no really orthodox flight pattern. However, close study of the most general flight habits of doves will give you tips which may often mean the difference between a good score and a poor one.

For example, watch especially closely that habit of slyly angling off, which a dove practices regularly on approaching a spot of which he is suspicious. He accomplishes this change of range so quickly and unobtrusively that as you swing on him you may discover that what was a perfect setup for a 2-foot lead has become a necessary 3-foot lead by the time you're ready to fire.

Almost always when you shoot at a lone dove and miss him, he will dive. This he does, I suppose, to gain momentum, exactly as does a hawk. It is a trick that causes untold waste of ammunition on the second shot. There is something about a miss that makes any gunner overanxious and annoyed so that he regularly slams off a second try before he actually knows the new flight angle of his bird. With the doves, the proper routine on a miss is to wait out the dive, wait until the bird has come up again and leveled off, then swing on the new angle and take him.

If you are at a feeding field and see a flock coming in, you can be reasonably certain that when you fire the flock will leave in a different direction from which it came in. Thus you can plan roughly where your angles for second or third shots may be. And you can be pretty sure, too, that as the whole flock takes off on its new course it will go through a short interval of desperately trying to gain altitude. During this interval, remember, when the birds are rising, they are certain to be concentrating on that endeavor alone, with no time right then for fancy flight tricks. In other words, this fast, rising flight will stay fairly even as to course, and this is a good interval in which to pound away. Once the birds have gained what they consider sufficient altitude, their barrel-rolling, sideslipping antics will begin again.

The most important single flight item to note well, however, is that a dove in flight is forever changing his pace. You will never see a mourning dove actually coasting on spread wings, unless you could call the intervals between wingbeats coasting, or think likewise about the break in speed a dove makes when he circles and prepares to alight. A pheasant, a grouse, a quail will give you perfect opportunities for coasting shots, but the mourning dove's wings are constantly maneuvering when he is aloft, and for every wing maneuver—especially when he is under fire—his pace changes. Obviously, your computations must change with it. If you know these things, you then begin to consider each shot presented to you as an individual study in lead, swing, and angle. By doing this, and not attempting to relate general conceptions to what, with doves, will always be a series of individual performances, you keep alert, you're never surprised, and you eventually get to the point where you can hang up a good score.

A word should be said about dogs. To my way of thinking, it is an unnecessary waste of time to attempt to utilize them in dove hunting. Once in a very great while you might run upon stubble or heavy cover in a feeding field where the doves will sit tight, especially if there's a wind to cover up the noise of your walking. And at such times a dog can be used to flush birds. I have tried it with a cocker spaniel, and both the dog and I had fun, but I see little point in it, for you can flush the birds to your own advantage much better by quietly walking them up yourself.

It is true that the right dog comes in handy for retrieving birds. It is also true that a great many dogs have about the same attitude toward picking up a dove as they have toward picking up a woodcock. The feathers come off a dove very easily, and whether this annoys a dog, or whether doves smell badly to them, no one knows. Some dogs will retrieve them without any sign of annoyance, and some want no part of it.

I recall one dog in particular, a big Arizona pointer named Danny, who belonged to a friend with whom I shot a good deal near Tucson one year. We took the big fellow along mostly because he raised such hob at being left behind. There were a lot of quail around the places where we hunted, and he was forever pointing them and being disappointed, since the dove season that year outlasted the quail season. Well, we would knock down a dove and Danny would watch it plummet with absolutely no interest. We would insist that he go after it, and this he would do. But not until he had been sharp-talked very sternly, and then not willingly but with tail and head drooping and every step such an effort that we had to laugh at him. He would search and search, all the time knowing exactly where the bird was. And at last when his master told him briskly to stop that nonsense and bring in the bird, he would pick it up as if it were both red hot and rotten. Forlorn and contemptuous, he would come plodding in, seventy-five pounds of dog acting as if four ounces of dove was more than he could possibly tote.

I had seen him fetch quail, and always he brought them in with his head high and tail wagging, brought them straight to his master, sat down with great dignity, and gracefully handed them over. The dove, however, was something else. He would finally mosey up within ten feet or so, but he wouldn't look at either of us. With a toss of his head he would spit out the dove onto the ground, turn his back, and sit down.

I broke a young cocker to retrieve doves one fall, and she didn't seem to mind. She would follow closely, took an interest in the shooting, and was eager to do her part of the work. But later, after she had got a taste of hunting where she flushed the game, she didn't like the doves. All told, I would say that a dog is entirely unnecessary, but if you have one which will retrieve doves without making a fuss, it certainly can do no harm to make use of it. I would not, however, force a good quail or pheasant dog to retrieve doves if they are as distasteful to him as they were to old Danny. I suspect that a temperamental dog might have his retrieving ruined thereby.

As to other equipment for dove hunting, little more is needed. A good pair of shooting glasses, I think, is important. Most of your dove hunting will be done in hot or at least warm, sunny weather, and a lot of it will occur when the sun is either coming up, or going down. You therefore have a sun-glare problem quite as bad as when you're duck shooting in bluebird weather, and tinted shooting glasses not only give more comfort and accuracy, but give you much needed protection during a long shoot.

What you wear in the way of clothing doesn't make very much difference. Certainly in the South it won't need to be anything more than a light shirt and breeches, and a long-visored cap to keep the sun out of your eyes. You should, however, give some thought to boots, even though they may be hot, because you may be doing your hunting in snake country while the season is still early and before snakes have folded up for the winter. I have never had the slightest snake trouble, nor have I ever felt that there was as much snake danger when dove hunting as when quail hunting, since you aren't working much in heavy cover for doves and are, in fact, standing or sitting still a good share of the time. But it doesn't do any harm to use caution. I personally wouldn't do any kind of snake-country hunting without having an emergency snake-bite kit along.

Aside from that, don't forget your water jug, and you're all set except for some gadget for carrying shells and birds. I've found that a regulation, inexpensive canvas trout creel isn't a bad shell and bird bag. It beats a shell vest for hot weather hunting, and there's plenty of room in it for a limit of doves—especially since the number of no-bird shells you're soon rid of when the flight starts always empties it in a hurry!

◇◇

Chapter 6

MOURNERS FOR TOMORROW

B Y ALL ESTIMATES and surveys available it seems certain that the annual legal kill of mourning doves at the present time is at least 15,000,000. Only the quail kill and the pheasant kill top that figure, the quail running somewhere around 22,000,000 and the pheasants somewhere in between.

I have always suspected that the kill of mourning doves runs much higher than officially reported. The nesting dove has always been a prime target of kids with air rifles. Many a quail hunter who fails to find an abundance of birds turns to the dove, open season or none. The poaching element in back-country sections baits many a secluded field, enticing doves by hundreds, and making heavy kills. From what I know of the past history of extravagantly illegitimate dove shooting in certain sections, and from the records of current arrests for violations, it seems clear that the gross annual dove kill may actually crowd upward nowadays—what with the tremendous increase each season in the number of hunters afield—toward the 20,000,000 mark.

When we hunters harvest that large an annual crop from out of the flocks of a single species, no one can question the fact that the bird is tremendously important on a national scale. Knowing these figures, it becomes all the more curious that so little has been done in the past to assist the dove, and also, knowing these figures, the dove himself becomes all the more remarkable. You can still see fabulous concentrations in

161

the South in fall. If the dove can do this with so little assistance and such heavy gunning, there's no limit to what he could do with us fully behind him. He could be *one* game bird of which posterity might always be certain!

Now it is true that the dove appears to be doing nicely, regardless of our inroads. But small studies here and there have shown that appearances are deceiving, at least in certain sections, and that it is time we took some very definite thought of the dove in his relation to conservation and the national wildlife picture.

It is doubtful that illegal shooting alone is an important enough factor to make or break the dove as a game bird, but examples of it dramatically point out what can happen to a bird which habitually concentrates its numbers during open seasons.

Not long ago it was common practice in the Southeast and South to hold regular festivals of dove shooting over baited fields on the large plantations. At a single authentically re-corded shoot of that time, a session lasting one day, 8,000 doves were killed! One especially bad effect of such slaughter was to get hunters in many places in the habit of thinking of the dove as a practice, or target bird. No attitude could be more wrong, or dangerous. We have no room in the present-day economy of nature versus civilization for practice birds, unless it be a bird such as the crow. And the real danger of the practice-bird attitude is that it fosters lack of respect for both the game laws and the target.

With the old-time festival dove shoot established, the dove began to decline over almost the entire nation, for those huge southern concentrations were partly made up of birds that had migrated from who knows where. The Migratory Bird Laws, which placed the dove under federal control, brought some relief. But the habit remained among many gunners, and still today the old scenes are often re-enacted. Such practices serve to illustrate dramatically the fact that a bird which gathers in heavy concentrations must be approached, as far as protection and conservation measures are concerned, with somewhat different considerations from those attended the ground dwellers. Violators can do untold damage to the national dove crop over a wide area by even a single day of unrestricted slaughter in a very small section.

Within recent seasons the dove has flared forth rather violently once more as a bird of dissension, and has finally drawn enough attention so that at present a rather pretentious dove survey and study, which is to last several years, is being made co-operatively in eleven states of the East and Southeast. There have been other dove studies of restricted scope in the past few years. H. Elliott McClure did several seasons of work in Cass County, Iowa, on a co-operative study backed by the Iowa State Conservation Commission, the American Wildlife Institute, and the Fish and Wildlife Service. This dove-management study turned up many useful facts, as did also one carried out by George C. Moore and Allen M. Pearson in Alabama, also co-operatively backed by several state and federal agencies. Some other states, also, have made small surveys. But none of those restricted studies can mean much on the overall conservation picture for the simple reason that the dove is migratory and also breeds in all states under greatly varied conditions. What the dove requires for abundant survival can only be learned finally, as with the ducks, by projects carried out over wide territories, so that all the facts that need to be known can be *known*, not guessed at, so that seasons and bag limits and shooting regulations may be set more intelligently and with more certainty of reasoning.

In the past several seasons there has been much disregard of law and order by rather large groups of dove hunters in certain areas. Oddly, it may be that the final outcome will be all to the good because of it. One of the best examples occurred in Mississippi during 1947. The seasons, set co-operatively by the Fish and Wildlife Service and by the states fell that fall as follows: Tennessee, Sept. 1; Arkansas, Sept. 16; Mississippi, Oct. 16. Naturally, hunters in those portions of Mississippi nearest to the other two states in question felt that this was a stupid arrangement. Tennessee and Arkansas hunters would get the best shooting, before too much southward migration and too much harvesting and working up of land had interfered. When September first arrived, even though the Mississippi season was not to open for a full six weeks yet, hunters there got out their guns and began shooting. And they continued right on through to the end of their *own* season. Obviously, this was a protest against what those hunters considered stupid handling of hunting regulations by state and federal authorities.

During the 1948-49 season, Georgia and the federal authorities had practically modern warfare over dove-hunting regulations. Hunters there claim the season opens and closes too early. They don't get shooting until after the peanuts and other crops are harvested, when, with feed scarce, the birds gather in shootable numbers instead of staying scattered. Consequently, hunters observe the season fairly well, but baiting is rampant. During the 1948-49 season armed federal agents equipped with spotting planes really cracked down on Georgia.

I was there. I heard the talk of both the federal men and the local hunters. I must say in all fairness that I was not well impressed with either the attitude or the knowledge of the federal agents. What local hunters want is the right to bait fields, register shoots, and have legal supervision to see that limits are observed. I'm just broad-minded enough, and curious enough, about such experiments to believe they might have something.

All told, it appears that what we are witnessing is a tremendous amount of newly awakened interest in the dove as a game bird to fill the bags of the ever increasing legions of hunters, and to replace some of our declining game birds. But what we are discovering is that we don't know enough about the dove to handle him properly on this new and larger scale. There is altogether too much confusion about the setting of dove seasons. The federal people first set a season period, from which each state may elect to take so many days, either as a split season or all at one time. These season periods are established on the basis of the past year's kill, and on meager survey information that has come in from federal operatives during the current nesting season. Each state then battles out its own solution, choosing those periods which it supposes to be the best for its own interests.

The result, of course, is that when you look over the federal dove season recommendations and then the final state regulations you get the most conglomerate picture it is possible to conceive, with seasons running in bordering states seemingly without rhyme, reason, or even plain common sense. Naturally, the hunters who get the short end are angry. And they want to blame someone.

Not knowing enough about the dove, the men responsible for setting seasons *have to guess*. All this guessing, of course, is bound to foster shortsightedness, and error. As an example, some few years ago in Texas there was a season set for the whitewing in the sections where it was plentiful, and another season set in these same locations for the mourning dove. This was done in all good faith, to give hunters the benefit of two dove seasons, and to take pressure off one species while the other absorbed the inroads of its harvest. But in the shooting excitement little thought was given to careful identification, with the result that literally hundreds of mourning doves, which were illegal game during the whitewing season, were killed and left to rot where they fell, the gunners being dubious about taking a chance on picking them up and being apprehended.

Along with the necessary guessing because of lack of real knowledge, and the honest mistakes of the wildlife biologists, there is too much of politics connected with conservation departments in some of the various top-notch dove-hunting states. Mississippi, fortunately, is beginning to get her situation somewhat better in hand. So is Tennessee. Texas has done pretty well. Georgia is in tough shape. Several other southern states have no reason to point the finger at Georgia.

All of which may not seem to have much to do directly with you and your dove shooting, but most certainly does. We are finally realizing that the dove is important, and also that we must begin managing him. We are rather suddenly realizing, too, that we must have some intensive study of the dove as a game bird before we can manage him. And, in feeling around slowly for facts about him, we are discovering that the dove is just as much a problem child when it comes to management as he has been a bird of contention and dissension for centuries. That is the one basic and elementary reason why no one has wanted very much to tackle his case in the past. This angle can best be illustrated by comparing the problems involved in dove management to those involved with other game birds.

Look first at the quail. Suppose you have a section of land in a geographical region well adapted to bobwhite. Theoretically, if you have a healthy stock, provide adequate food and cover, keep down the predator element, and restrict your shooting to a sensible harvest, you can perfectly control the number of quail so that continuing abundance may be had.

Now have a look at the ducks. We set up refuges. We plant them to abundant duck food. We allow no shooting. We see to it that nesting conditions are correct, and do our best to cut down predators. Consequently, the ducks soon catch on that here at our refuges they don't get bothered or killed, that they may feed, or raise their families with a minimum of annoyance and danger. Presently we have rafts of ducks using the refuges. By spotting these refuges along their migratory flight lanes, we assist at least a breeding stock of ducks to get through in good health from border to border. But the only reason we are able to make such a refuge system work is that ducks, happily, are water birds. Thus, their habitat possibilities are definitely restricted, and we use these natural restrictions to the duck's advantage.

When we compare the dove situation to these other examples, it is immediately easy to see why the dove is hard to control and assist. Paradoxically, the fact that his nesting sites are completely scattered has saved the dove from the colonial destruction of the passenger pigeon, yet these habits have at the same time made it practically impossible for us to control the doves. We can set up a dove refuge if we like, with abundant food, good nesting sites, and plentiful water. However, except in barren and arid regions of the Southwest, we still have no guarantee that the doves will use our refuges. Breeding as they do in all forty-eight states, a few here, a few there, we cannot entice or restrict them. The dove is simply too much of an individualist.

I do not think, however, that we should give up. It is very possible that we may be able to learn, eventually, how to *improve* habitats which the doves have already chosen, so that a better dove crop will be consistently forthcoming. So far that possibility is an almost closed book, and will remain so until exceedingly detailed studies and experiments in numerous areas have been completed and evaluated. However, each dove hunter can equip himself to assist the doves in some small amount merely by understanding as much about them, as he can. Let us therefore have a close-focus look at the mourning dove and what is thus far known of him. By becoming better acquainted with him and his whimsies at home we may without further confusion know better how to approach him to our best future advantage in the field. As Mabry Anderson, southern writer and conservationist who has fought for the dove for years, once said: "If you don't care for the sport, leave the birds alone, (but) sportsmen interested in the perpetuation of this sport should at least learn about the life history of their target."

Let us therefore begin from scratch by noting that the mourning dove—of which there are two subspecies in the U.S., eastern and western, so alike as far as we hunters are concerned that we need make no differentiation between them here—has been and is sometimes still known colloquially as the sharptail, the Carolina dove, the wood dove, the wild dove, and the turtledove. This last is a complete misnomer, and has a curious origin of errors. In Europe there is a dove rightly called the turtledove, a bird rather similar in appearance to our mourning dove. The last half of the scientific name given to this European bird long ago was *turtur,* a Latin word which attempted to describe the softly cooing voice of the bird. Somehow this Latin name was mistaken by Europeans as having been intended as "turtle" in English, and so the bird became known as the turtledove. Early settlers in America, seeing the mourning dove, confused it with the species they had known in England and Continental Europe, and so gave it the same name, which has stuck in many places. It is interesting as an aside to note, too, that there are several places in the Bible where the translators made the mistake of using the word "turtle" instead of "turtledove." For example the passage: "And the voice of the turtle was heard throughout the land." Turtles are of course voiceless, and what was meant was the cooing of the turtledove.

The scientific name of our mourning dove is *Zenaidura macroura,* and it too has an interesting and rather distinguished origin. It seems that one of Audubon's best friends—in fact, a patron of his—was Prince Charles Lucien Bonaparte. Bonaparte had a very beautiful and shapely wife whose first name was Zenaida. And so, when the scientists got around to giving the final present-day classical name to the beautiful and shapely mourning dove, which Audubon had painted and studied, the wife of Prince Charles received the honors. Zenaida was changed to *Zenaidura,* for in Greek *oura* means tail, and of course the long, wedge-shaped tail of the mourning dove is his most important identification tag. The last half of the scientific name, *macroura,* comes also from the Greek, and indicates that the bird's tail is very long. And so sciencewise, our mourning dove becomes the American dove with the long, pointed tail, and as shapely and beautiful as Zenaida, wife of Prince Charles Bonaparte. Perhaps scientific names, after all, are not quite the nonsensically tongue-twisting monikers they appear to be!

Surely the mourning dove is so well known that a color description of it hardly seems necessary, and yet I have often wondered as I examined a particularly perfect, healthy specimen how many gunners have paused to note the conservative yet almost indescribably beautiful and delicate shades of coloring, especially in the male. The female is colored the same, except that she is somewhat duller in shades, and she is also as a rule a bit smaller than the male, yet the sexes are very difficult to distinguish—impossible to distinguish in flight—from among a limit of birds, without opening the body cavity and making a really scientific case of it.

A healthy, well-turned-out male mourning dove is roughly

12 to 12½ inches in overall length. Some will weigh as much as six ounces, which puts them definitely in the weight class of the average quail, although studies have shown that the average weight of healthy mourning doves of either sex runs around four to four and one half ounces. When they go below that for adult birds, getting down around three ounces, they are definitely runts, neither as agile on the wing nor as palatable on the table as the average four-ounce birds.

If you were to pick out general distinguishing colors, you might say that the upper parts of the bird are pale gray to gray blue, the under parts reddish fawn to pink buff. There is a great variation in these shades among birds even from the same section, some dark, some very light. I have shot birds in the desert areas of the Southwest which were so light that they gave a first impression of being cream colored. Elliott McClure turned up an interesting fact about these color variations while working with doves in Iowa. Some injured adult specimens were taken by him, very pale in color. When he took them indoors and kept them out of the sun for a few weeks while trying to get them in shape again, they soon became as dark as the other birds. Some of this color was no doubt due to a change of diet, but a good share of the pale birds taken, especially in the hot, dry regions of constant bright sun are without doubt simply faded.

The back of the head and neck of the dove is usually highly glossed with a metallic purplish or bronze sheen, and there is a distinctive black spot on either side of the head just back of the eye, this often glossed over with blue. The bare space about the eye is pale blue, and very often the feathers above this are a beautiful glossy green, shading into fawn color on the forehead. The bill is black, the feet and legs deep pink. There are a number of black spots on the wing coverts, and the dark flight feathers are edged with a fine border of white.

You could not possibly closely examine the dove without discovering that it is illimitably more beautiful in every detail than you had ever thought it to be before. Yet it is the tail of this gray bullet that has always most intrigued me. This marvelously designed rudder is longer than the wing, and is composed of fourteen rather narrow, tapering feathers so strongly graduated pair after pair that when the bird is perching the tail comes to a startlingly sharp point. The long center pair of tail feathers is similar in color to the gray of the dove's back. The next pair, a bit shorter, have a dusky bar across them, and the tips are pale. This same system continues with each progressively shorter pair, the dusky bar becoming black and broader and the feather tips white for an inch or more, until the seventh pair is reached. The outer web of this pair is entirely white. Thus the dove at rest, with tail sheathed, gives an overall appearance of pink-buff and gray, but the moment it takes flight the beautiful tail is spread with the white and the black bars strikingly shown. It is truly the mourner's badge of distinction, the graduated formation and artistic design unlike that of any other of our species.

As we have noted previously, the mourning dove is an extremely adaptable species. It therefore has many advantages over the ground dwellers, which require especially certain types of cover, and which are always choosy as to altitudes. In addition, since the dove is migratory, and also extremely mobile and flexible in its feeding habits, it is able to cope with adverse conditions with which the ground birds cannot. It is entirely correct to say that the mourning dove ranges throughout the whole of North America. It is seen now and then in Greenland, and in Alaska, all across Canada, breeding regularly and in some abundance in the southern portions, from British Columbia to Nova Scotia. When you think of it further as breeding in every one of our forty-eight states, in Mexico, in the West Indies, nesting all the way from sea level up to as much as 12,000 feet, in temperatures ranging from the sizzling hot Sonora desert to western mountain regions where the nights get frosty even in midsummer, you understand immediately that the dove is a fabulously hardy little creature and therefore a game bird about which it is possible to be optimistic for the future.

I well remember, one fall a few years ago, a small flock of doves that had slowly come together near my home in Michigan. They were feeding in a cut-over cornfield near by, and as that fall was a fairly warm one, they stayed on long past the time when they should have been heading south. Presently we had a radical weather change, with some snow. The doves took refuge in a small willow swale, roosting in low bushes. I visited the place again in December, and the flock was still there and apparently in good condition. Luckily, though the winter was a fairly cold one, we did not have deep snows in the open fields. Those doves actually made it through the winter, as far as I could tell, without any great loss in their numbers, and when spring came several pairs were cooing away in the orchard, ready to nest again.

That is not to say, however, that the dove can brook all adverse weather conditions. I suppose that particular flock was slowly conditioned to its ordeal. During the winter of 1940-41, which was a severe one in the South, thousands of doves froze to death. I believe, however, that this 1940 debacle and its aftermath points out an extremely important lesson in dove management. In any state where there is an open dove season there will be birds that were raised there, and birds that have migrated. Evidence so far at hand regarding dove migration leads to the belief that birds raised in a certain locality will return to it to nest year after year. Therefore, when great inroads are made upon southern winter concentrations, the breeding stock which is left will scatter, come spring, to many places. The result is that the birds have a better than even chance of making steady recovery.

After the 1940 southern freeze-out, with of course a gunning season to deplete the stock further, surveys showed that there was an alarming drop in the national dove population. The federal hunting regulations for the following two falls were drastically revised. Result: The dove made a sensational comeback. The lesson, as I see it, is simply this: The dove can stand a sensible harvest, but since he is bound to have periodic adverse influences other than gunning, the hunting harvest and how sensibly or insensibly it is handled will always be the crucial management matter. If we are willing to concede that point, and all points relative to it, the dove can and will do a very great deal to take care of himself.

While the dove breeds in all our states, from what we know thus far it appears that the ranks thin out generally as one moves farther north. There is every reason to believe, therefore, that of the gross number of doves raised in the southern U.S. there is always a shootable surplus. But what, exactly, is the shootable surplus in the South? How many doves do we have, and how many can we take each year? Those are the questions that have to be answered before we can set management policies with a sure hand.

Many northern hunters who agitate for an open dove season will tell you: "We raise the doves and the southerners shoot them." This is of course much less than a half-truth. A lot of doves do breed in the North. But if the dove season in Mississippi, let us say, opens September first, it is doubtful if the North furnishes more than a very insignificant percentage of the doves which fall to the guns. They will be almost entirely local birds. Even if the season opened much later, probably fifty per cent, at a rough guess, will still be local birds. Any such northern attitude is wrong to begin with. We don't raise the doves. We do nothing except observe them in our fields. They cost us nothing.

By all fair standards, the North has a better variety of game birds than does the South, which has only the quail and the dove. In most northern states, though the gross number of doves raised may run into millions, it is doubtful if their numbers in many areas during fall would be of an amount to make a dove season worthwhile. If we want to shoot doves, transportation facilities southward are nowadays swift and economical, just as they are northward for the southerner who desires pheasants.

It is my belief that we will never build up our northern dove population to a point where hunting will be justified. Thus, one of the simplest steps we could take toward shrewd dove management would be to draw a cross-country line separating dove-hunting territory from non-dove-hunting territory. McClure, who did the Iowa dove study, contends that this line should be such that there would be no dove hunting above the southern borders of Virginia, Kentucky, Missouri, Kansas,

Colorado, and on across Nevada and central California. There would be some loud objections, perhaps justified. But let me show you what it would do for the dove.

The entire North would become breeding ground only, a vast refuge which would pour thousands of doves into the South each fall. No matter what happened adversely as to weather conditions, etc. after migration, there would always be some to come back. The untouched reservoir would continue to fill in fall any voids made locally in the South. Southern seasons might then be arranged so that always the shooting pressure would be at peak not when only local birds were available, but when both flight birds and local birds were abundant. The South would thus be harvesting a sensible share of its own crop, and filling out the remainder of the bag with northern birds. Pressures would balance.

Let us go back to further details of the life history of the dove. We may see by his nesting and migration habits what other considerations must be examined, if we are to hold his economy at its peak continuously. In the southern states, the mourning dove begins his courtship as early as January, and in the North, around the Great Lakes region, in early March. Cooing is the predominant portion of the courtship, although the male will at times indulge in short circular flights, snapping his wingtips together to impress his spouse. Since paired doves seldom choose the same tree in which another pair has decided to set up housekeeping, there is rarely any trouble between males, unless it happens that some upstart tries to take over the favorite cooing perch. After the female has indicated her willingness to co-operate, her mate calls her to the nesting site, taking the initiative in choice of location. The love-making continues with the female placing her bill in his, and vice versa, and with both birds caressing each other's heads with their bills. Though most birds forget about love-making after mating, the dove continues to display its affections on through the entire nesting season.

No one seems to know positively whether or not doves habitually mate for life. In captivity, the same pairs continue each year to mate. And there is some indication that in the wild, whenever possible, mates are carried over from year to year. However, during fall migrations the birds flock together indiscriminately, and it is quite possible that mates of the previous nesting are often separated and choose new mates for the next season. Barring accidental death to one or the other, pairs do remain constantly mated throughout each entire nesting season.

The breeding season of the dove is a very long one. Doves have been found in condition for breeding as early as December, and commonly nest as late as the following September. It is fairly well established that exposure to certain light rays controls the breeding capabilities of birds. In fact, birds artificially exposed have been induced to mate long before they ordinarily would in the wild. In most latitudes, October and November are the sexually dormant months. It sometimes occurs that nests have eggs or very young squabs as late as mid-October in the Deep South, but the sharp decline in the number of birds capable of breeding after early September indicates that all but a small percentage have entirely cleaned up their family affairs by November.

It is from studies which have produced this kind of information that we may make direct applications to hunting practices aimed at better dove management. For example, while the Alabama dove study was being made, it was found that over a third of the adult birds killed there during early September had left nestlings behind. It has been fairly well substantiated that when one parent dove is eliminated, the remaining one finds it impossible to feed the nestlings, and that they therefore also succumb. The final conclusion reached was that since the dove is not a highly productive species, viewed as to number of nestlings each pair is physically capable of bringing to maturity during a season, the take by hunters each year should definitely be held to no more than 35 per cent of the total population, and preferably to somewhat less than 25 per cent. If a season opening on September first accounts for a portion out of the gross kill of 33⅓ per cent of birds which leave squabs to starve, and if it should be that this figure is the average all across the South, then we are currently taking, by early season openings, far more in potential birds than our 25 per cent.

Many dove hunters will tell you that the dove nests twelve months out of the year, and that the discovery of eggs at hunting time is a negligible factor. Studies have shown, however, that the nesting *peaks* in various latitudes are reached in May, June, and July, slowly declining thereafter. Since it takes roughly six weeks from eggs to young doves completely on their own, it is obvious that all doves that begin laying even as late as mid-August would, if killed during early September, be leaving nestlings just hatched, and if killed shortly after September fifteenth, would be leaving squabs that still needed some care. Giving up of traditional early opening dates everywhere would unquestionably be extremely beneficial. We need more information, of course, but it is certain, at least, that the months of November, December, and early January would see very few, if any, nesting doves killed or nestling doves left to starve anywhere. McClure's Iowa study showed almost 22 per cent of the young still in nests September first. Less than 2½ per cent of young birds, however, left the nests after October first. The inference by comparison is obvious. The percentages may not be the same in other localities, but the *idea* is worth weighty consideration.

The percentages of late squabs also has another important meaning to gunners. The Alabama dove study showed that 95 per cent of the immature doves in the bags of hunters prior to November twentieth weighed less than 3½ ounces. Certainly those birds were of little use to anybody. Obviously, the later the season, the more birds that will have gained adult weight to make the bag worthwhile.

As with all other doves, the mourning dove builds an extremely flimsy nest, a mere platform of twigs barely strong enough to support the squabs as they grow. In fact, studies show that wind and bad weather are the most destructive agencies as regards nest losses. This, of course, is something we cannot control. However, the studies already made of dove nestings do show possibilities for certain aspects of simple dove management, and as usual emphasize the need for further studies over wide areas. Some of the study correlations are so interesting, and point out so dramatically the main relationships of the nesting birds to their environment—which must be known and understood before real progress can be made—that I believe we should look at a few of them here.

Two centuries ago, the dove was abundant in the southeastern portion of the U.S. Then, as the forests dwindled more and more with the increase in settlement, the dove began to increase westward. It is predominantly a bird of the forest edges, a bird that feeds in the open and nests in areas where trees sparsely cover the land. The cutting of the forests and the working up of the land encouraged the dove by manufacturing for him a more and more perfect habitat. As recently as fifty years ago, doves in the Northwest were plentiful only in the sagebrush regions. The rise in abundance there has closely followed in direct proportion to lumbering. Throughout all of the dove's range in America, the most vital reason for its increase with the growth and spread of the human population was that man by cutting the forests released the dove from the restraints caused by competition for proper nesting sites.

Now take a brief look in closer focus to see how we can relate this same dove-mankind relationship to better dove management. Western Iowa is a habitat well suited to doves during nesting time, a country of rolling hills, farms, and wood lots, with excellent feeding conditions and, except for some severe summer storms, good nesting weather. Cass County, where McClure's study was made, embraces roughly 370,000 acres. Of this, nine towns cover roughly 20,000 acres, and about 2,400 farmyards (not farms) cover roughly 6,000 acres. Keep these land percentages in mind now, because they are important.

To show you what one single midwestern county does in dove production, during the three years of the study an average of some 73,000 doves laid an average of some 500,000 eggs per year. Doves nest several times each season, laying two eggs each time, rarely three. Of the annual half-million eggs, various accidents and predations accounted for about 50 per cent. Thus, if this condition is average throughout the country, the annual dove *potential* is always half waste. Of the roughly 250,000 eggs left, however, that same 73,000 Iowa doves successfully brought to maturity almost 200,000 youngsters! In fact 85 per cent of the total of *hatched* young were successfully got out of the nest in good health.

Now go back to the land percentages. Here we find the man-dove relationship at an intense peak. The farmyard area amounted to only 1.6 per cent of the total county, yet it produced 20 per cent of the birds. The towns equaled but 6 per cent of the total land area, yet 65 per cent of the new bird crop was produced in their trees. Thus, the remaining 92.4 per cent of the county produced but 15 per cent of the bird crop, or about one bird to ten acres. Undoubtedly the reason is the existence of proper nesting sites in villages and farmyards, and the availability of abundant food. Of course, doves will nest in greatly varied places, in vines, on the top of a stump, even quite often on the ground. But their choice, from several studies, appears to be large trees not too heavily foliated. It is from all such facts brought together by tedious and patient study that we can eventually work out ways and means of improving habitats in especially productive areas. If a single midwestern county can produce 200,000 doves annually, and if by proper tree planting, control of uncongenial competitors for nesting space, etc. we can boost that figure another 50,000 or 100,000, then we have indeed done something to be proud of. Unquestionably we could do just that, not only in one county but in whole states.

Predators, luckily, do not seem to be too much of a problem. In the South, the worst predators were found to be bluejays and flying squirrels. In the Midwest, bluejays again topped the list, with fox squirrels second. Both not only destroy eggs, but kill the young as well. It seems therefore entirely sensible to me that since the dove is economically far more valuable than the jay we might begin a program of controlling the jay, and also the smaller, nongame squirrels.

I have spoken several times of the dove as hardy. One of the best proofs of this—and a facet of the dove case history which is extremely lucky as regards possible management—is that fortunately the mourning dove seems to be practically immune to serious diseases and parasitic infestations. The mortality from such causes is so small when figured as a percentage of overall mortality that they are negligible from a management viewpoint.

Thus management practices are in many instances somewhat self-suggestive, not in the preventive category, but rather in the nature of general assistance. For example, the planting of favorite dove foods in submarginal land areas that have proper nesting places along with readily available water and grit might well increase dove production over rather large areas. We have already found that this can be done with quail. If we are capable of producing congenial and safe nesting habitats, then one of the quickest rises in dove population would immediately be effected by the raising of a greater number of successful broods per season. It seems to have been rather well established that with the long nesting season a very high percentage of breeding pairs attempt as many as five or six nestings per year. But of these an average of never more than three is successful. This, to be sure, is pretty fair production. If, however, we could make certain heavily dove-populated areas so congenial and safe that the average nest success could be jumped to *four* broods per season, we would gain a tremendous new potential breeding stock. Some researchers feel sure that even the nestlings raised early in spring mature quickly enough to raise a brood of their own in late August. If it is true, then conservation measures which helped to assure the success of early nestings would have a fair chance of gaining a double bonus of new birds late in the season.

Now let's go back and pick up our pair of birds just beginning to nest in the spring and follow them through their summer and fall routine. We find them very casual fellows about their nest building. They spend perhaps an hour or so early each morning, the male bringing nearby twigs and the female weaving them carelessly together. When the sun begins to get high, the birds tire of this work and leave it until the next morning. Thus several days are required to get their excuse for a nest ready for the first egg. Sometimes as much as a week passes in nest building, and often the female then waits a day or so before laying.

The second egg is laid the day following the first, but incubation begins with the first egg. One squab therefore gets a head start on the other, for the first egg hatches on the fourteenth day, the second in the same length of time after it was laid. During the incubation period the female gets the best break, for the male relieves her around 8:00 A.M. and she gets the whole day off, until about 5:00 P.M. She then returns and sits out the night in comfort while the male gets a bite to eat and then to bed on a perch near the nest.

The youngsters are covered with soft yellowish down, which begins to disappear and be replaced by pinfeathers within a few days. They grow rapidly, their wing feathers forming much faster than their tail and body feathers. Each day they are fed pigeon milk several times by both parents, who perch on the nest edge and often allow both nestlings to thrust their bills into the parent larder at the same time. For a day or two this food regurgitated by the parents is made up of very tiny seeds, but soon the young are taking grains as large as corn and soybeans. At eleven to fourteen days, the fledglings are encouraged or forced by the parents to leave the nest. But they still get a few days of loving parental care and weaning while they learn to seek food for themselves. And meanwhile the industrious adults have usually begun thinking about another brood, either in the same nest or in a new one which is built immediately.

The old birds take the youngsters to their favorite feeding and drinking places, and here they meet other immature doves from nests in the vicinity. Since none of them fly as well as their parents, the young begin flocking together rather automatically, and in many instances flocks of fifty or more, all young birds, may be seen hanging around together in late summer and fall. This, of course, is an excellent arrangement of nature's, for it not only keeps the youngsters from having to compete directly with older, stronger birds in flight and in the search for food, but also gives them a perfect opportunity to choose mates of their own age later on.

Yet that is the least startling evidence of nature's marvelous planning toward the future of the species. A study of the sex ratio of doves shows how perfectly their lives are adapted to their species habits. Almost without fail, each pair of squabs raised at a single nesting is of the same sex. Thus, since these two birds are to be thrown together for some time after leaving the nest, there is little danger of inbreeding. Two males will eventually find in the flocks of young birds two females which have little chance of being young of the same parents.

In addition, the percentages of males and females among doves are practically fifty-fifty in the wild. Grouse, and also quail, sometimes have more males than females. Some other species show more females than males. The interesting observation here is that these other species lay large clutches of eggs, while the dove normally lays but two. If the sexes weren't approximately 50 per cent male and 50 per cent female, since pairs mate for the season and each male services but one female, there would soon come to be an unsatisfactory sex balance and poor propagation of the species. Besides, this fifty-fifty sex ratio has a very definite and fortunate bearing on the dove harvest taken by hunters. It is impossible to make a kill all of females or all of males, what with the sexes flocking together indiscriminately. The laws of chance balance the bag. In this respect it is interesting to note that the dove has a definite advantage here over such birds as grouse and quail. You cannot ordinarily tell sexes of these birds in flight, either, but though the laws of chance may keep the kill fairly even, the new birth rate of sexes may be far out of ratio and possibly cause a serious decline at times.

Young doves do not have their entire adult plumage until they are from three to five months old, but by this time most of them have begun, or even nearly completed, migration. In fact, southward migration of the youngsters begins from the northern portion of the U.S. as early as July and continues raggedly on through summer and fall. The adult birds, which are not willing to leave until the completion of the nesting season, and which are somewhat better adapted anyway to adverse weather conditions, do not migrate in force until the period beginning in late August and continuing on into October. Dove migration is not, however, the swiftly paced phenomenon of such species as waterfowl. They feed as they go, never seeming in any particular hurry, and from what is presently known of the process they may make as little as five miles a day and usually no more than twenty or thirty, unless storms and poor feeding conditions encountered along the way force them to do longer spurts.

Let us see now what effects these basic migration habits have upon hunting and conservation. Since the young begin migrating in July, more and more young follow as they come out of the nests and gain strength. Thus, with birds dropping down into the northern U.S. from Canada, and this process continuing and growing on through the summer, the peak abundance of birds over most of their upper range is reached in August. A survey in Nebraska showed that by September the doves in that state were only 24 per cent of the number that had been tabulated in August. This seems to me to be a rather certain indication that states such as Nebraska could never have an entirely successful open dove season.

However, we are still probably overlooking, as hunters, the most significant facts tied up with these migration habits and percentages. Wherever we open the season early, heavy shooting tends to hasten further migration. By opening seasons late in the South, there is a very good possibility that over a period of years the habits of the birds would change considerably. Unmolested, their migration would not be hastened. More important over a long period of years, since the heaviest shooting pressure of later seasons would always be upon concentrations that had been early migrants, it is possible that killing of these earlier migrants would tend to build a strain of doves with a higher percentage of *late* migrants.

So little dove banding has been done, comparatively, that nothing very definite can be assumed about dove flyways. It is generally believed that the dove population east of the Mississippi (the eastern subspecies) migrate into the Southeast and the Gulf States, the bulk of birds finally wintering in a rather narrow stretch of territory close to the Gulf. The population west of the Mississippi (the western subspecies) migrates first into Texas, New Mexico, Arizona, southern California, with the bulk of birds finally dispersing farther southward, into Mexico.

It is now quite definitely known that the eastern subspecies of the mourning dove has been slowly declining over the past decade. But it is just as definitely established that the western race has held its own quite well. Plainly, the less dense human population west of the Mississippi has meant less hunting pressure on that subspecies than on the eastern. And plainly, with the bulk of western birds taking haven in thinly populated sections of Mexico over the winter, while their eastern cousins must make a stand against continued heavy shooting along the Gulf, whatever other factors may influence the ups and downs of the dove, hunting is the most important.

Changes in farming practices do of course affect the doves. They prefer to feed in fairly open fields with ground cover not too dense or high and with trees at no great distance. When grain crops are clean-harvested and the land plowed immediately after, fall dove concentrations are not likely to occur. When such a practice takes hold over the greater share of an entire agricultural state, then no doubt the doves eventually change their migration routes to some extent. The perfect farm practice from the dove's point of view is the harvesting of crops in such manner that waste grains are left where the doves can get at them. We cannot, of course, expect that farmers throughout the country are going to alter their methods merely to assist the doves, but we can expect that those who are enthusiastically interested in the dove as a game bird will by knowing such facts give the birds the benefit of the doubt whenever possible.

The main reason I have tried in this chapter to point out these different facts, attitudes, and thoughts aimed at a better knowledge among us of dove habits, life history, and conservation is that I often wonder if we who hunt the dove really appreciate to the fullest extent just what we have in this little gray bullet as a game bird which we can easily *keep in abundance*. Quail, nesting as they do on the ground and leading their young about the fields, are at the mercy of all manner of predators which the dove escapes. Further, the cat or squirrel which destroys a quail nest very likely gets a whole season's production at one killing. The dove's prolificacy is budgeted by his several nestings. If the feed peters out on a limited section of quail or pheasant range, the entire population may be destroyed. The dove working the same range simply moves to a better scene of operations. If the water hole used by several quail coveys dries up, they may be done in. The dove flies off twenty miles and drinks his fill. Where severe cold kills the pheasants, the dove treks to the sunshine states. Yet with all these advantageous features, he is neither competition to our other game birds when he occurs in their habitats, nor half as much trouble and labor for us. Where intense agricultural practices utilize every square foot of land, the dove thrives while the other game birds are rooted out. Conversely, lands which have deteriorated to such an extent that quail and pheasants can no longer survive upon them are often entirely suitable for the dove. Indeed, as a game bird, he is a bird apart, filling a place no other species can fill, filling it easily, and with no perplexities or temperamental insistencies upon particularly specialized conditions.

Let us therefore begin to think now, while there is ample time, in terms of proper management and harvest. Let us be certain that we treat the doves of today in such fashion that in later years, looking backward, we do not have to picture them as having carried on their nest-time cooing in the spirit of mourners for the doves of tomorrow. If we handle them properly, the doves, as I have prophesied before, will be here when all the other game birds are long, long gone.

Chapter 7

PACIFIC MOUNTAINEER

D URING THE SUMMER of 1820 Long's expedition to the Rocky
Mountains was pushing its way slowly into the rugged
ranges of what was one day to become Douglas County,
Colorado. Near the present site of the village of Castle Rock,
some miles south of Denver, a member of the party hunting
along a stream that today bears the name of Plum Creek shot
a bird unknown to American ornithologists of that period.

It was a bird of the high, pine- and oak-clad mountain peaks
and valleys, a gregarious fellow with striking deftness of flight,
whose deep and resonant, booming, owl-like *coo* during nesting season, heard even a full quarter-mile distant, filled the
great sweeps of the quiet valleys and the austere mountains
with what was to man a strangely thrilling yet disquieting
feeling of loneliness. It was a bird whose migrations and constantly erratic meanderings in search of adequate food supply
brought its legions together in fabulous concentrations at
times, in the vast western wilderness regions. Now here, now
there, shifting swiftly and afar as the crop of acorns, pine nuts,
or wild berries gave out or was replenished, this restless, itinerant wanderer was to seem, one day, to the settlers who
finally swarmed throughout its habitat, a wilderness character
uniquely mysterious in its comings and goings; one season a
dozen birds stripping the few pampered, freshly planted fruit
trees; next season birds awesomely abundant; and the next
apparently forever gone.

185

This smoothly molded, plump-breasted bird with gorgeous bronze purples and wines and metallic greens in its plumage, a soft gray, squared tail with wide band of dusky black, a white half collar at the back of its neck, yellow legs and black-tipped yellow bill—this bird was eventually to live a violent history of struggle for existence against the need of the swarming western pioneers for food, and against their greed as they collected for financial gain what seemed then to be the endless bounties of nature. This same bird would win the battle, by a frighteningly close margin but not without the help of the white man who had almost destroyed him, and this same swift-winged, graceful mountain comet would also win, eventually—as if by man's apology for past treatment, when man finally found time to become acquainted with him in more leisurely and sporting fashion—full stature as one of the finest and most exciting game birds known to the Far West and the Southwest.

In 1823, three years after the Plum Creek bird had made fatal acquaintance with civilization's western progress, a naturalist named Say described this type specimen for the first time and gave it the name it bears today, *Columba fasciata,* the band-tailed pigeon. For years previous to Long's discovery of this exceedingly beautiful native American pigeon—a bird as large as or larger than our domestic and homing pigeons, sometimes weighing as much as a full pound—undoubtedly the Spanish colonists along the lower West Coast, and the Russian settlers farther north, had known the bandtail well, as a prime source of food when its great concentrations swept through the coastal mountains and valleys during migration time. And native Indian tribes from Puget Sound to Mexico had for centuries undoubtedly gathered and smoked bandtail breasts by the thousand each fall, much as eastern Indians had done with the passenger pigeon, to help tide them through the winters. Later, though the ancestors of our present-day gunners treated the bandtail very poorly—as indeed do some few so-called sportsmen of this generation—it is, in its way, to their honor and ours, that we came finally to discover in him a dynamic quality less material but far more thrilling than his use as food.

For that reason we set about to undo as far as possible the harm to which his kind had so long been exposed.

Somehow, perhaps because of his erratic habits, the mystery of his mountain wilderness retreats, and his wary, untrusting nature, I think of the band-tailed pigeon, or blue pigeon, or blue rock, or wild pigeon, or white-collared pigeon, as he has been variously and colloquially called over the decades since we first knew him, as a most romantic game bird. Nor can I think of him, as far as my own relationship with him is concerned, without always going back in memory to that relationship's very beginning, to a few scattered houses, a post office, and a general store. This collectively goes by the name of Macleay, Oregon, a quite inconsequential and sleepy little gathering of habitations dropped beside a winding, fir-lined road some eight miles east of Salem, the state's capital. I think, too, that there could be no better place for us to begin the detailed story of the bandtail, since this is as good a vantage point as any from which to look about us with a long and intimate view over the most important portions of his bailiwick.

If you stood on the top of the hill just west of Macleay, and faced straight *east,* you could see proof that the Cascades, fifty or more miles away before you, lie like a great north-south barrier that runs from border to border of Oregon, blocking this coastal third of the state quite completely from the other two-thirds east beyond their big hump. Many a bright, hazeless morning I stood on that hill, during a summer that seems somehow a long time ago, the summer when I was fifteen. I knew the towering Cascades were there without question because, with the light good, far off to the northeast, perhaps seventy-five miles, Mt. Hood could be seen shining in snowy splendor, and to the southeast, far-off Mt. Jefferson glowed plainly with the same white-cold midsummer flame.

Behind me, west roughly fifty miles, lay the gleaming Pacific, bathing the feet of the well-forested Coast Ranges, mountains much lower than the white-peaked Cascades. I draw this picture in detail, for the geography of it is important to bandtail hunters the length of the Pacific Coast.

East of the Cascades, the bandtail never was plentiful. A few of his numbers spilled over from time to time into Montana and Idaho, and long ago even as far east as North Dakota. But the Cascades formed an effective block, the tops of their high peaks lacking in food and nesting sites which would appeal to a pigeon, and the country immediately at the foot of their eastern slopes too bleak for this bird of the mountain forests.

Between the Pacific Coast Ranges and the Cascade barrier, about midway, lies a great valley, its pleasantly up-and-down foothills fir clad and nowadays cut into farms where hops and prunes and cherries and wheat and all manner of important agricultural products are grown. Good straight lumber still comes out of these foothills, but among the stately firs are venerable oaks that have not a straight three feet of board in any of their ancient limbs. For our purposes, the oaks are perhaps more important than the firs. Indeed, long ago, before the coming of the white man and his agriculture, they were for this same purpose more important than the titbits from the farms of today. For each fall these gnarled and giant oaks, hung thick with mistletoe, scattered acorns profusely within the wide circles of their branches.

This is the Willamette River Valley, lying like a great, green, well-watered productive tunnel, with openings north and south. North the valley meanders widely, until at last the flow of the river is swallowed in the turbulent west-moving rampage of the dynamic Columbia, which leads to the Sound and its islands with their hundreds of acres of seed pea fields. On across the Columbia, other valley systems with their clear streams dart here and there, the valleys reaching on northward, on across Washington, losing themselves finally, farther north still, in the awesome green and white mountain ranges of British Columbia, the northernmost outpost of the bandtail in summer, and where, as this is written, legal shooting may still be had with him in fall.

A pigeon winging down from British Columbia can go slicing southward through these high valleys and their foothills, swinging along past Georgia Strait and Vancouver, feeding full on peas and fruit along the Sound, looking down on Seattle, Portland, Salem, sliding easily down through this natural topographic tunnel, casting about in the Coast Ranges or dipping a bill of salt water from the Pacific—but blocked on the far east by the Cascades.

From Salem on south, this Willamette Valley is an open highway, stocked bounteously with those favorite bandtail foods: elderberries, acorns, pine nuts, fallen grain, and, unfortunately for the best interests of the bandtail, nowadays cherries and other fruits on which he often works such havoc that he brings agriculturist wrath upon his head. The straight-south course centers down past Albany, Corvallis, Eugene, and when the Willamette peters out at its creek-fed southern source, other valleys—the Umpqua, the Rogue—continue the highway. Roseburg, Grants Pass, and thence into California.

Here, to the east, the great deserts of western California and Nevada lie, bereft of any item which might draw the bandtail in consequential numbers. Thus the Cascade barrier is replaced, and the species held to the western two-thirds of our longest West Coast state. South—south—following the acorns, the manzanita berries, the lucky strikes in the orchards and the farm fields, skirting the western edges of the high desert plateaus, the trail leads on—following the Shasta—the long, straight pass down the Sacramento—the Russian—past San Francisco and down the San Joaquin. The high, dry mountain air, the firs, pines, redwoods, the high-valley ranches, creeks, rivers, oak groves—these are the special pleasures of the bandtail, and the places where the eager gunner must search and be ever alert for the unpredictable hobo flocks.

Down, finally, in Monterey and San Luis Obispo counties, along the flow of the Salinas, in the vicinity of King City and Paso Robles especially, there are usually extra-special spots in the oaks and on the farms for good feeding, if the season has been right, and here, too, is a congenial stopover for a few weeks, where the press of winter has been safely outdistanced. Here is the hunter's dreamed-of hot spot. Then, perhaps in late December, with the sun growing ever warmer as the southward movement picks up again, the birds drop on down into

San Diego County. All the way they are blocked to the eastward once more by the Imperial Valley and the desert regions of the Lower Colorado. Some of the flocks continue on into Mexico, into the secluded, brooding mountains. But the great majority of our true West Coast tribe winters here and there in southern California.

This, then, is the main migration trail of our Pacific Mountaineer. Nesting everywhere along that trail, but ever and ever more abundantly as the flocks move northward in spring, they have always been there, their habits curiously fashioned by the geography of the country. In days long gone there were millions, perhaps billions of them, so that they were in their way the western counterpart of the passenger pigeon. When that bird was on its way to doom in the East, the bandtail was being mistaken for it by many a pioneer. For decades—and even yet today—people confused the two. An excited report crops up that the passenger pigeon is not, after all, extinct. It has simply moved west to the seclusion of the mountains. A great flock of the birds has been sighted along the West Coast— the would-be naturalist having failed to observe that this pigeon has a perfectly square fantail, like our homing and racing pigeons, instead of the long, slender, wedge-shaped, graduated tail of the passenger pigeon and the mourning dove.

But as I have said, the bandtail knows something about the fringes of extinction, too. He, too, was trapped and slaughtered by millions for the market, some decades ago. It was not that his nesting habits were as tightly colonial as those which helped to doom his eastern relative. True, he is exceedingly gregarious, reasonably so even at nesting time, but in this habit, as in all his habits, he is most erratic. Thirty pairs may be found nesting in close proximity. Or again, single nesting pairs will be scattered over thousands of acres, consorting only at well-stocked feeding grounds. It was the search for food that led the bandtail to market, for, come early fall, birds in British Columbia started southward, picking up recruits as they moved, the flocks growing, growing until at times they darkened the valleys. It was, you see, these north-south valleys of which I make so much, with their restricted areas where food was abundant for the mobile legions, that brought them at that time so easily and with such compact concentration to the traps and the guns, and which bring them to our guns today. Funneling southward, always adding new legions, they squeezed in great hordes into the high valleys, through the mountain passes, and along the coastal beaches, until actually at times the greatest share of their entire populous empire might be trading from feeding ground to feeding ground over a space of what is today no more than a couple of counties. The situation is exactly the same today, except that the pigeon population is greatly diminished.

Except in a very few scattered instances, the bandtail lays but a single egg, as did the passenger pigeon. Their nesting period is long, and it is suspected—although not fully proved—that in the southern part of their range they may raise two or even three broods, but in all of the northern portion of the range normally only one brood is reared per season. Obviously birds with such habits could not possibly keep up with the inroads, of the pigeon netters especially. And also a great deal of the netting and gunning was carried on during the northward spring migration, when the birds were congregated in the grain fields.

Since the sex ratio in birds that raise but one young at a time can easily be thrown out of balance, even without man's predations, this danger added to the bandtail's difficulties. When many birds were trapped during nesting time, catches were bound to be predominantly either males or females, depending upon the time of day the catch was made, for one bird or the other would always be at the nest during specific hours, as with the mourning dove, the males from about 8:30 A.M. to 5:00 P.M., the females the rest of the time.

In the late 1880's and the early '90's, up in that same great tunnel, the Willamette Valley, Corvallis trappers were taking birds as many as twenty dozen, twenty-five dozen, thirty dozen, all in one sweep of the sprung net. The birds were packed and shipped by steamer from Yaquina Bay to ports such as San Francisco and Portland. And, on south in California, in the coastal-mountain pigeon paradise of the Salinas

Valley near King City and Paso Robles—or again in locations such as Mount Palomar, the mountain named for its early-day concentrations of bandtails and now famous for its mammoth telescope—the same thing was going on, with thousands of gunners aiding the slaughter day after day.

Some of these gunners were market hunters, but for the most part they were sportsmen. However, there were no bag limits, and since the birds were so plentiful no hunter considered his shoot successful unless he knocked down at least thirty to fifty birds. Of these, the large, old birds, called stagers, were not favored, especially if there was any possibility that they had been feeding on acorns. The bandtail is an extremely active bird and therefore requires a great amount of food. It is amazing the huge amount which each bird will consume each day, when the food is plentiful. Birds gathered beneath the oaks will stuff their crops until they fly with extreme difficulty, and of course the tannic acid in the acorns soon imparts a bitter taste to the flesh.

Thus, many old birds were left where they fell, while the hunter went on to kill more, trying to pick the smaller, younger, more tender birds from the flock. These he could tell easily once he picked them up, for the feather quills and the legs of young birds are always flexible. From the Spanish, hunters had learned the trick—which bandtail gunners of today should remember—of removing the crops of the birds immediately as each is picked up. In addition, it is an excellent plan to draw the bird immediately, and, as the Spanish did, to cut away the neck and the backbone. Later, as soon as birds thus treated are brought home and plucked, washing the inside with soda and water will help to eliminate the possibility of birds wasted because of a bitter acorn taste.

Added to the slaughter of the market netters and the undisciplined sportsmen was the great number of birds taken for trap-shooting purposes. The bandtail was especially prized as a trap bird, even more so than the passenger pigeon had been in the East, for it was so exceedingly wild, and so swift on the take-off. It was common practice for bandtails to be mixed in with domestic pigeons during a shoot, especially if the man running the traps wished to handicap a certain shooter. A man might make a good straight run on domestic pigeons, but when a bandtail suddenly burst out at the clang of the trap, he was almost sure to miss.

By all these attacks upon the main portion of the entire bandtail population of America, which gathered and stayed about in these same sections for weeks at a time, another few years would have wiped them out completely. But, luckily, just at that time, people had become aroused and alarmed by the great decline of the passenger pigeon and other native birds. In 1913 the Federal Migratory Bird Law saved the bandtail. With what seems today to have been unusual conservation wisdom for these times, the lid was clamped on tightly. The bandtail was placed on the completely protected list, an act stipulating that none might be killed until the first of September, 1918, at the earliest. Without that brilliant piece of legislation, and its particular application to this special case, unquestionably this chapter would be written now only in the past tense, and solely for its historical interest.

The 1918 stipulation was actually continued for twenty years, until 1932, as far as general hunting was concerned. By 1924, however, the birds had made their comeback on the Coast to such an extent that many cherry farmers were complaining loudly of damage to their crops. Permits for destruction of such flocks were made available to California fruit growers, and six years later Washington (and Arizona, of which we will hear more in a moment as regards the bandtail) followed suit. I suspect, however, that the crop damage was used by gunners itchy to have the bandtail on the game-bird list again, as a wedge to a full open season. For by 1931 so many permits had been begged that for all practical purposes the season *was* open, and during a portion of the breeding season, at that.

Now if we leave the coastal flyway momentarily and drop down into Mexico, where, incidentally, excellent bandtail shooting may be had, we see an interesting aspect of ecology, which tells the remainder of the bandtail story as regards his range. There is an abundance of the species in Mexico, part of the population made up of the true type, *Columba fasciata*, and part composed of an almost identical subspecies which never does come up into U.S. territory, except now and then a straggler. The bandtail legions fan out over nearly all of Mexico, and even on south into the highlands of Guatemala and northern Nicaragua.

Think now of this tribe of mountain birds, thousands of years ago, beginning a northern migration, beginning to form the tribal habits which we find among them today. And keep in mind that as this tribal movement northward begins, the birds are spread out clear across upper Mexico. In migration, they move north now in a long, sweeping east-west line. But presently this line comes up against the desert barrier of the Lower Colorado. The line is split by this barrier, its one portion squeezing in together and following the West Coast route we have just described. The other portion, however, on the eastern side, finds sanctuary in the high mountains and plateaus of southeastern Arizona, and of New Mexico, and spills over raggedly into the edge of western Texas.

As it moves on northward, Texas is deleted as uncongenial territory. But the mountains of New Mexico and Arizona are full of pine nuts, acorns, and nesting sites. And for those birds that still have an urge to travel, Colorado is intriguing territory, with a few scattered birds crossing west into Utah and Montana. Thus we complete the survey of the bandtail's U.S. bailiwick: British Columbia, Washington, Oregon, California for the coastal tribe; and for practical purposes, only Arizona, New Mexico, Colorado for the splinter tribe.

In states such as Utah and Texas the birds are now so sparsely distributed that hunting them would not be worthwhile. The few that find sanctuary there are better left for breeding purposes. In Colorado, a season was finally opened in twelve southern counties, in 1944. But the small bandtail population, and the fact that the birds congregate too compactly at isolated feeding grounds, made the good sense of a Colorado season highly questionable. Since that time, Johnson Neff, U.S. Fish and Wildlife Service biologist, has done a detailed study of the Colorado bandtail, with the resultant advice that these birds—whose sex ratio appears to be far out of balance—be given full protection from now on.

However, when the Colorado flight moves southward to join those birds that have spent the summer in the western three-fourths of New Mexico and the eastern two-thirds of Arizona, sportsmen get a chance at them. In fact, after the fruit-grower permit difficulties in 1931, it was decided to open a season in the five important states: Washington, Oregon, California, Arizona, and New Mexico. This was done in 1932, and has continued. But while the bird has held up fairly well under the shooting pressure, it is still a source of worry to the conservationists. It would, in fact, be quite unfair both to the bandtail and to sportsmen to write of this grand game bird as if all were well with him. His erratic temperament, his habit of rearing but one youngster per nesting, the fact that he follows the food supply so meticulously and that agriculture has so changed the ecology of his original habitat, make him a problem bird not only to those of us who wish desperately to keep him abundant, but also to those many fruit growers to whose crops he is at times exasperatingly destructive. Without question we *can* have the bandtail as a game bird as long as we want him, which is to say, as long as he doesn't upset agricultural economics too drastically. But this is a species that must have thoughtful and exceptionally delicate handling, if he is to stay permanently abundant enough to keep him on the game-bird list.

It has always seemed to me that the five western states that have open season can feel justly proud of the bandtail, for they have in him a marvelous game bird found nowhere else in the country. And when I so constantly compliment this species, I do so with a most nostalgic feeling, for my association with him over a gun barrel goes back a long way, to that summer when I was fifteen, in Oregon. That is an age, I'm sure, when shooting is at its romantic and thrilling best, simply because it is new. Who gets the thrill, in middle life, from a clean shot on a duck, a pheasant, or a grouse, that he did from the very first one he ever saw, and shot, as a kid? My first bandtail sighted was thrill enough, but the first one that fell to my gun I could never forget, and for several reasons, not the least of which was the stern lecture that came with it.

I had stood on the hill just west of Macleay, Oregon, that morning, looking away off at shining Mt. Hood, drinking in all of this atmosphere of strangeness which, to a lad who had never traveled previously and had been reared in far-off Michigan, was something, let me tell you. I had heard the bass cooing of a pigeon, and I was trying to locate it. And then, presently, I saw the bird, sitting on the limb of a dead tree at the edge of a fir-bordered wheat field.

In later years I was to learn, of course, that this was a typical bandtail habit. But at that time I didn't recognize this bird as a wild pigeon. In the mountains, when scattered flocks are passing through during hunting season, a clearing or small opening in the oaks and conifers, especially one where a dead stub stands, makes a perfect place for the gunner to conceal himself. As the birds feed here and there on pine nuts or acorns, it is a sure bet that they will come eventually—one, two, three or more at a time—to rest at the dead tree site, where a good view may be had of any danger lurking in the surrounding forest. But concealment, for the hunter, is paramount, for bandtails have most remarkable eyesight, and a jittery wariness undoubtedly born of their wilderness habits. You can hunt in good bandtail territory when a flight is on, and watch flock after flock swerve to keep out of range of your gun, unless you wear camouflaging clothing and keep well hidden and still. This is quite different, in general, from hunting mourning doves, and it is altogether different in that with the bandtail you get shooting a great share of the time in the forest, which makes it much like shooting doves on a woods pass, except that the bandtail will often fly higher, and will swerve and roll until he makes you dizzy as he follows the contours of the mountains or the treetops. His flight habits in general are, it seems to me, even more unstable than those of the dove, and his wide fantail makes it possible for him to rudder himself instantly into new and difficult angles.

He is, in other words, perfectly fitted physically to his mountain habitat, and centuries of flying in mountainous country have made of him a most unpredictable target, one which utilizes every air current, which literally falls down the sky banking a mountainside. In fact, in this respect the bandtail displays a unique habit often startling to the gunner who is unfamiliar with him. A bird may be sighted perching on a fire-killed tree in a forest opening on a steep mountainside. From here he can survey great sweeps of country, while he rests and digests his dinner. The tree he'll choose will be the tallest one he can find, and he'll be perching on some topmost branch, in the really big timber perhaps upwards of 200 feet above the ground. As the hunter approaches, let us say that the bird senses danger. Sometimes, oddly, he will duck down and flatten himself against the limb, like a squirrel, hoping that the hunter will pass without noticing him. But when danger gets close and he feels he's been spotted, he will fall out of the tree, and with wings either almost folded or completely folded against his body, jettison himself down the mountainside exactly like a stooping hawk! If the wings happen to be not quite folded, the wind whistling through them makes a sound like a falling bomb, and can be heard from some distance away.

I would not try to estimate average bandtail speed when the bird is in full flight. I only know that his take-off is exceedingly swift, much more so than that of the homing pigeon, and that when once aloft and under way his pace is tremendous. That fact, added to his often rather high flight, his size—fifteen to seventeen inches in overall length—and plump, compact body, makes of him a target that takes a lot more killing than does the dove. In addition, range is much more difficult to judge in mountainous country, and again size plays a part by making the birds appear closer than they are. I can't feel that gun *gauge* is terribly important, so long as a man can shoot and can judge range and discipline himself accordingly. Anything from a 20 to a 12 is fine. But I do think when it comes to loads a bandtail hunter should use nothing smaller than number 7½ shot with a heavy powder charge, and not fret if all he can get is the same load in number 6.

When I sighted that first bandtail of mine, I had with me my first gun. It was a single shot, bolt action .22, heaven knows how ancient, and most inaccurate on its own, notwithstanding the assistance I gave this same quality by my inexpertness. I crept toward the dead tree beside the wheat field, but before I was within anything like reasonable range the bird sensed danger. I am positive he had not seen me. But a bandtail, along with his keen eyes, has as acute hearing as any game bird with which I am familiar. And this, used in conjunction with his telescopic eyes and his extreme natural wariness makes him harder to approach than a deer. In fact, deer hunters in the mountainous West could tell many a tale of big bucks put to flight by a warning from the bandtail. Often a hunter stalking a deer will hear a clap of wings a hundred yards ahead of him in the thick forest where a bandtail is feeding, and then a moment later the crash of his deer bounding away. Quiet as the hunter has been, the alert bird has heard him, and, in flushing, has given the characteristic bandtail danger signal. This same warning wing clap is what puts an entire flock of feeding bandtails to flight when one of their number senses danger. And thus, since each bird is always alert and jittery, a flock is especially difficult to approach. Each one acts as a sentinel for all the others.

My bird gave one clap of wings, then fell out of the dead tree headlong and with wings folded. But he had little room to fall, and as he zoomed upward again, I shot. At that instant the air was full of pigeons. The flock for which he had been apparently acting as sentinel, birds which I had not seen as they fed on fallen grain in the wheat field, had instantly heeded his warning. Needless to say, I missed, but I remembered this incident so thoroughly in later years that it stood me in good stead when I had adult opportunity to contact these fellows at a feeding-field shoot. I had learned, you see, that a hunter who expects to stalk feeding bandtails must be exceptionally cautious.

Trembling with excitement and disappointment, I stood watching the disappearing flock, realizing even then what amazing adroitness of flight these birds possess. They raced down the field, hurdled the tall trees at the far end with a zooming upward burst of speed beautiful to see, then turned and came back low on the far side, following the land contours, the knolls and low ridges which dropped away toward the creek in the valley, the whole flock taking each hurdle with a flowing ribbon of flight. This habit the initiated bandtail gunner knows well—how a flock will come whipping down a valley, sweeping in roller-coaster fashion over each hummock and ridge, gaining momentum as it dips into the depressions, losing momentum on the upswing. The smart hunter knows, too, that his best stand is often at the top of a low ridge, where he can take the birds when their speed is momentarily broken by their upswing. And he knows, too, that low-flying flocks which have had to run a barrage of guns down a valley course will begin to make toward higher ground when thoroughly frightened, intent on getting up where their fine eyes can spot the guns. These shrewd bandtail habits the clever hunter plays to his own advantage, and thus they're excellent little items to keep in mind.

I watched the birds swing back, surprised and trembling again to see that they were going to come right over me. I loaded the ancient .22. I threw it to my shoulder, and as I shot I closed my eyes. But when I opened my eyes again, after the shot, a bird was actually tumbling out of the flock. And what's more, when I picked it up and got over my excitement enough to examine it, I found it drilled neatly through the neck!

I knew now that this was no homing pigeon. Its white collar, worn high up toward the back of its head, its cape of iridescent green, the gray and slate-blue of its back and wings and lower parts, and the rose-pink of its upper breast—what a beautiful prize it was to behold. I spread out the wonderful wide gray tail with its dusky band. And then suddenly I heard a sound and looked up and there was my uncle, whom we were visiting in Oregon, coming up to me from out of the firs where he had been cutting wood.

I started an excited flow of talk. But he cut me short with a wave of his hand. "You, young man," he said gravely, "will have to pay dearly for that bird. That's a band-tailed pigeon, and it was probably nesting, and besides that they're fully protected by law. If there's one thing I can't abide, it's a game poacher. You come with me. We're going straight to the sheriff!"

That was only the beginning. My uncle was a man who loved the outdoors, who had lived in lumberwoods for many years, who had hunted and fished all his life. Later I realized, of course, that he was only bent on impressing upon me that if I was going to be a hunter I would have to know what to shoot and what not to shoot, and that I should know beforehand what was legal, not just shoot at the first living thing I saw. He knew, of course, how it was with a kid, but he intended to impress this lesson upon me with severity. And he did, especially since I was greatly in awe of him and his quiet ways.

He lectured me all the way home, showing plainly and emphatically his disgust with me. But now and then he would almost forget and fall to telling me details of the bandtail's life history, describing at one moment how the birds built their flimsy nests of large twigs in the pine and fir trees, or how sometimes in the mountains they nested in wind-eroded holes in the sandstone of high cliffs. And then at the next moment he was full of anger again, explaining to me that this bird was undoubtedly a male, and would be needed to help care for the young squab hidden somewhere in the forest. The parents, he explained, continually looked after the squab, taking turns, for roughly thirty days, before it was able to fly away by itself. He told me that he knew a man who had found young bandtails in the Southwest as early as February, proving that the parents must have started nesting in December, when there was still snow in the mountains. This he used to work up my sympathy, and then he went on to say how diligent the birds were about trying to keep their race against man, their only real enemy, running in their favor, how undoubtedly their breeding season continued way on through until August and September.

In the light of how little is yet known of the bandtail, it is amazing to me that my uncle by his own observations knew at that time so much about their habits. He told me how, in fall after nesting season was over, the white neck ring on the males began to be less conspicuous, and he said further that though male and female birds look very nearly identical you can tell them apart a fair percentage of the time by the fact that the white neck ring of the male is larger and more clearly white. This fact has since been rather well substantiated. Also it has been established that the breast of the male is very distinctly of a purplish raspberry hue, that of the female less distinct and more gray.

But all of these digressions had no real effect upon dampening my uncle's basic anger. When we finally arrived at his home he didn't pause, but took me across the road, where lived the sheriff—who, I learned later, was a hunting crony of my uncle's and no officer of the law at all—and after due deliberation of the most grave sort this makeshift officer agreed only to jail me instead of giving me a stiff fine. But at last, when my uncle had finally told him how it would complicate matters to have me in jail, since I was supposed to return to Michigan soon, he relented and let me go scot free with nothing more than a final fifteen-minute reprimand.

I'll tell you, they had me scared. The bandtail, however, tasted delicious after my aunt had cooked it that evening, though I ate it in silence, under the stern eye of my uncle, not daring to give the least clue to the excitement I felt with every bite.

For the sportsman who desires to get good bandtail shooting, there are several necessary items to be borne in mind, the most important of which is not to be too optimistic about what the hunting is going to be like during any season, until he is actually into the birds. The ups and downs of this bandtail proposition are very much like duck hunting, except that where ducks follow specific flyways, the flight lanes of the bandtail are entirely governed by the food supply en route. In this they follow exactly the system that the passenger pigeon followed. The general north to south migration may be on in full swing, but while it is occurring there may be just as much trading back and forth from east to west, the birds working southward meanwhile but always scouting good feeding.

As with the ducks, temperature and weather control almost entirely the time at which the migration will get under way, and how swiftly and with what concentration it will move. For example, bandtails in Washington may begin to get restless in late summer and early fall. If a sudden cold snap occurs, the birds will start south immediately, and there will be a very good chance that hunting will be excellent, for the abrupt movement will concentrate the birds in areas of abundant food supply. The same movement will occur if cold rains and windy weather come, whether early or late in the season. But there is also another type of movement which must be considered by the gunner who wishes to be successful with the bandtails, and this is the vertical migration that always occurs as the weather becomes cooler in fall. Remember that the bandtail is a bird of the mountains. As soon as the weather cools or rains come to the upper altitudes, the birds will begin to work downward from the high forests, dropping down into the protection and greater warmth of the valleys. In all probability, too, feeding conditions will be better in the valleys, for frosts will have come early to the 8,000- and 10,000-foot altitudes, destroying whatever berries there are to be had. And too, grain harvesting in the lower agricultural valleys will have left plentiful scattered waste grain upon the ground.

Thus, if you know that the bandtails usually pass through a certain portion of your proposed hunting state during their fall migration, the best bet as a rule will be to watch for them in the valleys and, if they do not materialize except in small scattered bands because the weather is still exceptionally warm, then you may conceivably get good shooting by taking to the big timber on the high slopes. Here, among the oaks and pines, there may be scattered flocks which have begun to work downward.

However, as I have emphasized, the bandtail is most erratic, from the hunter's point of view, though completely logical in his habits from his own point of view. It is almost impossible to predict what sort of season you'll have in any specific locality until the season is actually under way. If the birds are usually in evidence each fall in a certain territory, undoubtedly they will be again, *if* the season has been congenial to the grain, fruit, and acorn crops. If the crop seasons have been poor, without question the main concentrations will not materialize at all. The birds will simply pass on through. Logically, too, the hunting will often be less predictable in California or southern Arizona than in Washington and Oregon—depending of course upon the date of the opening. This is because there is every chance that the farther south the birds travel, the better the weather will become over a wider territory. They will have moved into the warm valleys in the Northwest to avoid inclement weather in the high altitudes. But if the feed is poor in the California valleys but good in the mountains, chances are the temperatures in the California mountains will not be uncongenial enough to keep the birds from the high reaches.

You can get a very good idea of this unpredictability of the bandtail by taking a look at the records of a few random seasons. For example, during the early 1920's the birds were hardly seen at all in the country surrounding Los Angeles. Much of this may have been due to a drastic drop in the bandtail population. Yet that does not explain the whole matter. During the spring of 1927 there were suddenly thousands of bandtails calling their rumbling owl-like *who-who* mating calls throughout the San Jose hills near Pomona. The previous spring not a single bird had been noticed there. And, the following year, 1928, only a few dozen birds showed up in place of the thousands. Again the following year, no birds were in evidence, and this situation continued until 1933, when numerous huge flocks suddenly put in an appearance once more. As it happens, these are spring records, but the comings and goings of the bandtail in fall are just as whimsical. It is easy to see what this can mean to the hunting.

During the fall of 1947, I was in the East, rushing to get my work caught up so that I could make a hurried trip to California specifically to shoot bandtails. Knowing that the birds usually are most abundant during December—when the season is on—in southern Monterey County and northern San Luis Obispo County, I had my plans laid to establish headquarters somewhere in that general vicinity. The oaks and crop fields near King City and Paso Robles seem always to be favorite hangouts for the birds when the flight is good, and so I looked forward with much eagerness to a sojourn in Monterey County and some wonderful warm-weather shooting.

Unfortunately—or perhaps fortunately—it was impossible at the last moment for me to make my proposed trip. Meanwhile I had had discouraging reports on the crop of acorns, manzanita berries, etc. in Monterey County and indeed throughout northern California. A little later, when I had written to J. S. Hunter, chief of the California Bureau of Game Conservation, bemoaning the fact that I had been unable to come out, he made me feel much relieved by replying that I certainly had missed nothing. The bandtails had passed over almost all of California in a great rush, finding feeding conditions not to their liking. My chosen district saw hardly any birds at all. Farther south, in San Diego County, the main flocks paused for a short time, but hunters in general were completely disappointed, and in all probability the majority of the birds wintered that year in Mexico.

Since the food situation during migration makes bandtail hunting always something of a gamble, the various state conservation departments and the federal Fish and Wildlife Service have tended more and more toward giving hunters a break as to seasons. I mention this to show that often the criticism hunters level at their lawmakers is quite unfounded. A summary of seasons since 1932, when the bandtail once again appeared on the game-bird list, shows that there has been a steady trend toward opening the season at the time most advantageous to the hunter, the weeks when there is the best average chance that the birds will be most abundant. For example, over the years since 1932 the season openings in Arizona have moved steadily back from December to September, in New Mexico from November to September, in Washington and Oregon from October to September. In California they have always been during December.

Whether or not this setting back of seasons is a proper conservation measure, I am not prepared to say. Surely if we are to have the bandtail as a game bird at all, it is logical to have the seasons set at a time when hunting the birds is worthwhile. And so I am inclined to agree with the idea, and to feel that if the bandtail population balance is, or becomes, too precarious other measures such as shortening of seasons and reduction of bag limits should be utilized, or else a closed season be put into effect every other year.

Johnson Neff's detailed study of the bandtail on the Pacific Coast tends to show that seasons at present give the gunner a good break, at least as good a break as can be had with such an unpredictable species. In all localities the birds begin to flock together noticeably toward the end of the breeding season, and to stay bunched up from then on during migration, following the food supply. In Washington as a rule this flocking and movement reaches its peak in late August and early September, the birds pausing here and there for several weeks at a time near some watering hole or feeding location. In Oregon the time is roughly the same. If the season is perfect as to weather, the peak may be reached in Oregon perhaps a week later than in Washington, say about September first to tenth in Washington, and September seventh to seventeenth in Oregon.

Judging from what is currently known of bandtail movements, California appears to have two, the birds along the coastal slope of the mountains in northwest California beginning their flocking and migration about the same time as those in Washington and Oregon, while birds in the Sierra may not move much southward until on toward December. They do, meanwhile, migrate vertically, dropping down toward the 2,500- to 5,000-foot levels. In Arizona and New Mexico the migration is shorter and thus likely to be rather erratic, especially since weather conditions in the lower levels are usually warm. However, in these locations reports over the years tend to prove that flocking and migration begin at about the same time as in the Northwest. For the prospective bandtail hunter who wishes to be successful, all these facts are important.

Likewise, knowledge of the range of greatest general abundance in each state is good equipment for the hunter who isn't familiar with the bandtail locally. Coastal Washington and the

Puget Sound area, the coastal and near-coastal belt of western Oregon, the counties previously mentioned in California, along with the mountains of Del Norte, Siskiyou, and San Diego counties—these are the hot spots on the Coast. In Arizona, areas such as the mountains around Flagstaff, the Pinaleno Mountains, and the vast territory along the rim country of the upper Salt River are good, and in New Mexico locations such as the wild, rugged terrain of the Burro Mountains near Silver City. On the whole, however, bandtails are where you find them, and any nonresident of the bandtail country who is planning a hunt should definitely contact people locally familiar with conditions.

Luckily, a few scattered flocks do winter, or remain for most of the winter, in various places throughout their summer range, some few even sticking it out as far north as Washington. Thus, if a season is such that the concentration of birds doesn't pause to give hunters a real chance at them, there is always the possibility of getting at least a little shooting with the strays who forget to migrate. But it must be kept in mind, too, that areas where concentrations—and therefore heavy shooting—are usual during migration, may often fizzle out during seasons when food is abundant everywhere. The shooting pressure influences the birds to avoid these special danger spots and to scatter out over a wider area.

One thing which is entirely certain is that nobody can tell you to go to any specific spot at any specific time, and promise you that you'll be on a flyway where the shooting is tops. To date so little is known of flyways—if indeed the birds have definite routes at all—that such information is of no importance. Banding may eventually assist in settling the question, but so few band-return records exist to date—the Fish and Wildlife Service files in 1940 contained only five—that they mean nothing.

The most popular kind of bandtail shooting in the past has always been pass shooting, but it is a somewhat specialized kind of pass shooting, since most of it will occur in mountainous terrain. As with the mourning dove, the best flight times will be from dawn until about 9:00 A.M., when the birds are going to feed or from feed to perch, and again in late afternoon when they travel from perch to feed or feed to water and roost. A perfect setup for the pass shoot would be about as follows. Let us say that you know a section where a north-south ridge separates two valleys. In the valleys there are grain fields or other feeding locations, or, if the country is entirely wild, fairly open oak flats. Somewhere along the ridge there is a notch, or saddle, giving access to either valley without the necessity of the birds flying over the hump. Such a mountain pass will invariably attract birds in flight. If they are shot at in one valley, they will fly through the pass into the other valley. Or, if gunners are stationed in both valleys, they will constantly trade back and forth, or set courses up and down the valleys. Where such stations have suitable cover for the hunter, the shooting is always excellent, and fast.

You will probably think it strange, therefore, when I say that if I were to have the job of conservation management of the bandtail at the present time I would outlaw pass shooting entirely. Not that it isn't a fine sport. It is little short of terrific, and when a concentration of birds is in the vicinity you would think time had moved back a hundred years to the days of fabulous abundance. I can best tell you why I feel as I do by going over a few pertinent facts, the first of which is that bandtail-pigeon hunting is an activity entirely different from that to be had with any other American game bird, and therefore it should be most important to us to do our level best rigidly to preserve an adequate breeding stock of these birds. From all available surveys, statistics, and observations, the bandtail situation seems to be about as follows: Washington and Oregon, fairly well-founded suspicion of slow decreases in population; California, population just holding, with neither increase nor decrease except locally and seasonally; Arizona and New Mexico, possibly slight and very slow increases, but actually not a large enough population to allow much hunting if the number of hunters increases in the future as it has in the past few years; Colorado, probably a slow increase in the southern counties, which can eventually help the Arizona and New Mexico hunting, if the birds get a break.

From these observations we can see that the balance is a very delicate one. Now let us see what happens in pass shooting. The terrain is brushy, rough, and with many steep slopes as a rule. The birds take a lot of killing, and fly so swiftly that they make extremely difficult targets. Hunters do not judge range accurately, and when there are many birds and many hunters the excitement of the constant barrage and the constantly flying birds makes for careless, long-range shooting. Consequently, a very great number of birds are crippled and lost in the brush. Where a mourning dove would hit the ground stone dead with one pellet, the bandtail will hobble off to die. Where a crippled mourning dove, or one shot dead at long range, would be relatively simple to find, the bandtail falls in brush and is difficult to locate. In addition, the up-and-down terrain influences many hunters to leave both crippled or dead birds where they fall, with no attempt to retrieve them if they happen to have fallen in places where they would be hard to get to. During one season in California, wardens and conservation men checked just such a pass as I have previously described, when birds were abundant and shooting was heavy. The consensus of opinion was that as many as five birds were lost, crippled or dead, for every one picked up. On one Sunday during that season 6,404 birds were checked out in the bags of hunters at that particular pass. Assuming that the estimate of loss was correct, the total figures would indicate roughly 36,000 birds killed on that one day, with only 6,000 utilized. That, to my way of thinking, is nothing short of scandalous—and the hunters whose bags were checked on that day admitted it themselves. However, we all know that when there is open season on a bird, we will hunt it, all of us. And, knowing this, if we also know that pass shooting on bandtails, because of the geography, is terribly wasteful, we should discipline ourselves by law since we can't seem to do it by individual conscience.

This instance of which I speak is not the one exception which proves the rule. Numerous other examples could be mentioned. One in particular occurs regularly near Corvallis, Oregon, at the Pigeon Butte pass, long a popular bandtail shooting ground. Reliable estimates have put the loss in cripples there at a minimum of 60 per cent of the birds downed. A bird that lays one egg, normally raises one brood per season, lives in such a restricted range, and concentrates the bulk of his numbers in fall, can't stand such losses forever. It is, in fact, amazing that the bandtail has done as well as he has.

And while we are discussing this phase, I want to mention one other facet that is so very often overlooked. When game birds of any kind are extremely plentiful during any specific season, the number of hunters who go out after them also increases proportionately. In the case of the bandtail this means that a concentration of birds because of good feeding conditions in an area will mean a concentration of hunters. It will not necessarily mean, as we have seen, that the bandtail is generally more plentiful that year, but only locally so. It may, in fact, be conceivably at a low population ebb that season, yet the shooting pressure will be greater simply because the feed is good and has drawn the birds and therefore the hunters.

This hunter increase, which always occurs with any game-bird population upswing, unquestionably teaches us that we have two kinds of hunters: those who are enthusiasts of the bird in question, who would hunt that particular bird whether they had much success or not simply because they are addicts of that particular kind of shooting; and those who like to hunt and don't care much what, just so they can shoot, or shoot at, *something*, to get in on the gravy.

Now I am not saying this in criticism of the latter group. They have their rights and I can easily see just how they feel. I have been guilty of the same attitude, too. But we have made new policy along those lines in the case of the ducks, by requiring those who wish to hunt ducks to pay for the privilege by purchase of a special license, which is to say, a duck stamp. In many states, we buy our fishing license, and then if we want to fish for trout we must buy another special trout license. Everywhere we must do the same if we wish to hunt deer, or bear, or antelope, etc. I think this special permit idea is an excellent one. And since the bandtail is a very special fellow who needs help and study, I am convinced that he should be reserved for those who are specifically enthusiastic about him as a bandtail pigeon and not just as general game. And the way to settle who is a bandtail enthusiast and who is not is to let each hunter prove it by the purchase of a special bandtail permit, perhaps for one dollar. The fellows who just want to *hunt*, and who wouldn't bother with bandtails unless they were very abundant, probably wouldn't spend the dollar, but the fellows, rich and poor, who took extreme delight in being out in the mountains after bandtails, whether the bandtails were there or not, would gladly lay down their dollars. And the money could be earmarked strictly for study of and assistance to the bandtail. The Fish and Wildlife Service people working with bandtails have studied ways and means of driving flocks away from cherry and other crops to which they are sometimes destructive during summer. Rather than issuing permits for killing these birds, since they are itinerant anyway, some of the special license money could be used when and as needed to protect the agriculturist from pigeon depredations. And such usage would in its way help to better the relationship between sportsmen and ranchers. To my notion, if they aren't worth a dollar extra a year for the privilege of merely watching them fly before a gun, even if you never draw a feather, then they aren't worth having on the game-bird list at all.

Of course, my views are bound to bring the cry that special licenses are in their way discriminatory, that they keep the game for the wealthy sportsman. That's a perfectly silly argument, and I've heard it so many times applied to the duck-stamp situation that I'm weary of it. We have to get over the idea that natural resources are ours to be taken just as we like. In today's world, getting our share of them is a *privilege*, and privileges are never for free. The man who can afford transportation to the hunting grounds, a gun, a box of shells, a pair of boots, and the time to go hunting, can afford another buck to pay for the *special* privilege of carrying on his activity with band-tailed pigeons. If he doesn't want to pay, then let him hunt rabbits, for obviously he doesn't want to shoot bandtails in *particular*, else he'd be willing to sacrifice some other small item of daily bread or comfort to save the necessary dollar.

There is one other side to this matter. As has been said, the food of the pigeons has a great effect upon the taste of the flesh. Anybody who has ever hunted bandtails to any great extent will tell you that a great many birds shot by the average hunter wind up in the garbage can. The real enthusiast not only likes to hunt the birds, but to eat them as well. I do not believe in killing game just for the sport of shooting, unless use can be made of it. As a matter of fact, I am personally dead against the much-touted "plinking" sports, such as the shooting of woodchucks, for that very reason, unless it is a really necessary measure of predator control. The special license might conceivably eliminate some hunters who consign their birds to the refuse heap. I have already touched on the matter of preparing bandtails so they won't be bitter, in case they've been feeding on acorns. But since the majority of pigeons, in California particularly, will have been acorn fed, I want to make one more suggestion, especially for the tyro bandtail hunter. If you aren't sure, don't cook the birds and then toss them out because you find them none too tasty. Make a point of cleaning them as previously noted; then, just to be sure, soak the breasts and legs for several hours by barely covering them with brine flavored with lemon juice, or vinegar. This is a guaranteed method of eliminating the tannic-acid taste from an acorn diet.

So much for my personal views, controversial as they are. And now to other methods of hunting, which all of this foregoing discussion leads to directly. The bandtail, it must be remembered, is very much like his extinct relative, the passenger pigeon. And if we go back to the history of that bird we are reminded that the methods of trapping for market, and often the methods of sport shooting, were based primarily on the fact that the birds decoyed well. The same is true of the bandtail to a far greater degree than most hunters realize. I have always said that decoying of ducks was not as good a sport as pass shooting them, and so I suppose the same should hold true with the bandtail. But it doesn't, for the simple reason that the bandtail is a much more difficult target than any waterfowl, because of his speed, his changes of pace, and his rolling, dodging flight. Thus, since the bird is completely congenial about coming in to decoys, and since the sport to be had is entirely as good as that to be had in pass shooting, I propose that hunters think first in terms of this method for the bandtail, for it is an approach by which the waste in crippled or lost birds can be cut to practically zero.

Let me describe for you a scene to show you how well it works. Suppose that we are in the Puget Sound vicinity of Washington. One of the famous bandtail shooting sites there is Whidby Island, where acres and acres of seed peas are grown and shipped around the entire world. The bandtail has learned that the agricultural pursuits of man can be greatly to his advantage. He has learned to delight in seed peas which have been wasted during the harvest. And, incidentally, they impart a delicious taste to his flesh, so that we may be sure our birds from such a section will be the very best for the table. Here on Whidby Island the local birds, and flight birds from British Columbia, have gathered in large flocks, working the pea fields. Hunters by the dozen have taken their places long before dawn, hidden in the oaks and the scattered conifers. They're going to do their shooting at these feeding fields. But we haven't been able to locate a site that suits us, for that kind of shoot. Actually, we're lucky.

The moment the guns start banging away near the feeding fields, great flocks of birds will rise, scatter, and sweep across the island. To be sure, they will keep returning again and again, trying for a chance to fill their crops in peace. They aren't willing to give up easily when they've discovered such a bonanza. But after the first few barrages, many of the shots at extreme range, the birds being so wary and not easily confused will circle high and almost always out of range. The feeding-field gunners may be lucky enough, a few of them, to get their ten-bird limits, if they stick with it. But you know how it is— like duck hunting when a lot of guns are shooting a marsh —everyone trying so frantically that no bird gets within range before he's driven off by some gun strainer.

All this we have divined beforehand. And so we've chosen a stand near an old dead tree surrounded by small firs a good half mile from the heavy batteries of guns. Near us there's some wheat stubble that is a good secondary feeding spot for birds that become discouraged in the pea fields. And there are no other gunners nearby. We have made some decoys, simply plywood or heavy cardboard cutouts shaped like pigeons. These we have placed here and there, half hidden, in the fir trees, so that the feathery branches disguise them enough to make of them reasonable facsimiles to birds winging over. We may even have been at this game for some years, and may have gone to the trouble of having several bandtails stuffed. A couple of these we placed on the bare limbs of the dead snag. Several more, along with more cutouts, we put in the stubble. We have painted the cutouts in flat colors to represent fairly well at a distance the general bandtail color.

Now put yourself momentarily in the position of the birds which are being driven from the pea fields. They come slicing down the sky, putting as much distance as possible between themselves and the guns. By the time they reach us they feel a little safer, for no shots are following. There is the barren snag, with a couple of pigeons perching in it. A closer look discovers the fact that the firs have a good scattering of "birds" perching safely in their branches. Out in the wheat stubble a few more are obviously feeding. Birds winging over don't come sailing directly in to alight. Oh, no. They're far too shrewd for that. But, like ducks, they do decide to have a closer look. They circle, dipping and banking gracefully at a furious pace, with the dawn sun glinting from their metallic capes. And then they are suddenly within range.

We rise from our brush blinds that we have placed in the shadows of the firs, and swing on our birds. If we're fast enough, we connect—and our birds go tumbling to earth in the wheat stubble, where we may easily retrieve them. Or, if we do cripple a bird, it falls where we may run it down with no trouble. We may even have a cocker or other retriever along for the purpose.

This kind of shooting should be begun very early in the morning. If a location is chosen, as this one was, some distance from a concentration of hunters, we are bound early in the morning to get birds coming *in* to the field and birds that have turned back without feeding. Thus, being hungry, they will be more amenable toward our decoys. They'll be looking for a place to sit down and wait a while, mulling it over, working up their nerve to try again. On the other hand, if they have had a chance to feed, they will be more easily driven away for good. If we have chosen a spot where there are no other gunners at all, then we should set up our decoys in scattered positions—assuming that there are several gunners in the party—some distance away from the seed-pea field where we know the pigeons will feed. At least one gun will take up his stand directly overlooking that feeding field. It will be his job to get what shooting he can, but primarily to keep the birds from feeding, thus sending them back to our decoys. After a few rounds, this fellow is relieved and one of us takes his place.

For this kind of shooting, if we're short on decoys, even a single bird, stuffed or cut out, placed on a dead snag in plain sight will invariably be sufficient to intrigue flight birds into attempting to alight. Often the flocks won't be large, for the shooting at the seed-pea field will have broken up the large gatherings and scattered them. But this is to our advantage, even if the birds come in only one, two, a dozen at a time, for fewer birds will therefore have located our shooting stand. And the real beauty of this decoy shooting is that it not only works to perfection, but that the birds are always in full flight, hurrying away from the scene of the shooting at the feeding location. If you have shot teal in the marshes, and think they're fast and tricky, you have a new experience coming when you draw on a bandtail whistling in to a decoy.

There are all kinds of variations on this type of decoy shooting. When you're shooting in the big timber, a dead snag in a forest opening will be popular, as we have seen, with every bird in the vicinity, and it will be a perfect place for a couple of decoys. Decoys placed at the edges of the oak flats in the valleys will also turn the trick. Or, if you're willing to sit it out patiently, the dead snag can *be* the decoy, bringing you one bird, or two, at a time off and on throughout the day. Personally I can't think of a more congenial and pleasant occupation for a day in the sunshine and quiet and bracing air of the big-timber mountains. I hardly think it needs to be said, however, that the real sportsman will take his birds as they are coming in, or as they dive out of the snag when frightened, and not allow himself to be tempted into blasting them as they perch.

I might qualify that last just a little. I ran into a team of hunters in Arizona one year who were rifle enthusiasts. With .22's, they went after bandtails that were feeding on pine nuts and acorns in big timber. They used the dead-snag technique, and placed themselves at ranges which would not only give the birds a real chance but would try their own skill as well. They were very enthusiastic about this shooting, and they did get birds. This plinking is not for me, mainly because I'm strictly a shotgun man and think a bird should be shot on the wing. But I must say in all fairness that undoubtedly it's good sport for the small-bore rifle enthusiast, and has the definite advantage of either killing cleanly or missing cleanly. Surely, with a bird as wary as the bandtail, plinking is not going to mean too unfair an approach, and will never destroy any great number of birds. It's an idea for those who care for it. And I might mention that for either shotgun or rifle shooting, the dead-snag approach either with or without decoy is an especially excellent way to hunt bandtails during the middle of the day, for they will always look for these perching spots during their resting and digesting siesta, after morning feeding and before the afternoon flight to feed, gravel, and water. In addition, my Arizona rifle enthusiasts felt that they had a good method for hunting the really big, thick timber. Birds feeding on piñon nuts in such places are extremely difficult to down on the wing with a shotgun, for piñon pines are small, low, scrub-like trees, from which the birds flush and go dodging off through the trees, hardly ever giving a shotgun hunter a chance to swing and lead them.

Besides pass shooting, feeding-field and water-hole shooting (the last I'm not in favor of), big timber shooting, and decoying, there is one other type of sport you may at times get with the bandtails which is just about the craziest kind of gunning imaginable—cliff shooting along the Pacific, at spots where the birds have gathered near the beaches. If feed is good in the nearby inland forests, and high, rocky cliffs overhang the beaches, it sometimes occurs that bandtails, which seem to need salt as do all other pigeons, will spend a certain portion of each day flying along the cliffs and fluttering up to peck at the damp salts on the rock face. Or, if you find the right location, they will come diving over the cliff face from several hundred feet above, like jet-propelled falcons, with wings folded, plummeting almost to the beach and then spreading their wings and sailing down to alight and drink salt water or waddle about the beaches picking up tiny crustaceans and salty gravel.

Nobody can tell you how to find the proper places. The best bet is to locate, in bandtail territory along the coast, spots which have all the requisites, and then to check them for pigeons when the migration is on. No one can tell you, either, how to hit these birds. You just try, that's all, the enjoyable part of it being that if you connect with a few you can be proud of yourself, and if you don't you'll have had marvelous shooting, at least, of a kind you'll get nowhere else in the country.

That last phrase is, indeed, a summary of my whole feeling of excitement and enthusiasm about this beautiful, swift-winged pigeon of the western mountain wilderness that I've called our Pacific mountaineer. And it is the reason I've spent so much of this chapter urging conservation measures in his behalf, and in trying to give many details of his history and habits. Unfortunately, the bandtail is not a bird which can be managed, as we say, by wildlife biologists even to the extent that the mourning dove can. He is, like our ruffed grouse, at heart a bird of the deep woods and the great forests, and he has never listened without high suspicion to the coaxing of man's civilization. We can assist him indirectly by practicing intelligent forestry, and by hanging on to those wilderness areas still left in the West. Aside from that, our only management possibility is by discipline of our guns. The bandtail has shown definitely and admirably over the past four decades that he can respond mightily to this discipline, especially since he is almost entirely free from natural enemies and disease, and so hardy that he can tolerate great changes in altitude and stay healthy while undergoing temperature variations from well over 100 to a dozen-odd degrees below zero. But he has also shown that without shooting discipline his place as a species upon the earth is indeed precarious.

Let us therefore take this lesson to heart. Let us continue permanently to have the dynamically thrilling sport the band-tail offers, a sport unlike any other on our continent. The inference should be obvious.

Chapter 8

DOVE OF THE DESERT

I WILL NEVER FORGET my first trip into the Southwest, and I will never remember it without immediately associating with it one of the grandest and most unusual game birds it is our privilege to hunt in the United States. Having been born in the Great Lakes country, I looked forward to my first sight of Arizona in particular with much excitement. I was not disappointed.

One of my first interests was in the many species of cactus. People kept telling me that I should be sure to visit the organ pipe forest—which has since become a fully protected area set up as the Organ Pipe National Monument—because there was nothing like it to be found anywhere else. The strange clumps of this cactus are restricted in the U.S. to a rather small area in the vicinity of the little town of Ajo, in the southwestern part of the state, and run from there on down and across the Mexican border.

As it happened, the day I planned to visit the section the dove season opened. Once I began to see doves whisking over mesquite and paloverde thickets as swiftly as our car was slicing along the ribbon of road across the desert, you could have wrapped up the organ pipes and pitched them all down across the border. However, the doves and the cactus together were that day to play an important part in my gunning education.

My companion and guide was a man who had lived in the

219

Southwest for many years. He had the patience of the desert itself, and he needed it, I'm sure, where I was concerned. From the moment the sun knocked the top off a yonder mountain and came blasting like a rocket across the gray desert just after our early departure, I was wanting to stop and get on with the shooting. For with the race of dawn over the desert, here came innumerable mourning doves right on Old Sol's tail, making him hump to keep ahead of them as they headed for water and feed.

When we had got well on down toward Ajo, I could stand it no longer. "Now dammit, Doc," I said. "Pull over here somewhere. This foolishness has gone far enough."

He chuckled. "You northerners are always in such a cussed rush. You can't kill all the doves in this country, anyway. Why don't you just relax till we get where we're goin', then you can shoot yourself blue on both shoulders."

"Just one shot," I pleaded. "Just to blood me."

At that he pulled the car over, making a great pretense of effort with his patience. He didn't unlimber his gun, but squatted in the shade of the car, flat crown cocked over one eye, rolling a cigarette and watching me as I stalked off into the desert a little way to wait for a shot at one of those gray sizzlers.

I did little waiting. Here came a bird, rather high, and, it seemed to me at a distance, merely coasting along. The flight appeared not labored but of a slower, more deliberate and lumbering fashion than I mentally matched to the mourning doves I knew. And the bird appeared exceptionally large. I had heard that the western mourning dove is a bit larger as a rule than our easterners, and, since I naturally didn't want Doc ribbing me about my barn-door shooting after I'd made him stop, I decided it might be advantageous for me to swing on this slow bird. Only when it had got within range and I started swinging, I suddenly realized that here was a fooler for sure. Slow? That bird knew where he was headed and he wasn't kidding!

I remember feeling strangely puzzled, because there was something about this bird in flight that didn't click off "mourning dove" in my mind. Then he was swerving—it seemed to me he acted far less bold in his approach than the dove—and I was frantically trying to hang a proper lead out in front of him. And then I had done it, prettily as if I had really known what I was doing. He came hurtling down into a head-high patch of furry looking, every-which-way cholla, spiking himself belly down and fully spread-winged on its countless thorns.

Before I had reached out to retrieve my bird I knew that here was the most peculiar mourning dove I had ever seen, if indeed it was a mourning dove at all. The tail was squared, its center feathers dull brownish gray on top, but those to either side lighter gray for two-thirds of their length, followed by a dull black band, and with their long tips white. The upper side of the spread wings showed a wide band of white running from edge to edge across their center portion. The bird was definitely heavier and larger than any mourning dove; the bill had a noticeably more downward curve.

"Now what," I said to Doc when I had walked back and held the bird out to him, "have I got here?" At that time, aside from my tyro's knowledge of the mourning dove and my Oregon experience with the bandtail, I knew nothing much of our dove species except that we had once counted passenger pigeons by the billions.

Doc answered me briefly in his best below-the-border manner: "*Paloma de pitahaya.*"

"Indeed!" I said scornfully. "Now tell me in Yankee."

"Well," Doc said, "that means doves of the cactus, or cactus doves. Since you've gone to college, you'd probably call it a white-winged dove. Or you might, like some old-timers, call it a whitewing pigeon. To us here in Arizona—and in Texas—it's simply a whitewing. I've always felt, like most hunters who've had experience with 'em, both on the wing and on the table, that they're a better customer than the mourning dove from both angles. Matter of opinion. They're different, anyhow. And there's such a little bit of territory where you can find 'em in the U.S. that they've always excited me. Now get in the car and let's go. I want to show you something more than those organ pipes."

What Doc had in mind, as I was soon to learn, was to show me whitewings and organ pipes together. In the section that is now the National Monument, and where shooting is now prohibited, the organ cactus grows in great clumps, the numerous shoots of each clump upwards of eight inches thick and anywhere from five to twenty feet tall, and the plants scattered so profusely that they form a veritable forest, a weird and unusual landscape indeed. Oddly, this species almost never grows anywhere except on the southwest exposures of fairly low mountains and benches, up to about 3,500 feet elevation. Their blooms, the petals of which shade from brownish green to greenish white, to purple and maroon, appear during May and June, which means that the fruits mature late in summer.

The red, fleshy fruits, or cactus apples as they're sometimes called, are not bad eating. In fact, Papago Indians regularly harvest them in large quantities. Out in the Growler Mountains west of Ajo we found the apples in abundance, and from here on around to the south of Ajo, where several springs—now inside the Monument—are located in this exotic forest, they continued so. But the important part of the picture is this: everywhere you looked there were *innumerable* whitewings, perching in the cactus and the brush, flying high, flying low, trading constantly from place to place seemingly without plan or direction, all of them intent upon gorging themselves with the ripe fruit.

Doc pointed out to me the blood-red droppings of the birds, colored from their cactus-fruit diet, and later on, near a spring where we did some shooting, he called my attention to the ground. For several hundred yards around the spring it was littered with shotgun shell cases of all sizes and vintages. How many years some of them had lain there no one could tell. But it was obvious that here was—and long had been—a favorite shooting ground for those who knew the whitewing. And it was obvious, too, that the organ pipe and the whitewing enjoyed a close relationship in nature, one undoubtedly of value to each. In fact, it has since been fairly well substantiated that the late-fruiting organ pipe is often responsible for stretching the rather short nesting season of the whitewing in Arizona, for it provides food at times when other natural foods may be lacking. And no doubt the doves are responsible for furthering the interests of the cactus, too, by dropping its seeds in new ground.

This day with Doc is one I'll never forget, especially since, as I was to learn later, we were very lucky in finding the birds so abundant. I've never seen that many at any other time. And the season now, of course, is not altogether advantageous to the gunner. The whitewing concentrations don't stay long after nesting, and they have such a short distance to move into Mexico that you're lucky to catch the big flights even with the season opening as early as September first.

This bird, you see, is really a foreigner. Although it appears by the thousands each summer in U.S. territory, we are in the position, so to speak, of borrowing them from Mexico. Our southern boundaries lop off just a wee bit of the northernmost portion of whitewing range. And, as the bird is essentially a desert species, only a few small areas along the border form suitable whitewing habitat. He thrives on torrid temperatures and arid tropical environments. Undoubtedly this is what eliminates much of the high mountainous terrain along our southern border as congenial territory for him.

Beginning in California, along the western side of the lower Colorado, you find a few birds. I believe this is a fact not generally known among sportsmen. This situation comes about because California makes no distinction between whitewings and mourning doves so far as game laws are concerned. Therefore, whenever California's game laws are studied by non-residents, or even by residents living outside the Imperial Valley and the lower Colorado River region, they miss the inference that either dove may be shot during the special season set for that section. The regular mourning-dove season farther north opens at a different date. As a rule, when the Imperial Valley season opens, a limit may consist of either mourning doves or whitewings, or both, but, if both, the limit must apply to the aggregate. Whitewings are never found in unusual abundance west of the Colorado, but at times fair shooting with them may be discovered.

When you cross the Colorado and enter southwestern Arizona, however, you enter one of the two special domains of the whitewing in the U.S. If you drew a straight line from west to east, beginning at the Colorado and ending in Prescott, about a third of the way across Arizona, then continued the line from here on a straight southeastern tangent, down across the Tonto National Forest and the San Carlos Indian Reservation, until you bumped up against the border of New Mexico, you would box in for all practical purposes the nesting range of the whitewing in Arizona. In this area, the main summer distribution centers in the following locations: 1) a wide region surrounding Phoenix and running from there in two directions, the one northwestward up and around the rim of the Harquahala Desert and on to the Colorado River, the other southwestward and down the Gila River Valley to the Colorado near Yuma; 2) a solid concentration to the west of Tucson, and a larger one from Tucson south to the Mexican border. There are, of course, other good whitewing sections in our boxed-in portion of the state, but these areas, with perhaps one more added near Sonoyta, on the border far to the southwest of Tucson, are the main ones.

Eastward, into New Mexico, the bird is nowhere abundant enough to make shooting feasible. All of the border country is too high, most of it above 3,000 feet, to intrigue summer whitewings from out of Old Mexico, and though it might seem blistering hot to a human, it's too cool for these cactus-fed customers. But Texas, in the vicinity of the Rio Grande Valley, is a different story. Here the whitewing flourishes in the mesquite and blackbrush—or did, and would, except for the inroads of agriculture and gunning, which have made it necessary drastically to restrict shooting at present.

That ties up the U.S. gunning possibilities with this wonderful desert exotic. Not much territory, to be sure, as far as the majority of our hunters are concerned, but well worth a thousand miles of travel each way for even as little as a three-day shoot. Or so I choose to believe, and there are many

enthusiasts who do just that every year, for whitewing shooting is of a different cut in many ways from regulation dove
shooting. Not necessarily *better,* but, as Doc said, "different
anyhow."

As this is written, the season in Texas allows three days
only—September 17, 19, and 21—and on those days shooting
only from 4:00 P.M. until sunset, which gives the birds a chance
to eat and drink on the morning flight, and by staggering the
days keeps them from being immediately driven below the
border. This season at present applies only in the following
counties: Cameron, Hidalgo, Starr, Zapata, Webb, Maverick,
Kinney, Dimmit, La Salle, Jim Hogg, Brooks, Kennedy,
Willacy, Val Verde, Terrell, Brewster, Presidio, Jeff Davis,
Culberson, Hudspeth, and El Paso. The remainder of the state
is closed. In most of these open counties, the mourning-dove
season is open on the three whitewing days, to avoid the snarl
of doves illegally killed in error. But the main mourning-dove
season in these counties does not open until later, when the
whitewings are long gone into Mexico. This is an excellent
conservation measure. The same effect is gained in Arizona by
opening the whitewing and mourning-dove seasons together
on September first. The whitewing season then runs for only
fifteen days, but the mourning-dove season continues. However, since by September fifteenth almost every whitewing has
migrated, the possibilities for illegally taking whitewings mistaken for doves is almost entirely eliminated.

For those who may be interested, the scientific name of the
whitewing is *Melopelia asiatica,* and the species is arbitrarily
divided into two subspecies, eastern and western, the birds of
Texas being supposedly of the eastern subspecies and those of
Arizona and California of the western. For all practical purposes, no gunner need make any distinction between them.
The whitewing has a wide range below our borders, covering
most of Mexico and on down to Panama. It is abundant in
parts of Cuba, Haiti, Jamaica, and the Bahamas. It also has
been recorded as a straggler within our borders in Florida and
Louisiana.

There is probably no other dove whose flights, even in the

present day when the whitewing is in a somewhat precarious position, are so reminiscent of the passenger pigeon. And, oddly, the whitewing as well as the bandtail had its page of history that matches on a less violent scale the slaughter of the passenger pigeon. Strange it is that this sort of misfortune should have followed civilization's discovery of the passenger pigeon, the bandtail, and the whitewing, all the species that had restricted ranges, and yet have missed in good part the mourning dove, which is so much more widely distributed.

In early days along the Rio Grande and in Arizona, the whitewing was awesomely abundant. Without question there were millions and millions of birds in the race, which had over the centuries established itself in these sections now included in the U.S. We know now that whitewings born in one section will return to it for nesting. We know also by observation and logic that good feeding, nesting, and watering conditions were what drew them in the beginning. And it is important that we keep these facts in mind as we take a brief look now at the history and habits of the whitewing in the U.S.

Picture these tropical doves, long ago, wintering in southern Sonora, and from there on south throughout Central America. There are literally billions of them. With the coming of February and March, they begin to migrate northward. The birds that have wintered farthest north in what is now Sonora will undoubtedly move, many of them, to the northernmost limits of what they consider congenial territory. And probably every year a few adventuresome fellows will push on past the place where they were born. In what is today Arizona, for example, they found the great deserts stretching on and on to the vicinity of the present Phoenix, and so, over the centuries, an abundant race of whitewings became established upon them. Here and there were streams and springs. Nesting sites in the great mesquite and cactus forests were abundant. Food was bountifully existent. These birds—this race of them—were truly of this country, and the birds with which they may have consorted during the winter down in Mexico never did come up into this northern range.

Presently man's civilization began to discover this civilization of birds. Man followed the river valleys—the Salt, the Gila, the Santa Cruz—and it was along such bottom lands that the whitewings were concentrated. They seemed, therefore, to be even more fabulously abundant than they were. Where the old San Xavier Mission, built several centuries ago, now stands, a little way from Tucson—which itself is one of the earliest settlements in the U.S.—whitewings by tens of thousands were making their daily morning flights from their nesting colonies in the great mesquite forests in that section, out into the desert to feed and drink. These flights, usually high and swift, and seemingly endless as flock after flock passed overhead, were undoubtedly watched by rugged fathers and their followers who raised gleaming white San Xavier from out of the barren desert. And unquestionably thousands of them never returned to their nests, but were utilized as a staple item of food by these same pioneers.

By the time Arizona had collected an appreciable number of white men, the cactus dove had become not only a main entree on the summer bill of fare, but had made itself an enviable place on the list of birds of sport. In fact, early in this century, whitewing shooting was the main hot-weather diversion of Arizona's outdoor-minded population. Hundreds of citizens took their stands late every summer afternoon along the flyways, and it was the usual thing for each gunner, if he could shoot at all, to knock down anywhere from fifty to a hundred birds before he quit.

This had not gone on long before the word had spread. Wealthy sportsmen from the West Coast, and even from as far away as New York, where game laws were beginning to cramp the style of the big-bag enthusiasts, began to flock to Arizona during the summer months, to get in on the fantastic shooting. The San Xavier Crossing, still a famous flight lane near Tucson and still just as popular today with hunters each fall, saw well-equipped camps established and sports paying good prices to lads to retrieve their birds for them. As far north as the valleys of the Santa Maria and the Bill Williams River, the northwestern limits of whitewing range, the shooting was just as heavy. The Cave Creek and Wickenburg areas, still favorite spots in the central northern portion of the range, the big, solidly established whitewing colony in what is today called the New York Mesquite Thicket on the Santa Cruz River south of Phoenix—a colony still one of the largest in Arizona—were hot spots for the wealthy big-town sports and the native hunters. And, before the sport hunting had more than barely established itself, market hunters began to see possibilities. San Francisco and Los Angeles began to receive shipments of thousands of birds.

But all the time something else was happening which went unnoticed by those who said the whitewing would always be so abundant that shooting could no more than put a dent in its numbers. Agriculture was getting a start in Arizona. The portions of southern Arizona most advantageous for crop raising were obviously those which already supported the best vegetation, and this of course meant that land was swiftly cleared in places where the most water was likely to be. The great mesquite forests, always favorite nesting grounds, were slowly cut and burned away. River bottoms were cleared of brush; natural waters and springs were often diverted.

It has been established through painstaking research of wildlife biologists that the worst predator of the whitewing in the U.S. is man himself, not only because of his gunning, but because the whitewing is not the farmyard nesting bird that the mourning dove is. When cutting of wood in the mesquite thickets disturbs nesting colonies, they often fail to bring off their broods. In addition, the whitewing nesting season in our territory is extremely short as compared to that of the mourning dove. Contrary to popular opinion, the majority of cactus doves in our territory seldom raise more than one brood—sometimes two—of two squabs per season under normal conditions. Further, the whitewing is not the grain feeder on the whole that the mourning dove is. He is more wary and sticks closer to his desert foods.

Thus can we begin to see what happened to the fabulous whitewing population that the pioneer knew. Since it is only for nesting that these doves stay for a few weeks in our country, it is obvious that once the major portions of their traditional nesting sites were destroyed and disturbed, their watering places often taken over by man, and crops grown where once desert foods abounded, the entire routine of the U.S. tribe of whitewings was completely upset. They could not adjust swiftly, and especially they could not bring forth numerous young during such a short season under these new conditions.

That is not to say, of course, that the whitewing in the U.S. is doomed. Far from it. Birds are still reasonably abundant in both Texas and Arizona. In Texas, cutting of the blackbrush in the small area originally inhabited by whitewings and plowing up of fields almost drove them out for good, or rather almost brought that race to extinction. But now we are seeing something in Texas that augurs well for the future of the birds there. Whitewings are spreading out over a much wider area than they inhabited before the coming of the white man. Counties far from the southern tip of Texas, counties where the whitewing was always unknown, now report more and more birds every year. Holding down of the gunning season has allowed them to hang on while making adjustments from their traditional ways. They now swarm to the grain fields to feed avidly as they once blanketed the tangles of arid-country vegetation. And along the Arizona-Mexico border whitewings by thousands may often be seen in grain fields during the short migration season.

In Texas, not only did agriculture run the whitewings out of house and home, but, curiously, it brought a predator little known previously along the lower Rio Grande, the purple grackle. This bird, which followed the opening of the country by the plow, delights in a meal of doves' eggs, and, since the whitewing is more colonial in its nesting than the mourning dove—not from choice but because of the small suitable areas in its arid habitat—the grackles found it possible to wipe out many nesting attempts on single raids.

The whitewing has been a difficult problem for the Fish and Wildlife Service. First someone would claim that it was nearly extinct, a half truth, for millions still swarm below our borders. It was our tribe that was in trouble. Again, when the gunning seasons were held down, many sportsmen who happened to have good shooting cried "Nonsense!" at the study-project men. As I've said, the whitewing comes closest to the passenger pigeon in his awesome flights. He flies high and swiftly and in loose flocks, one following another, until you think when you watch a flight that it is never going to end. But during the time when hunters see these flocks, they sometimes forget that they are seeing practically all the whitewings in their area concentrated during a migration which begins abruptly and has a very short distance to travel.

The high flight of this dove annually saves him from much overgunning, and makes for some of the grandest shooting any American gunner will ever experience. Here again, the bird shows that he is a product of his environment. In arid country the distance between a water hole and a good roosting site, or between roost and feed, may be very great. Thus these doves habitually take their time about starting off in the morning. They know the flight will be a long one, and since they don't mind the heat as much as the mourning dove, you always see the mourning doves begin to fly out first, then half an hour later the whitewings begin to pass over. And, being lazy in their way like many another desert species, they stay at their feeding longer, so that the two species may use the same flight lanes but seldom will you see them flying together. And of course it is always the food and water problem of desert country that keeps whitewings in rather compact concentration.

This last has a curious bearing on the history of whitewing hunting. Some years ago the season in Arizona was traditionally during summer. Gunners claimed that as soon as midsummer rains came, the birds headed for Mexico. And they proved it by showing how birds would be swarming at a desert tank, then almost entirely absent after a heavy rain. What actually happens, of course, is that once heavy rains have left puddles where the birds can drink closer to their nesting sites, they temporarily scatter, abandoning the tanks to which they formerly swarmed. Nest counts in such areas during rainy seasons finally proved the point. The cessation of summer hunting was an excellent measure. Thousands of parentless squabs were left to perish from the summer shooting. And early and late shooting to avoid the severe heat was seriously upsetting the sex balance by taking a preponderance of males that had left their mates at the nests.

Primarily the cactus dove is for the pass shooter. And let me tell you he calls for a real knowledge of lead and swing! For when the flights begin, they are really *up*. No gun is too large, no charge too punchy, and the gunner's eye must be good to drop them consistently. The one prime rule is to choose a stand where the birds will come down in the open. Otherwise you lose many, for with a fast, high bird the fall is long, and you don't always get clean kills. One of the common criticisms you hear of whitewing shooting these days in Arizona particularly is that the flights are too high to reach. Often, however, this is the fault of the hunter who doesn't know his birds.

To wit, when you see a heavy flight of whitewings begin to pass over, you have a frantic urge to get under it no matter what and blaze away. It's sport, to be sure, and tremendously exciting. But quite often it is just as unproductive. The point to keep in mind is that your stand will always be more important, as far as your bag of birds is concerned, than the number of birds in the flight. When these birds are flying high they are not so inclined to follow land contours. They fly straight and fast, especially if going from water to roost late in the day, or from roost to feed in the morning. Thus, a stand on a rise or knoll, even if it has but few birds passing over, will usually pay off with the whitewings better than one under the main flight on level ground.

Traveling *toward* water, whitewings usually fly lower, especially if they must travel uphill. And very often if not too heavily shot at they will pause here and there to rest in the bushes. This is a good thing to know when you pick a stand, for the time of day will govern which way the flight will be going, and likewise your choice of stand. But no matter what flight or stand you choose, you always have to remember that the whitewing in the U.S. is a skittish little critter. A man hunkered down at the edge of the brush will cause him to dive and swerve and flare, falling all over himself in his escape gyrations. However, a man going unconcernedly about in the open, walking, especially where men may be working in grain fields, will get little attention, and therefore quite often better shooting.

I can't say that I believe too strongly in shooting right at the tanks, although I know it is popular. A bird that flies upwards of twenty miles for a drink when temperatures are scorching ought to be allowed to have it. Besides, it has been well proved that sometimes all cactus doves from an area of almost a thousand square miles will concentrate at the single tank in their vicinity. Tank shooting may thus equal over-gunning, and may conceivably tend to discourage the birds from using a great area.

On the other hand, shooting along any particular flight but at sporting distance from the tank, so that missed birds can drink in peace before going to roost, seems to me legitimate practice. Years ago there was a watering place in the Sand Tank Mountains southeast of Gila Bend, Arizona, where white-wings came by thousands. They nested in the area because of its good cover, and water. The place was—and the general locality still is—a hot spot for whitewing hunters. Now a man-made tank replaces the old watering hole, but I feel that such spots should be inviolate. You can often see several thousand birds in the vicinity during nesting. If we keep in mind that the water, primarily, is what holds them year after year and brings them to this entire area to nest, we may well reflect that by doing our shooting some distance away, under the high flights, we may make that pleasure last a lot longer.

We might also take a potent lesson from this very tank. Man-made watering places near good nesting sites in the large old mesquite thickets—which the birds like much better than second growth for that purpose—will unquestionably give us better whitewing hunting in years to come. The birds don't mind flying long distances to feed, if they feel secure about water. Besides, such tanks scattered over the desert are in-expensive, and invaluable to quail and all manner of game.

If you think you are going to "walk up" whitewings very

often as can be done fairly consistently with mourning doves, you'd best forget it. Mexican whitewings may be tame enough to be hunted thus, but our birds have known concentrated barrages for too long. Our cactus doves just aren't walk-up birds. But you can get feeding-field and roost shooting if you happen to be located in the right places. The reason I hold that pass shooting is the major whitewing sport is that scattered feeding grounds that make long-distance flights necessary also make long-distance trips necessary for the average hunter. If you're lucky enough to get the birds at a grain field in either Texas or Arizona, however, during the peak of migration, you can partake of some of the craziest shooting I know anything about.

The whitewing appears slower in flight than the mourner. But he takes a big wing bite and is a fantastically wild flyer when you plug away at him as he skims in to his feeding ground. When cover is such that you can get right out into the middle of a field, well, your guess is as good as mine as to how to hit the birds. You try it. That's all I've ever done. You'll get your limit, without doubt, if the birds are plentiful. But you'll burn a lot of useless powder. You'll kill a bird that is burning his wing feathers doing six-sided loops through the low cover, and then along will come a single who appears to be just drifting by without concern. This easy one you'll miss cold, and then you'll be so exasperated you'll begin missing the tough ones you've just learned to hit.

Off some little distance from a roost edge, if there aren't too many hunters around, you can get wonderful late-afternoon shooting of a quite different sort. Here you can catch the birds letting down, coasting on set wings—a whitewing habit that differs radically from mourning-dove flight—coming in low and looking easy. These fellows won't flare, however, when you fire. If you miss, they'll dive. Again, you try to hit 'em. Don't ask me how. Then, if you want the superlative of wild shooting, get yourself right into a whitewing roost. You can get good cover for yourself in such a brushy spot, and whang away to your heart's content. Someday someone will write a whole book about this hunting. It's worth a whole book. And the author will tell you exactly how to hit these crazy birds from a roost stand. Be sure not to read the instructions, for you may be certain the author won't know what he's talking about! In all the wingshooting world I know of no bird flight to equal in calm determination and detachment the high, straight pass flights of the whitewing, nor do I know of one which can even compare with the fantastic frenzy of it when you catch the birds low and unaware.

Indeed, if you have never hunted this cactus dove, you have a surprise in store for you. There is no other American gunning like it. You can take a man who has hunted every other U.S. game bird and put him to shooting at whitewings, and he will tell you that he has never tried anything even remotely approaching this, or witnessed anything like this. I've seen that happen. It is without question one of the greatest shooting thrills still left in the U.S. today.

In Texas nowadays, of course, you get no morning shooting. To my mind, afternoon shooting is best anyway, although it's hot work, even when you sit quietly with your water jug and let the birds do the hardest part. But you have to make it a point always to be on time. Usually you find it necessary to get your birds in an hour or not at all. Sometimes, in fact, your shoot will last only twenty or thirty minutes. That few minutes, however, packs a wallop that many a whole day at other wing-shot work can't touch. We can keep this wonderful shooting, too, if we carefully watch our limits and our seasons, protect what is left of our ancient and traditional whitewing nesting areas, grow new ones for them, and see to it that watering places near these areas are furnished for the birds.

Chapter 9

AND LO, IN THE EVENING —

IF YOU EVER WRITE a book, you will understand the strange feeling an author has when he sits down to begin a last chapter. Don't ever let an author tell you that he doesn't get a lonely, empty sort of feeling when he tries to end a book.

You don't write a book in a day. You *live* with it for a whole year, or more. And when you live with this kind of book twenty-four hours a day for so long, two things happen to you: you squeeze from memory every detail of every experience you've ever had with its subjects, turning them in your mind and living them over again; and you come to feel that day after day as you work you are, so to speak, talking to and associating with the same crowd, your readers. Shoot the breeze day after day with the same gang for that long, and you come to know them mighty well, just as they come to know you.

To me, it's exactly as if we had been hunting together for a long time, spinning talk while waiting for the flights to begin. That's the feeling. And now we come to the place where the flights and the talk and the high excitement are over. It is evening. The bags are full of plump birds. Shoulders are beginning to ache and turn a bit blue from the many misses. The birds we didn't get have returned to their roosts, straight and sure as the one that came winging back to Noah in his Ark, long ago.

We stow the empty guns in their cases, peel off curiously light shell vests, and drain a last drop of tepid water from the

235

jugs. The sun spreads a last sly wink of promise over the quiet landscape and ducks down behind the far horizon.

Someone says, "What are we going to do with these birds? It's mighty warm, you know."

"Spread 'em out loosely in the trunk of the car," one of the boys answers, "so they'll air on the way back."

There's no talk as we start the drive. Full satisfaction is a quiet thing. No one knows that better than a dove hunter. If he's had shooting at all by day's end, he's had full measure of it!

Finally someone says, "Gad, man, but I'm starving. How about stopping for a snack somewhere?"

The driver looks around and grins. "You're forgetting the birds," he says, and smacks his lips. "I'm just rightly nursing my hunger, thinking how good they're going to taste!"

That does it. There's a fair sort of argument under way in no time about how a dove should be prepared for the table. Naturally, I have to have my say on the subject, too, before the time comes that we break up for the evening and say "So long, and good shooting!" For the shooting is not the whole of dove hunting, not by a skilletful! There is no finer eating in the world than a bag of doves properly prepared. It has been said with a fair degree of accuracy that dove hunting is water-fowling in miniature. The comparison carries through in the eating, too, for though doves have a distinctive flavor of their own, it is best described as a "ducky" taste.

As with any game bird, of course, the quality of the chef's work when it reaches the table depends a good deal on what care the game has had up to the time it reached his hands. But there is quite often a particular problem in doing right by the game after the hunt where doves are concerned, for such a great share of dove hunting is done in warm, or even very hot, weather. When any bird is shot on a warm day, simply picked up from the ground and stuffed into a game pocket or bag with others, the meat will taint or sour rather quickly.

The best plan is to lay your birds out in the shade, if your stand is conveniently located for this. They shouldn't be stacked in a heap, and of course you should keep your eye alert to see that ants or other insects don't get at them. As soon as the shooting slacks off, the crops should be taken out. This is a simple operation. Dry-pluck an area over the crop until it is clean of feathers, then make a small break in the skin and pull the crop out. The crop and its contents, especially if the crop is full, lying against the upper breast meat, are usually responsible for soured meat in the bird. Taking time to remove the crop will greatly assist in avoiding this.

If you are on a trip where you must stay out over night and hold your birds over without refrigeration in warmish weather, I've found a plan that works quite well. One caution, however, before I begin on it. Don't take anyone up on his offer to hold your uncleaned and unplucked birds over for you in a deep freeze. It's a good way to ruin them, and to make the final cleaning a big mess, regardless of how many deep-freeze salesmen tell you the contrary.

Since the nights will usually be cool, or even nippy, the birds should be drawn after the hunt, preferably after dark so the sun doesn't get at them. Leave the feathers on, but open the abdomen neatly below the end of the breast bone, and remove the entrails. Unfortunately, this usually means you have to dispose of the giblets, for there's no way to keep them well. But you can leave the tiny hearts attached and in place, and use them later in the gravy. Don't try to clean the body cavity too thoroughly, and never wash it out with water. Just wipe it a bit with a clean cloth, or paper. Now shake salt heavily inside the body cavity. When all the birds have been treated thus, loop them by the heads, singly, along a long, stout string, spacing them three inches or so apart, and stretch the cord between two trees.

Be sure no birds on either end are near enough to tree trunks or branches to be reached by furry prowlers, and that the birds are far enough above the ground so no shrewd night character can jump after them. Foxes and coyotes can jump higher than you'd imagine.

By hanging your birds feet down and salting them inside, you will allow the body cavities to drain well during the night, and the meat to cool out. Next morning early, if you have extra jackets, or even blankets, in your car trunk, you'll find that beneath them the temperature will be very cool. Spread the birds beneath and heap on as many coverings as you have for insulation. Keep the car trunk in deep shade during the day and the coolness will hold pretty well. I've kept birds for as much as three days thus with no spoilage, airing them again each night.

Of course, when you're coming right in with your kill, none of this care is necessary. On a shoot that begins in the morning and is to last until evening, follow the crop-removal routine during lulls. But on an evening shoot, obviously you can bring the birds right home and go to work on them as is. If you can wait on the eating part, and the birds are clean shot, it's a good idea to dress them and lay them in the icebox for a day or more before cooking. But don't freeze them. Put them low down where they'll just stay fairly cold. It brings out the flavor and hardens them up.

A dove, and that includes bandtails of course, should be plucked dry. The feathers are set very lightly, and come off easily. But the skin is exceedingly tender and will tear unless you are careful. To my way of thinking, a dove doused in boiling water to scald it before plucking is an ill-treated bird, and a skinned dove is worse than no dove at all. To be sure, dry plucking takes a little more time. But the game should be respected as much in table preparation as on the wing.

After the dry plucking is completed, singe the birds very lightly and quickly. Too much time over a blaze will bring the fat out and make them oily and the skin more tender than ever. After the singeing, simply wipe your birds clean with a damp cloth. Don't go soaking and scrubbing them in water. They're probably cleaner than the guys who shot 'em, anyway.

Now comes the separation of sheep from lambs. If you have a big party of hunters and several limits of birds, no doubt you'll have enough so you'll want to cook the tender young birds one way and the tougher old birds another. The bills and feet of the youngsters will be much softer than those of adult birds, and their leg bones will break more easily. You can of course sort the birds while plucking, if you like. Feather quills of birds of the year will be softer and more pliable, and the youngsters will have more pinfeathers.

Bandtails, as I stated in detail in Chapter 7, must be handled a little differently from mourning doves and white-wings, if they have been feeding heavily on acorns. And most of them probably have. Keep only breasts and legs as a rule, and treat the meat as described in the bandtail chapter. There's little meat on the other parts, anyway. With mourning doves and whitewings, however, I am a proponent of opening the birds by splitting them down the back. It's easier, neater, and cleaner than drawing them through an abdomen slit. You can use the method whether or not you have previously opened and salted them in the field. After heads and feet are removed, simply lay a bird breast down, neck facing from you. Grasp it with your left hand from above, set the point of a sharp knife close against the neck, and cut back toward you, severing ribs on one side close to the backbone. If you cut carefully and only through flesh and ribs, you'll not cut into the entrails and will be able to lay the bird flat open and get at the insides with ease and dispatch. Later, if you choose to cook the birds whole, a single quick stitch, or a toothpick, will close each and hold it in shape.

There are as many ways to cook doves as any other bird. We can't cover every one, but I'll set down a few. Perhaps you can take inspiration to go on from there, concocting recipes of your own. Always remember that preparing game in new and unusual ways can be a fine hobby in itself, and that the eating should be as exciting as the hunting. Too many sportsmen are satisfied simply to throw birds half cared for into a skillet, cook them carelessly, then tear away at tough meat and call it good. It's just as easy to make them *really* good. Most of us males can turn out a better job on game cookery by far than our womenfolk, if we make a point of it, although it would make me uneasy if I thought I'd be quoted.

If you like fried birds, there are a couple of ways to turn the trick. Frying is of course the simplest and quickest method of preparing them. And I have always liked at least the season's first batch fried because that way you get the plain game taste, with no tampering. For deep frying, try to pick the younger birds. Older ones are inclined to be a bit tough prepared this way.

Deep fry the birds whole. One good way is to dip them in either milk or evaporated milk, shake on salt and pepper, then roll them in flour, or in cereal such as cornflakes. Have plenty of fat, and have it boiling. You can of course use bacon drippings which add a pleasant taste, but I prefer tasteless grease such as one of the vegetable compounds. Simply drop the birds in whole and cook until they are brown and crusty.

For gravy, drain the excess cooking fat, and to the settlings in the bottom of the cooking pot or skillet add a big chunk of butter and at least a tablespoon of flour. Stir this mixture thoroughly, add milk as desired according to how thick you want the gravy. Keep stirring so it won't stick. The giblets, simmered in butter and then added to the gravy, finish the job.

To my way of thinking, a better though longer frying method is as follows, especially if you aren't good at telling young birds from old. Put a lot of butter in a deep iron skillet for which you have a tight fitting lid. Roll the birds in flour, salt and pepper, and when the skillet is quite hot, drop them in. Let them brown in the butter, turning them, keeping the heat just so the butter doesn't burn. When they are well browned, since doves usually have little fat on them, add about a half cup of water. Now cover the skillet tightly, and turn the fire very low. You can even put the covered skillet in an oven heated to about 250 degrees, or you can transfer birds and liquid to an earthen roaster and put it in the oven. Pack the birds snugly.

Just let the covered receptacle simmer away for about an hour, or at least until the birds are tender. By tender I mean until the meat is almost ready to fall away from the bones. Add whatever water you need to the liquor left when you take up the birds, thicken it a little with flour, and you have doves and dove gravy that really taste like cooking straight from the old homestead. Naturally some hot biscuits have to be ready to go with this.

Broiling is another good way to handle doves. This calls for whole birds, of course, and is most easily done when the birds have been split down the back as described earlier. Either lay them out flat, breasts up, on the broiling grate, or, if you are cooking outdoors, put them in a wire mesh broiler, breasts toward the coals. They should be greased with butter or cooking oil first. See that the fire is hot, and sear the birds well. Then lower your flame, or rake coals out of the campfire to bring the heat down. Turn your birds frequently, and don't forget to baste them quite often, with butter if possible.

See that they broil slowly, and never poke them with a fork to test tenderness. You let the juice out if you do. Many people insist on having all fowl broiled extremely well done. Doves are delicious that way but inclined to be dry. Try them sometime broiled as indicated but just a little rare. Salt and pepper them as soon as they come from the grill, dip a bit of butter over them, and if you can get your hands on a jar of tart, perfectly clear quince jelly, serve it with the birds. Never mind a lot of fancy trimmings. This is real eating that shouldn't be mixed up with a lot of other tastes.

When you get to birds that you know definitely are going to be tough, it's time to think in terms of pies and stews. Band-tails on which only breasts and legs have been saved taste mighty good this way. Of course you can also use young birds if you wish. The stew is the easiest, an excellent way to whip up a quick meal in camp if you plan beforehand to have the ingredients along. The birds should be cut up, dropped in a deep cooking pot and just covered with water. Don't salt them. But if they have little fat, put a chunk of butter in the water, or, in lieu of that, a small chunk of bacon. Cover them and let them boil slowly until they begin to get tender. Now add whatever vegetables you wish, or have at hand—carrots, peas, onions, potatoes, celery—in whatever quantity you wish, depending upon the amount of meat in the pot. Now add salt and pepper, more butter, and let the pot cook very slowly until the vegetables are done. That's all there is to it, and you have a whole meal.

There is another concoction which I suppose would be called a stew that I've eaten many times and of which I've never had enough. You take birds that have been fried the slow way—not deep fried—and for which you have made rich gravy. You can either put the birds into the gravy whole, or break them up. Heat the birds and gravy together, and add whatever seasoning in the way of vegetables that you like, such as diced onions, tomatoes, etc. Or, if you wish, dispense with the vegetables. If you do use them, let them get fairly well cooked, then add a lot of noodles, and cook them slowly. Remember that this will be a thick stew, so keep the fire low and stir the stew occasionally. This is an excellent way to use fried or roasted birds and their gravy left over from the day before.

To make a dove pie, boil the birds first in just enough water to cover them. Let them simmer slowly, until they're tender. Meanwhile line a deep dish with pie or biscuit dough and have your top crust made, too. Now lift the birds from the broth, put in carrots, peas, celery, cooked mushrooms, potatoes if you choose, and perhaps a bit of onion. The vegetable combination isn't too important. Go according to your tastes. Simmer the vegetables until they are tender, thicken with flour, drop in a hunk of butter. Put the birds in the pie dish, pour in the stew, lay on the top crust, and bake the pie in a medium-hot oven until the crust is brown.

You can vary all of these basic recipes, or use them as foundations upon which to build new ones. For that matter, if you want to have a look around in the cook books, you can find innumerable fancy ways to prepare your birds. Maybe some of them will appeal to you. I have even seen recipes calling for sour cream to be poured over a perfectly good and innocent dove after it was ready to be eaten. Personally I can't think of anything worse, or a quicker way to ruin a bird. In my opinion, game is supposed to taste like game. The chefs who do their damnedest to allay what is spoken of as a "gamey" flavor, whatever that is, do nothing but try to make everything taste alike. There's no reason to attempt to make a wild duck, for example, taste like a tame duck, nor to try to force a wild dove or pigeon into tasting like a loft-raised squab. You can even find recipes for serving doves with cabbage, stuffing them with sauerkraut, and pouring over them all manner of hideous sauces. If you will take my advice, and treat them kindly and simply on their way through the skillet, you'll have a much better meal, and it will taste like nothing so much as the very birds you brought home.

About as fancy as I'm willing to get when it comes to dove cookery is a recipe I take credit for inventing several years ago. It's a pretty fair little concoction, if I do say so, and I hereby give up my great secret for the first time. When I was a kid at home we very commonly had fried apples as a substantial vegetable dish. I supposed, when I grew up, that everybody ate fried apples, and was surprised as time went on that most people I talked food with had never even heard of them.

One time the subject came up when there were doves to be cooked. In my mind I began putting the taste of raw sliced apples with their skins on, fried in butter, with the taste of dark, well-browned dove breast. The upshot was that I floured the doves and browned them whole, in butter, using a hot flame and cooking them for only about five or six minutes. I then turned the fire way down, arranged the doves with breasts up so if there was any sticking it would be on back and ribs. Salting and peppering them lightly, I now laid apple chunks, skins and all, thickly over the birds, filling the deep skillet to the top. Putting in several spoons of water, I sprinkled brown sugar heavily atop the apples, dotted the whole with chunks of butter, and dropped in a very few caraway seeds.

You cover this dish tightly and let it simmer on a slow fire until the doves are tender and the apples done. Then serve it with the apples laid out in the center of the serving dish, the birds gathered around them, and the juice dripped over the whole. There, my friend, is a meal to make you lean back from the table in peace and full satisfaction, the perfect meal with which to end a successful day of dove shooting. Come to think of it, it might not be too bad a way to end a book.